THE

EVERYTHING

TOKEN

'Just like the dawn of the internet and social media, the early days of NFTs were filled with a lot of noise. Now that the dust has settled, the businesses that truly know how to use this technology are leading the way into a new digital era. *The Everything Token* cuts through the clutter and lays out a blueprint of what you can learn from that top one per cent of companies that are using NFTs right' Gary Vaynerchuk, Chairman of VaynerX, CEO of VaynerMedia, and creator and CEO of VeeFriends

'Web3 offers many new opportunities – including NFTs, which have countless use cases. Kaczynski and Kominers share valuable insights from their in-depth research and experiences with NFT communities on how businesses and brands, whether incumbent or upstart, can use them' Chris Dixon, founder and Managing Partner of a16z crypto

'NFTs were a mystery to me. Thanks to this book, both the economics of NFTs and how businesses can use them are now in sharp focus and no longer mysterious. It helps, too, that the book was so much fun to read!' Paul Milgrom, Shirley and Leonard Ely Professor of Humanities and Sciences at Stanford University and Nobel Laureate in Economics

'This framework for mastering the next wave of disruptive digital technology will be the industry standard for years to come. Simply put, *The Everything Token* is a must-read for business leaders' Jeff Charney, CEO of MKHSTRY and former CMO of Progressive Insurance and Aflac

'You can't ask for savvier or more enthusiastic guides to the potential of NFTs than Kaczynski and Kominers' Alvin E. Roth, Craig and Susan McCaw Professor of Economics at Stanford University and Nobel Laureate in Economics

'You might have dismissed NFTs as irrelevant to your business, but *The Everything Token* does a great job explaining how this technology can be a game changer for customer engagement and acquisition. It's a terrific learning tool for companies looking for success in Web3' Adam Brotman, Co-CEO of Forum3, former CDO of Starbucks and former Co-CEO/President of J. Crew

ABOUT THE AUTHORS

Steve Kaczynski is a communications and marketing professional with over fifteen years of experience, including stints in leadership at Progressive Insurance and Nestlé.

Scott Duke Kominers is Professor of Business Administration at Harvard Business School and a partner at a16z crypto. He co-leads Harvard's Crypto, Fintech and Web3 Lab.

Both advise entrepreneurs and established firms on NFTs, Web3 and marketplace design, and are avid NFT collectors and creators themselves.

THE

EVERYTHING

TOKEN

How NFTs and Web3 Will Transform
the Way We Buy, Sell and Create

STEVE KACZYNSKI

AND

SCOTT DUKE KOMINERS

BUSINESS

PENGUIN BUSINESS

UK | USA | Canada | Ireland | Australia
India | New Zealand | South Africa

Penguin Business is part of the Penguin Random House group of companies
whose addresses can be found at global.penguinrandomhouse.com.

First published in the United States of America by Portfolio/Penguin,
an imprint of Penguin Random House LLC 2024

First published in Great Britain by Penguin Business 2024

001

Printed and bound in Great Britain by Clays Ltd, Elcograf S.p.A.

The authorized representative in the EEA is Penguin Random House Ireland,
Morrison Chambers, 32 Nassau Street, Dublin D02 YH68

A CIP catalogue record for this book is available from the British Library

ISBN: 978 – 0 – 241 – 69203 – 5

www.greenpenguin.co.uk

MIX
Paper | Supporting
responsible forestry
FSC® C018179

Penguin Random House is committed to a
sustainable future for our business, our readers
and our planet. This book is made from Forest
Stewardship Council® certified paper.

To our families,

both centralized

and decentralized.

CONTENTS

PART I

THE NEXT

DIGITAL

REVOLUTION

Introduction

PLANET OF THE APES

In March 2022, one of the then-hottest startup companies on the planet raised $450 million in an oversubscribed investment round valuing the company at $4 billion. Investors were champing at the bit to fund Yuga Labs, a unicorn startup whose premier product was . . . digital pictures of cartoon monkeys!?

The pictures weren't made by a famous artist. In fact, while their individual visual features had been hand-drawn, the images themselves were created by a computer process. An algorithm randomly combined features like fur, clothes, and facial expressions into an image looking something like this:

Popular sites like Quora and Reddit were flooded with people asking versions of "Why would anyone pay real money for a random picture of a monkey?" Some commentators pointed out that the pictures technically weren't of monkeys at all—they were of apes, which are a different kind of primate—but that didn't do much to clarify why anyone would think they might have value.

Even more baffling, in a world where most consumer startups race to acquire as many customers as possible and tout their "total addressable market," Yuga had only created ten thousand of the images, *and committed to never produce any more.*

The whole premise seemed ridiculous. But even more absurd on its face was that the pictures weren't quite the product at all. Indeed, they were publicly available for anyone to view or download on the internet. What Yuga had really "sold" was just a series of digital records—*non-fungible tokens (NFTs)*—which associated specific people (or rather, their computer accounts) with specific images in the collection.

That's right: investors put hundreds of millions of dollars into a company that had sold ten thousand digital records linking computer accounts to public primate pictures.

Moreover, while Yuga had *created* these digital records, it didn't even control them. Unlike the tech platform behemoths that closely guard every bit of their data, Yuga's NFTs were stored on a public decentralized computer network called a *blockchain*, so once they were created, the NFTs were in effect out of the company's hands. Yuga couldn't control who bought, sold, or traded them—much less the market price. And the public nature of the blockchain meant that wherever the images went was tracked for the whole world to see.

The whole phenomenon left many observers scratching their heads. The images weren't much like the type of art that people often paid millions of dollars for—and again, to the extent that anyone "bought" or "owned" one of these images at all, what they actually got was the digital record, i.e., the associated NFT. People could buy and sell NFTs just as they might trade Pokémon cards or oil futures, but NFTs are otherwise quite different—after all, with futures you eventually own the commodity, and with Pokémon you get a card that can be used to play a game.

Some thought NFTs were at best a bizarre fad, and at worst some form of gluttonous excess—another ridiculous thing for people who already have everything to spend money on. (Plus, as a way to do business, blockchain-based products themselves were often met with deep skepticism, owing to the speculative nature of the emerging crypto industry, as well as the fact that some people associated cryptocurrencies with money laundering and fraud. More on that soon.)

To be fair, you might be thinking, *if a company can successfully sell a product that bizarre, they must be doing* something *clever . . .* but that just kicks the banana a little bit farther down the road.

Why would anyone *pay money for a digital record associated to a picture, primate or otherwise?*

It's because what they were buying was, in truth, far more than just a digital record. The NFTs were the foundation of what was emerging into an incredibly successful digitally-native, community-based brand—one of the first of its kind—called the Bored Ape Yacht Club.

Having one of the tokens was your ticket in: NFT holders "owned" their Ape images and were even given the right to use the associated intellectual property in their personal business ventures. Meanwhile, Yuga Labs was continually building new rewards and features on top of the NFTs—everything from holders-only online games to live events like an annual music festival. Yet that comprised only a fraction of the activity around the tokens: both holders themselves and third parties introduced their own forms of utility and benefits for the Bored Ape NFTs—everything from exclusive products and merchandise to large-scale immersive puzzle game experiences. Thus as the Bored Ape Yacht Club's public prominence grew, token holders shared in that success, both because it raised the value associated to the individual Bored Ape NFTs (there were only so many of them, after all), and because it expanded the range of valuable opportunities available to holders.

As a result, for many, being a Bored Ape NFT holder became part of their personal identity and way of life. They integrated their Ape images into their digital profiles—which helped raise brand awareness—and they plastered Bored Ape posters on their walls. The network of Bored Ape Yacht Club holders became a true club, a global community of brand enthusiasts, many of whom went out of their way to help one another, and in effect became a decentralized marketing arm for the Bored Ape brand. And in parallel, Yuga Labs evolved, introducing new types of products and experiences built around the Apes, with the NFT holders benefiting from exclusive or preferential access.

All of this made more and more people want to "Ape in" and join the Club—and that, along with royalties collected on NFT secondary-market sales, increased the company's revenue streams at Ape-neck speed. The excitement was so palpable that Yuga Labs made $90 million selling a second NFT collection—Mutant Apes—just a few months after launch. As new people joined the Club, the opportunities afforded by the network grew—and people took it upon themselves to organize everything from local Bored Ape meetups to weekly online "Mutant Monday" celebrations.

The feedback loop from token ownership to community brand-building took Yuga from a small startup to a multibillion-dollar unicorn in less than a year. That growth doesn't seem to have been an accident, either. Even as the broader NFT market experienced ups and downs in 2022 and 2023, Yuga continued to sustain success through NFT sales, secondary royalties, merchandise offerings, partnerships with major brands, and sponsorships for live events. In one instance, Yuga created a short-term gaming experience that expanded its holder base by 40% and raked in $2.2 million from in-game microtransactions. Shortly after that, a digital-physical merchandise partnership with Gucci made $5 million from the sale of a limited-edition pendant. And, in March 2023, the company added a fine art line that generated roughly $16 million in revenue. And these examples aren't exhaustive—in just its first years, Yuga's total revenues reached hundreds of millions of dollars.

This consistent growth alongside recurring revenue streams made Yuga so attractive that top gaming executives from Activision Blizzard (creator of World of Warcraft, Diablo, and Overwatch) and Epic Games (creator of Fortnite) joined the company to be a part of its magic. And meanwhile, numerous celebrities, established brands, and product entrepreneurs Aped in, acquiring Bored Apes and featuring them in everything from music videos to streetwear—driving yet more attention to the brand as they did so.

NFTs made all of this possible. And perhaps ironically, they are able to create such massive and wide-ranging value because they do something simple extremely well: *defining digital ownership.* In this book, we're going to teach you what that is and why it's important. And then, we'll explain how NFTs are already changing the way we engage and do business. It's not just startups like Yuga Labs. Established brands like Starbucks and Adidas, sports leagues like the NBA and the NFL, and web platforms like Shopify and Ticketmaster are all leveraging NFTs to improve upon their existing business models.

Yuga Labs, just described, provides one case study, and through that and a series of others we discuss in further detail, we'll demonstrate the role—and inevitability—of NFT technology in our everyday lives. And we'll show you how to harness NFTs' power for your company.

BUT WAIT—AREN'T NFTS CONNECTED TO CRYPTOCURRENCY, AND ISN'T CRYPTO A SCAM?

We get this question a lot, honestly. Especially when popular cryptocurrency exchange FTX imploded in November 2022, many people we know were saying things to us like "Wow, too bad—I know you've been pretty into NFTs, but I guess that whole industry must've just collapsed, right?"

It's true that when we were writing this book, the world of crypto had something of an "immature market" feel to it. Some NFT projects and companies *were* outright scams; many more were just poorly thought-out, overhyped, or otherwise unsustainable as they spent money recklessly trying to deliver on unrealistic promises. And as you would expect, much of that quickly came crashing down.

But you know what? The early internet was like that, too, in a lot of ways. When we first got access to the web, we were cautioned not to put in any personal information—and certainly never to share financial information like credit card or bank account numbers. But as the technology matured, it became safer, more reliable, and easier to use. Nowadays, we punch our credit card number into online payment systems all the time, and many people do all of their banking online. Moreover, people buy everything from clothes to furniture on the internet sight unseen, get into cars as directed by apps, and use online marketplaces to stay in complete strangers' houses when traveling.

And you know what else? Even today, there are still scams on the internet—the ubiquitous kind with fakes, phishing, and the like. But while we're constantly working to improve online security and consumer protection, we certainly wouldn't want to stop using the internet—just like we wouldn't eliminate consumer banking even though there are sometimes bank runs. That's because the internet creates value in so many ways that it's become essential in people's daily lives.

It's early days yet, but NFTs—and crypto, more broadly—have that same potential.

NFTs make it possible to create an effectively infallible record of who owns what in digital space. We'll get into how that works soon (it uses those blockchains we've mentioned in passing a couple times*), but for now let's just think briefly about the possibilities.

Prior to NFTs, if a company wanted to create a digital good for its customers, doing so was expensive, time-intensive, and filled with complexities like developing and maintaining the digital platform where the product lived. As a result, in practice, being in the digital goods business really only made sense for digital-first platforms like gaming companies, streaming services, online education providers, or megacorporations like Apple and Amazon. And even then, the manner in which consumers could buy and interact with digital goods was highly constrained—they could typically only use their digital goods inside of the platform that created and sold them, in very specific ways.

Provable digital ownership through NFTs allows practically any company to unlock previously unattainable brand value. They can issue digital goods that provide real value to the customer, whether it's through access to special events, discounts on their products, or even just simple, shareable digital collectibles. Companies of any size, and even individual creators, can now make digital goods easily, without spending a tremendous amount of time and money in the process. Moreover, these goods don't have to be tethered to any individual platform, and that expands their value by giving consumers the opportunity to use them flexibly across the internet. NFTs have simultaneously

---

*And crucially, these systems remained robust even during the most chaotic moments of the 2022 crypto crash.

improved the value proposition of digital goods for both the creator making them and the consumer purchasing them.

This is an incredibly powerful general-purpose technology. And like all such technologies, early exploration and experimentation featured a lot of misuse, poor ideas, and even malbehavior. But while that makes the current iteration of NFT products somewhat unpredictable, it doesn't diminish the opportunity NFTs create.

Even as the early speculative bubble around NFTs was popping, major businesses and new entrepreneurs alike were waking up to the possibilities that NFTs present to enrich digital and real-world experiences, change the way we connect with friends and family, and transform the relationship between consumers and businesses. You might be surprised to learn that you've already interacted with NFTs, perhaps daily, if you use social media platforms like Twitter or Reddit.* Both organizations have quietly made use of the technology to let users showcase cross-platform digital avatars. Likewise, many people are now receiving NFTs as they drink coffee, attend events, or play online games. As we'll discuss in the chapters ahead, regular usage of NFT technology in the next few years is a near inevitability, as its applications grow by the day.

In the early days of the internet, few people had the foresight to realize we'd use it to stream shows, play games, connect socially, and pay most of our bills. In fact, there's an old *Late Night with David Letterman* clip where the comedian pokes fun at Bill Gates, asserting

---

*Just as we were wrapping up this manuscript, Twitter was in the process of rebranding to "X." We've chosen to maintain the name "Twitter" here to ease the exposition.

that since devices like radios and tape recorders already exist, being able to watch sporting events on the internet was an unnecessary advancement. But nowadays, it's hard to imagine that anyone ever thought a Walkman cassette player could be a substitute for online streaming.

Similarly, digital goods have existed in some form for ages, but NFTs make them so much more powerful that they've become a completely new product category. As the technology surrounding NFTs evolves and matures, it has the potential to become part of almost everything we do online—and even much of our experience offline.

As we were writing this book, crypto adoption was growing, especially with younger demographics. The 2023 a16z crypto *State of Crypto* report showed millions of new active crypto user accounts and transactions since 2022, reflecting roughly a 50% increase in six months, as well as exponential growth in the number of new blockchain-based software applications (*smart contracts*, in the parlance of crypto), driven in large part by interest in NFTs. And even outside of crypto, digital assets were being bought, sold, and traded more than ever—even by children, who were regularly buying and trading items in games like Roblox and Fortnite.

NICE TO MEET YOU!

We're Steve and Scott, and we've spent much of the past few years embedded in NFT communities and helping launch NFT products. We're beta testers of sorts, of this brand-new technology—and we've seen its power firsthand. Steve even owns one of those expensive primate pictures.

But we haven't just been "going Ape." We've been writing, teaching, and advising companies about how and why NFTs work, and what they mean for the business world. We wrote the first *Harvard Business Review* article about NFTs in 2021, entitled "How NFTs Create Value." And since then, we've worked on so many parts of the NFT value chain that our learnings, well, fill a book.

Steve's a career marketer who's led multiple disciplines at Fortune 500 and multinational companies, and today he counsels startups, top brands, and the world's largest agencies on how to navigate the NFT world. Scott's a professor in the Entrepreneurial Management Unit at Harvard Business School and the Harvard Department of Economics. He studies the design of markets and marketplaces—and how new technologies can transform them. He's also on the research team at a16z crypto, a branch of the venture firm Andreessen Horowitz, where he advises a range of NFT creators, infrastructure developers, and marketplace builders.

And we're not just speaking to people who already know the landscape. We're helping legacy brands understand and make use of NFTs, and translating between cutting-edge crypto innovators and some of the biggest companies in the world. Steve works with Starbucks on its NFT-based rewards program, for example. Scott teaches MBAs and executives at leading tech and product firms how to build for this emerging internet era.

We wrote this book to explain how NFTs are transforming business and our day-to-day life. This is a brave new digital world—and whether you're an executive at a multinational company, a small business owner, or just a curious consumer, we hope you'll take away key lessons that will help you succeed.

So without further ado, let's peel that banana and formally introduce you to:

THE EVERYTHING TOKEN

Could digital "tokens" possibly be worth hundreds or thousands or even millions of dollars? The tokens themselves are just bits of computer data; shouldn't they be a dime a dozen (or perhaps even more appropriately, a penny a billion)?

The trick is precisely that these tokens *aren't* a dime a dozen—they're not random, arbitrary bits. Rather, each NFT is an individually distinct digital record, which can be linked to other assets or product features, and whose owner(s) can be consistently identified.

The term *non-fungible token* literally means what it says. Something is *fungible* when you can exchange one unit for another without a second thought. Dollar bills are fungible; so are grains of rice—for practical purposes, every one of them is just like any other. By contrast, each NFT is unique, just like in a litter of puppies. This makes them non-fungible—you generally wouldn't trade your puppy for another one! (The word *token* in context basically just means a digital object that a given user or account can have control over.)

Some NFTs come in editions with multiple copies of the same asset, like with trading cards: Two copies of a Charizard card in identical condition are equivalent from the perspective of most collectors. But for our purposes, a Charizard card is still non-fungible—especially relative to, say, a Pikachu card—because if you own one, you still own *your copy* of the card as a discrete asset, in a way we don't normally think of individual ownership of specific dollar bills, for example, even though each bill technically has a serial number.

Because each NFT (or copy thereof, in the case of editions) is individually distinct, the computer account that controls it can be consistently identified. This makes it possible to recognize an "owner" of an NFT in a way that was difficult or impossible in previous incarnations of digital goods: *The owner is whoever controls the token.* And NFTs can be linked to other assets or product features, extending the concept of digital ownership beyond just the token itself.

As we'll describe in more detail soon, the way NFTs work is similar to the way that the text on a deed to a house turns a dime-a-dozen sheet of paper into a record of ownership for a potentially quite valuable asset—which of course makes the deed itself valuable, too. You certainly wouldn't pay thousands of dollars for a random piece of paper, or likely even for a ticket to a local minor league baseball game (which is more or less a deed to a seat). But plenty of people would pay that much for the deed to a house.*

And just like with deeds, by making it possible to clearly establish and verify ownership—and potentially exchange it—NFTs enable

---

*Technically, people are generally paying for the *title* to the house (i.e., the right of ownership over it); the *deed* is just the document granting that ownership/title. We'll often use the term "deed" slightly casually to cover both meanings in this text, because NFTs correspond more closely to deeds, but often meld both concepts.

markets to emerge. NFTs have enabled trade in digital images and media files (such as those Ape images we mentioned), as well as new business models around everything from rewards programs to online education.

But NFTs go even further: Because they're embedded in software, many NFTs can take on functions over and above simple ownership. Owning a house might also gain you access to the local Rotary Club and public schools. Imagine that but for brands: owning a Nike .SWOOSH NFT can get you access to special Nike releases. Bored Ape NFT holders get free entry to "ApeFest," the music festival we referenced earlier. Even the Vatican has issued NFTs that give holders exclusive access to historical artifacts and documents.*

And just as neighborhoods often form a sense of community and collaboration, NFTs are enabling participatory brand-building of a form and scale that has never existed before. You're not just along for the ride—you're part of the action. Imagine if you could have a true stake in Star Wars and own a character in that universe. Or play a role in designing the next-generation Patagonia jacket. Or—in a very different context—contribute to a global network around your favorite social cause.

Moreover, like with the Bored Ape brand, while NFTs started out in the digital realm, they have quickly carried over to the physical world as well. This isn't an accident: by design, NFTs share some value with their holders, and thus encourage them to invest in growing,

---

*And of course, these sorts of benefits are typically carried over with the NFT if/when it's transferred to a new holder.

sharing, and enhancing the brand everywhere, both online and IRL. While writing this book, we tried to think of a title that properly encompassed what an NFT actually can "do." We worked off the prompt, "What current products and services can NFTs augment or replace?" The simple answer was . . . pretty much *everything*. This technology has the power to revolutionize multibillion-dollar industries and small businesses alike, enhancing current revenue lines and creating entirely new ones. And we're already starting to see completely novel NFT-native product categories—not just digital brands like the Bored Ape Yacht Club, but also new forms of digital credentials, subscriptions, and ownership records.

As we'll unpack, NFTs start with the simplest of structures—just an ownership record in a digital database—but we can build functionality on top of them in a way that creates surprisingly flexible value. NFTs can turn images into event tickets, and event tickets into brand anchors. They will usher in the next generation of customer loyalty programs, creating structures that benefit both businesses and consumers in new ways. They'll change the way we manage our work histories and health data. And they can transform simply owning a product into a close-knit community experience.

NFTs are the everything token.

2

Digital Ownership and Why It Matters

HOW DO YOU SELL A PIECE OF DIGITAL ART?

There's an old joke about an elephant: How do you put an elephant in the refrigerator? Easy—open the refrigerator door, put in the elephant, and close the door!

The point of the joke is that not only is the situation ridiculous, but the solution provided omits all the parts of the problem that actually make it challenging in the first place. How do you get a large enough refrigerator? Or do you just need to find a small elephant? Either way, how do you convince the elephant to walk in? And while you're at it, did you remember to reinforce the floor so the elephant doesn't fall through?*

Selling a digital artwork or music track is a bit like putting an elephant in a refrigerator: At some level, the process is so straightforward it doesn't bear explanation—all you have to do is find someone

---

*Plus, technically, in the most standard version of the joke, there's already a giraffe in the refrigerator that you have to remove before you put the elephant in!

who wants to buy it, agree on a price, and make the sale. But when you look at the problem more closely, there are all sorts of challenges.

When we sell something physical like a piece of jewelry or a trombone, we transfer ownership by transferring the object. But if Scott sells you a digital image he created, what does he "transfer" exactly? He can send you a copy of the image over email, but that still leaves a copy on his computer (not to mention one on a server owned by Google or Microsoft or whoever). And if he keeps the copy on his computer, what's to stop him from selling an identical copy to somebody else in the future? They won't know that you're the official owner unless he tells them, and the copy he would email them is indistinguishable from yours.

Perhaps you trust Scott to delete the image after he's sold it to you, or at least to not sell his copy again to a second buyer now that you're officially the owner. He's a Harvard Business School professor, after all, and it would be bad for his public reputation (not to mention likely illegal) to sell the same asset to multiple people while claiming he was selling it to each of them exclusively.

But if you resell it to somebody else, then they have to extend the same type of trust to you—and so on down the line. At minimum, this need for trust limits who can buy and sell from one another, and if the initial creator isn't well known, it might make it impossible for them to sell the image in the first place.

There's another solution, of course, which is to maintain a trusted record of who owns copies of the image. Note that this already transforms the idea of ownership somewhat—saying that you "own the image" in this context doesn't necessarily mean you're the only one who has a copy, but rather that an agreed-upon recordkeeping system says that you are in fact the owner.

That's what art galleries have done historically when selling digital artworks—establish a trusted record of who owns what. It's also essentially what happens in multiplayer internet video games, where the game's internal database keeps track of who owns which Roblox pet or Fortnite skin.

That pushes the trust problem onto the platform—you have to believe they're not going to enable some people to gain unfair advantages. It also limits how you can trade, and where—in Pokémon Go, for example, you can only engage in one-for-one trades of Pokémon with people nearby, and you have to conduct the trades inside their game environment. You can't trade Pokémon with someone halfway around the world, even if they have one you really want, unless you hack your GPS. And there's no way to trade Pokémon for something like Minecraft building materials, much less cash—at least not unless you trust your counterparty to send you the additional compensation off-platform as promised.

Even if you're not a gamer, it's likely you've run into a version of this problem in some other context. Most digital event tickets and gift cards, for example, have historically just taken the form of confirmation codes in emails—which means if you're buying one from someone else, you have to trust that they aren't selling a copy of that same email to five other people as well.

Selling digital goods seems like it should be easy, but precisely because of their digital nature, it's actually quite hard. We have to think about how to define ownership in the first place—and even once you've done that, you need a way to trust that ownership is transferred properly.

ISN'T THAT MORE OR LESS HOW WE SELL LAND?

Yes, in-deed! At least in the United States, when you buy a piece of land, you receive a piece of paper called a *deed* that declares you the owner. And the transfer is recorded in a centralized ledger called a register of deeds, so people can check who the owner is in case of a dispute.

But as anyone who has bought real estate knows, it's a megillah. There are a ton of complex documents and agreements to go through, and then you still need to secure a loan, get insurance, and sometimes have everything notarized. And even once you've done all of that, in rare circumstances it turns out that the original property right codified in the deed was messed up somehow, and there really are competing claims. That's why buyers are often required to purchase title insurance, which helps protect against that possibility.

"DIGITAL DEEDS"

An NFT serves as a sort of digital deed—a record of ownership that can be passed from one person to another. Often, we associate such records with other assets, just like we associate a physical deed with land or a car, or a marriage certificate with proof of nuptials. In that case, by convention (or sometimes by contract), holding the NFT represents ownership of the associated asset and whatever rights owners receive.

Why do that? First off, just like with deeds for land, using NFTs can simplify trading in an asset that is costly (or impossible) to move. A company called Midwest Tungsten Service sold an NFT representing ownership in a 14.545-inch tungsten cube weighing roughly 2,000 pounds. (The holder of the NFT has the right to touch the cube once per year, and/or "burn" the NFT—meaning it's deleted from existence forever—and have the cube delivered via freight truck.) And while this example is admittedly a bit wacky, it serves as proof of concept for using NFTs to manage ownership of physical property. In addition to tungsten, NFTs have been used to sell everything from fashion items to houses, and these sorts of applications will expand over time.

Moreover, and more powerfully, we can use NFTs to establish property rights over assets for which ownership would otherwise be difficult to certify, or even define—as with the case of digital art described above. NFTs do this easily and seamlessly.

Who owns the digital image we've pictured below?

It's whoever owns the associated NFT—and at time of this writing, that was actually Scott, according to the public record on the blockchain.

↑↓ **Item Activity**   ⌃

Event	Price	From	To	Date
⇄ Transfer		NFTBark	34202F	24d ago ↗
⇄ Transfer		MetaArtCollection	NFTBark	24d ago ↗
⛟ Sale	0.0754 ETH	MetaArtCollection	NFTBark	24d ago ↗
✦ Minted	0.0888 ETH	NullAddress	MetaArtCollection	10mo ago ↗

The NFT associated to this image was originally created by Gabe Weis, a noted digital and physical artist, as part of his collection called The Stoics. It was then sold to someone who goes by the pseudonym MetaArtCollection, who sold it to Steve (who goes by NFTBark), who sent it to Scott (whose digital wallet address is 34202F).

This all sounds completely intuitive until you remember that all of it is only happening digitally. If Gabe Weis had created a physical painting and sold it to MetaArtCollection, then it's natural that they could have later sold it to Steve, and he could have gifted it to Scott. But what does it mean when the underlying image is digital?

First, Gabe Weis created the image. Then it was associated to a digital ownership record—an NFT—through a process called *minting*. MetaArtCollection bought the NFT during the minting process, which means they sent money (in this case, the Ether cryptocurrency) to Weis, and Weis sent the NFT to MetaArtCollection's digital wallet.

Several months later, MetaArtCollection listed the NFT for sale on a public NFT exchange called OpenSea. Steve purchased the NFT from them—sending money in exchange for control of the NFT. And then, once Steve had control of the NFT, he passed it on to Scott.

NFTs eliminate the need for an art gallery or other intermediary to track this sequence of ownership and resale. Each transaction was secured cryptographically and recorded publicly. Anyone who wants to can look up who owns the token, and only the token holder has the ability to trade or sell it. Moreover, once such a transaction happens, ownership transfers immediately, and that, too, is recorded publicly (and when money is involved, it transfers at the same moment). And because both the NFT and the associated image exist as digital assets, it's especially easy to link them together. Such NFTs typically have direct connections between the NFT record on the blockchain and a copy of the associated image or other media stored somewhere else, usually on some public server. And moreover, as we'll discuss soon, because NFTs are embedded in software, it's often possible to give them functionality over and above just recording ownership.

NFTs have been used to sell some artworks at astronomical prices. XCOPY's "Right-click and Save As guy" and Dmitri Cherniak's "Ringers #109" each sold for over $7 million; and perhaps most famously, digital artist Beeple's "Everydays: The First 5000 Days" sold for $69 million.

But while we will certainly talk about NFTs that convey ownership over digital imagery and other media, this mostly isn't a book about the types of NFTs you'll find at Christie's and Sotheby's. Rather, it's about the types of NFTs that are already being owned and collected by ordinary consumers worldwide—and that you could create. We're talking about NFTs for event tickets, credentials like digital diplomas, and virtual goods in online games. NFTs are helping ensure that streetwear megafans get access to the latest apparel drops, and fostering online communities that never would have existed before. The multibillion-dollar consumer products, entertainment, and travel industries will change the way they manage ownership, product sales, and customer engagement because of this technology.

In short, NFTs will fundamentally shift the way we buy and sell . . . well . . . *everything.* And even some of the most straightforward NFT applications—such as creating digital souvenirs and collectibles—reflect tens if not hundreds of billions of dollars of value on their own. (The global collectibles industry had an estimated value on the order of $400 billion in 2022; ticket sales were estimated to be on the order of $80 billion by 2023.)

How can simple digital records be so powerful? It's because NFTs play a role in one of the most fundamental dynamics of society:

MAKING MARKETS

Markets can't exist without property rights. Conversely, when we gain a richer or easier-to-use way to create property rights, we can enable new types of markets. Once we start thinking about NFTs this way, applications jump out immediately—of course the now-ubiquitous use of NFTs in establishing property rights and creating markets for digital images and media, but also anything else that can be encoded as data.

Of course, there's nothing that says that people couldn't have created these types of markets in the past by building the right kinds of trusted intermediaries. But in general, they didn't—at least not at scale.

The reason all this activity is happening now is that NFTs make it so much easier. With NFTs, the trust in asset definition and transaction security that a buyer would typically have to give the intermediary is generally outsourced to publicly auditable, functionally immutable software, i.e., transaction-processing algorithms on a blockchain. And all the core infrastructure is standardized and ready to use out of the box—pretty much anyone can create NFTs, and once they do, those tokens will automatically fit in with a range of applications and platforms across the internet.

HOW CAN YOU *REALLY* CREATE INFALLIBLE DIGITAL OWNERSHIP?

Of course, for any of what we've just described to work, everyone has to be confident that the transactions are real and permanent. Steve wouldn't be willing to send money to MetaArtCollection—an anonymous stranger on the internet—unless he could be confident that once he got control of the Stoic NFT, MetaArtCollection couldn't somehow claw it back. Similarly, for MetaArtCollection to feel comfortable buying the NFT from Gabe Weis in the first place, they would have to be confident that it would not suddenly disappear or lose its association to the image. Again, this sort of assurance isn't too hard with physical goods because once someone has sold you a painting, they can't just walk into your house and take it back (at least not legally). But with digital assets, it's not quite that easy.

This is where blockchains come in. Blockchains are massive digital ledgers, the largest of which have already recorded billions or even trillions of transactions, as well as millions of associated software programs. They use cryptographic protocols to authenticate and securely record everything, and they're typically partially or fully decentralized in the sense that their records and activity are syndicated across many different computers run by a range of individuals and institutions. This means that like with the servers that propagate the internet, there's no one controller who can unilaterally distort the system's records or shut the whole thing down. Moreover, the computers that maintain the system are economically incentivized to keep everything running properly—and because of the way blockchain cryptography works, the older a record in the ledger is, the less likely it becomes that even a very targeted attack on the system could tamper with it.

Still, when presenting at the Innovation Summit of a Fortune 500 company, Steve was approached by one particularly skeptical business leader who asserted that everything is hackable, and thus it was hubris to claim that NFTs provide infallible digital ownership. We see where he's coming from; to the extent we've had meaningful digital ownership historically, it has often been pretty shaky, as the underlying software could just be reprogrammed or shut down at any given time. But that's one of the core reasons why NFTs—and blockchains—are revolutionary.

When something is put on the blockchain, it's given a *transaction hash*, which is a unique identifier that can be used to trace the item's origin. Each time that item moves, it gets a new transaction hash, which links the new owner to the previous one through the blockchain, so the item's history can be traced all the way back to its creation. But the real magic of the blockchain comes in *how* those items are moved digitally.

For an item to be transferred on the blockchain, it needs something called a *consensus*, which is a series of approvals from several individual computers that maintain the network. As an example, the top blockchain for NFTs at the time we were writing, Ethereum, had more than five hundred thousand validators run by individuals, corporations, and decentralized entities from around the world who approve the various transactions.

When a digital asset record is updated on the Ethereum network, it needs multiple approvals from randomly selected computers in that network of over five hundred thousand validators; by design, to control the overall blockchain, you would need to control more than two-thirds of them. One might surmise that a very wealthy person could still just take control of two-thirds of the world's validators for their own purposes. Setting the logistics of doing that aside (the entities maintaining the network would be unlikely to let it happen), at the time we were writing this, controlling just a single validator required locking up roughly $60,000, so the up-front cost to even have a chance at controlling over two-thirds of the network for one moment was

$20 billion.* And if the nefarious behavior were detected by the network, the bad actor could lose their privileges and their $60,000 per validator.

Indeed, so far, even with trillions of dollars of value having flowed through the Ethereum network, the system has held up without anything resembling a major hack on the underlying blockchain and its ledger records. (That's not to say that software *built on top of* Ethereum hasn't been hacked, however. But again, that's where improved software design will help crypto mature over time.)

As a result, at least with the major blockchains like Ethereum, people have come to rely on their digital ownership records as effectively immutable and infallible. It's similar to the way people in the United States tend to trust government records of who owns what land. It's not that nothing could ever possibly go wrong—all the registries of deeds could shut down, for example—but the system is stable enough for the vast majority of people to trust it for most purposes. The blockchain's reliability doesn't come from a centralized institution like the US government; rather, it's the result of a mixture of immutable software, decentralized control of the network, and incentive alignment among validators and users. That's a powerful formula, and it leads to systems that at least theoretically can run autonomously and sustain ownership even in the absence of stable institutions or legal enforcement.

---

*Technically, stopping a transaction from going through for a moment (instead of changing a transaction or ownership record) would require controlling only one-third of the validators—but that would still need a $10 billion investment!

What we've just described with blockchain-based ownership is very different from the way most classic software platforms manage ownership of digital goods. For example, the ledger of who owns which Kindle books is controlled centrally by Amazon; leaving aside risks from hackers, the company itself can unilaterally modify who owns what, and has done so in the past, as we'll discuss further in Chapter 5. To the extent that centralized platforms have obligations associated with the way they manage their ledgers, those are generally maintained through terms of service—which in practice means that users have to trust the platform, or else potentially go through complex and expensive legal processes if anything goes wrong. NFTs on blockchains replace this need for platform trust with decentralized, immutable source code.

Note that this doesn't mean that NFTs don't benefit from stable government and legal systems—to the contrary, having high-quality centralized institutions can supercharge what we can achieve with digital assets. But what's special about public, decentralized blockchains is that the ownership-record layer can be maintained without the need for third parties.

DIGITAL OWNERSHIP RECORDS ARE . . .
EVERYTHING

Because blockchains are computer networks, NFTs are fundamentally embedded in software. They can often be made programmable, and other software can be written around them. That means they can do far more than paper deeds can.

We'll say more about how this can be achieved later, but it's worth stopping for a second to reiterate this point: *While the specific problem NFTs solve is providing infallible proof of digital ownership, at their core, NFTs are software.* And just as we can build extensions on top of web browsers like Google Chrome to introduce new features, or use mods to add new items and world maps to video games like Minecraft, both creators and third parties can build on top of NFTs. This sort of composability has been the foundation of the internet and many of the most successful software movements in history—and NFTs generalize it to nearly every category of product.

As we mentioned earlier, an NFT that starts as just an ownership record for a digital image can later be programmed or adapted to also serve as an entry ticket for an exclusive event. It's unlikely that your house deed has ever gotten you into a private Madonna concert. But an NFT series called World of Women did just that for its holders.

3

The NFT Staircase

*O**kay, but what does all of that have to do with the expensive pri-*
mate picture brand?

This is another totally fair question, and honestly, we get it pretty often. Even once we understand how NFTs provide an objectively better software solution for digital proof of ownership, how does that connect back to the Bored Ape Yacht Club (BAYC) becoming a global phenomenon? Examining the secret sauce behind BAYC actually helps demonstrate many of the unique advantages of NFTs.

BAYC took off in mid-2021. After a year of Covid-19 precautions had kept many people isolated at home, people were spending more and more time on the internet—and the members of this unusual club came together in a remarkable display of online camaraderie. Although they were dispersed all over the world, they had a few things in common. They shared:

1. an interest in technology—they were, after all, incredibly early to the world of crypto and NFTs;

2. a curiosity about new markets and forms of intellectual property;

3. an affinity for the Ape images and a desire to see the Bored Ape Yacht Club grow to be something more than just pictures.

The BAYC founders fanned the flames, encouraging this group of online professionals to become, in many ways, a decentralized startup. They encouraged people to use their Bored Apes as their profile pictures on social media and to connect with others who had done the same. They then gave out community grants to start Bored Ape–themed businesses, funded real-world meetups to deepen connections, and featured particularly prominent BAYC NFT holders on their highly trafficked Twitter account.

The result was a club that even megacelebrities were soon lining up to join. Prominent Ape owners included pop music icon Madonna, basketball superstar Steph Curry, and comedian Jimmy Fallon. Yet other Apes were owned by everyday folks, or even undergraduate and high school students who had happened to buy early when the prices were relatively low.

And with celebrity engagement driving the brand into the public sphere (not to mention media coverage increasing awareness by asking versions of "What the heck are these Ape images about?"), the opportunity to leverage one's own Ape intellectual property became particularly valuable. That led to a wave of new Bored Ape businesses and IP licensing, putting the images on everything from burger wrappers and Old Navy T-shirts to canned water and high-end luggage.

Meanwhile, the Apes had headlined both Christie's and Sotheby's auctions, with one particular Ape image being resold for more than $3 million. Soon after that, another Ape appeared on the cover of *Rolling Stone*. By April 2022, the Apes were being featured in everything from late night TV to Adidas products, and the images themselves were selling for hundreds of thousands of dollars. Capping this off, in June 2022, rappers Snoop Dogg and Eminem performed a live premiere of a new music video featuring themselves as Bored Apes. You would ordinarily expect this to be at a marquee public event, yet this performance was in front of the crowd at ApeFest, a sold-out mega-party held at Pier 17 in Brooklyn that was open to Ape NFT owners and their close associates. And don't forget about that Yuga Labs capital raise—$450 million is nothing to sneeze at.

The story isn't just a fluke occurrence—it illustrates the *why* and *how* behind NFTs. By studying this example and many others, we've identified five core principles of successful NFT projects that apply across contexts and industries and put them together into a model we're calling *The NFT Staircase*. Here they are:

- **Ownership:** NFTs provide a verifiable and secure record of who owns what, typically complete with a full history of provenance.

- **Utility:** NFTs can also provide direct benefits to ownership, such as entry to a music festival or access to exclusive merchandise. This sort of use value creates a direct reason to want to own an NFT in the first place.

- **Identity:** NFTs offer functional utility, but people sometimes form connections with digital assets on a more personal level. They might display the image associated to an NFT on their social media feed, for example, or print it out and put it on their wall. Plus NFT ownership is often to some degree public by default—and so acquiring an NFT is frequently an act of affiliation with the brand that created it, just like wearing a branded T-shirt.

- **Community:** Once an NFT becomes part of one's identity, there is a natural opportunity for it to become something bigger. The resulting community is somewhat akin to a fandom: holders of a given NFT have shared goals and interests to connect over, just as Star Wars or New England Patriots fans always have something to talk about.*

- **Evolution:** An engaged community can then drive further utility creation and expansion in a way that builds upon the NFTs in a continual value loop, creating value for holders and the brand in tandem.

These five factors follow from one another: Identifying owners is necessary in order to provide them with utility. Then the better the utility, the more likely owners are to appreciate and engage with a given NFT, and the more likely they are to deeply integrate that NFT into their identity. The stronger the contribution of an NFT to someone's identity, the more likely they are to become an active participant

---

*Han shot first!

in the associated community. And then as an NFT owner starts to co-create with other enthusiasts, they in a sense become part of the NFT's brand—and help drive its evolution.

Of course, people might *acquire* NFTs for any one of these reasons individually, and/or in combinations thereof. You might buy an NFT because it gives you access to a particular event like a lecture or concert, but later display it as part of your digital identity on various social media platforms. Plus, because you literally own NFT assets, they can often function to some degree as investments—holding an NFT might give you a membership in a club with the potential option of reselling it down the line, just like you might with a physical collectible.

In short, as we explained in our *Harvard Business Review* article, "owning an NFT effectively makes you an investor, a member of a club, a brand shareholder, and a participant in a loyalty program all at once."

Some NFTs leverage only the ownership feature, making them more or less just digital deeds. Others simply pair ownership with a specific form of utility. And there's nothing wrong with that! But many NFT products have the opportunity to leverage the full feedback loop from ownership and utility to identity and community and beyond. And some NFTs do just that, in effect becoming digital brands anchored by their communities of holders. BAYC was a breakout success in the NFT market in large part because they accomplished this so successfully.

At a high level, the value of BAYC NFTs within our framework looks something like this:

- **Ownership:** This is table stakes, but all owners of a Bored Ape Yacht Club NFT have clear ownership of their magical internet monkey.*

- **Utility:** BAYC NFT holders have gotten access to limited-edition and exclusive merchandise; digital experiences like mobile gaming contests; and numerous free NFTs. More recently, BAYC holders have also been invited to high-end in-person events, including performances from musicians like Snoop Dogg, Future, Eminem, The Roots, Lil Wayne, and Beck, as well as comedic sets from top-tier talent like Aziz Ansari, Chris Rock, and Amy Schumer. These benefits, with values sometimes reaching into the tens of thousands of dollars, have come from both within and outside the BAYC ecosystem, and have been developed by Yuga Labs, BAYC holders, and third parties. And on top of that, BAYC owners are granted commercial rights to their Apes—so, for example, they can use them in business logos, license them to be used by toy companies, or have them star in a cartoon show.

- **Identity:** Through a combination of affinity for the BAYC art and seemingly continual utility rewarding ownership, many BAYC owners have come to strongly identify with their NFTs and broadcast them to the public. People shop for BAYC NFTs whose visual characteristics match their personalities, and may speak of having a "forever Ape"—the BAYC that is as dear to them as a family heirloom. Even megacelebrity Justin Bieber famously paid $1.3 million

---

*Yes, we know—apes technically aren't monkeys; they're a different type of primate.

in January 2022—way above market value at the time—for an Ape he personally identified with. Holders proudly set their Apes as their profile pictures on social media and wear BAYC-branded merchandise when traveling. Some have even gone further, feeling such a sense of attachment to the brand that they create their own clothing with their specific Apes on it. (Brazilian soccer player Neymar even had his Ape cast into a custom diamond chain!)

- **Community:** Identity attachment has led to and reinforced a strong BAYC holder community. It's a bit like rooting for a sports team: If you see someone wearing a hat of your favorite team, even if it's a complete stranger, you might have an instant affinity toward them. Seeing someone in Bored Ape Yacht Club merchandise is much the same—if anything, it's dialed up even more because in addition to loving the Club, there's a scarcity aspect as well. Only an elite few have access (and that access is very expensive), which has helped make the community even tighter-knit. It's hard to measure community engagement precisely—especially in a context like with the Bored Apes, where the total community size is capped at a relatively small number. But thousands of people attend BAYC events and use BAYC images in their social media profiles, and both of us personally know people who have found jobs and/or established major business deals through the network of Bored Ape NFT holders.

- **Evolution:** Unlike with most ordinary brands, BAYC's expansion has been heavily driven by its NFT holders' innovations and feedback—which has taken the brand in unexpected directions. As an example, the original company road map didn't have an in-person element. But after seeing holders spin up unofficial meetups across the world, BAYC first started funding these third-party events, and then worked with community members to develop its own. This sort of community-driven evolution plays a part in nearly everything BAYC does, from creating and managing its own cryptocurrency to use in the Bored Ape ecosystem to building a video game series around their intellectual property. And again, the community drives the brand, with BAYC holders building all manner of products, activities, and storytelling around their NFT assets. Each evolution creates new value for the BAYC NFTs and their holders, reinforcing the feedback loop.

The various forms of direct utility to BAYC owners provide a strong incentive to acquire the NFT, independent of the potential benefits in terms of personal identity or community membership. But then once you have the NFT and start internalizing the benefits, you might start to feel an affinity toward it—an affinity that might be supported by famous celebrities having acquired Apes. Similarly, gaining access to the community of holders can provide its own sources of value in ways that drive you to engage further, growing the value for everyone.

One might acquire a BAYC token just for the sake of being able to print the associated Ape image on T-shirts, for example. But then because you have the token, you go to ApeFest, where you pick up some limited-edition merchandise and make a couple of new friends. After heading home, you stay in touch with those friends by hanging out in the holders-only Discord chat room—and in some side-chat there, you meet a new sales contact for your T-shirt business. Now suddenly you realize the further value of being plugged into the community and become highly engaged—and so when new people "Ape in," you're the one who's welcoming *them*, and possibly turning out to be the business contact one of them needs.

In this way, all the different sources of value together feed back into the value of the NFTs themselves. The more valuable it is to be "a part of the Bored Ape Yacht Club," the more people want to own the NFTs. And because overall supply is constrained, this can also drive up the value of the NFTs in the market.

And the feedback doesn't stop there: In the case of the Bored Ape Yacht Club, token holders can sell their tokens whenever they want. This means that if the market price does go up, holders can potentially cash out that increase in value—if they want to—by selling their tokens to someone else.

With each one of those transactions, someone who values being a holder even more joins the community—with all the positive feedback that can create. And leading up to those transactions, the opportunity to internalize some of the overall increase in value provides a strong incentive to invest in growing the value of the community in the first place. It's just like how owning your house means you internalize the benefit of renovating your kitchen—you get the full use value for as long as you own the home, and then if you later sell, the sale price is higher because of all the improvements you put in. Plus, with most of sale transactions sending a percentage of royalties back to the parent company, unlike many other collectibles, the original BAYC creators benefit from a robust secondary market.

This is more than just monkey business—it's the core logic of a new value chain that NFTs are helping to enable, part of a new technology paradigm that people are calling *Web3*.

In the chapters ahead, we walk up the NFT Staircase, illustrating the power of an NFT strategy that leverages these different elements. We examine both real-world and stylized case studies illustrating the framework, and then explain how to apply NFTs in your business. But first, to more clearly understand the NFT value proposition, it's essential to provide a crash course in Web3 and show how it improves upon the technology eras that led up to it.

4

The Business of Web3

M ost people in the technology world think of the history of the internet in two phases.

Web 1 was the early internet. Widespread internet access arrived in the United States in the 1990s, expanding across the world in waves. Many people got their first email accounts and web browsers (AOL online CDs, anyone?). They started "surfing the web" in droves, checking out news websites and blogs. Eventually there were opportunities to participate in commerce—often first on businesses' individual websites, and then via aggregator platforms like Pricewatch, and then finally through marketplaces like Amazon and eBay.

Next came Web 2, the "social web." Social networks like Facebook, Twitter, Instagram, and Snapchat (and before them, the likes of AOL Instant Messenger and MySpace) made it possible for people to have two-way conversations over the internet—and, potentially, use these digital media to form deeper connections with one another. The social web changed how we viewed the internet entirely. It was no longer "read-only"—now suddenly everyone could "write" to share their thoughts, pictures, and life updates with the world.

By now many consumers understand and interact with both Web 1 and Web 2 on a daily basis. We get news updates in real time via Twitter, or daily on the *New York Times* home page. We post "Happy Birthday" on our friends' Facebook walls, search Google for all the things we need to know, and buy everything online from groceries to designer clothing. Even if today's companies providing these services were to crater (and they might—remember Yahoo! and Friendster?), new Web 1 and Web 2 companies would replace them and continue to be ingrained in our lives.

But now many forward-thinking entrepreneurs—including international tastemaker and musician Pharrell Williams, Reddit founder Alexis Ohanian, actress and philanthropist Reese Witherspoon, and Web 1/Web 2 powerhouse Gary Vaynerchuk—believe we've entered a third phase: Web3 (and they're so excited about that they removed the space between "Web" and the number). That's where NFTs fit in, and it's the stage we're focusing on in this book.

The idea of Web3 is that we can fundamentally disrupt the way business works by giving individuals a greater degree of ownership over their data and other digital assets. This gives people more control of their experience online, and at the same time it gives them a share of the pie—which incentivizes both users and platforms to invest in making the experience better for everyone. It's bringing consumers and their favorite brands closer than ever before in a way that creates more value for all involved.

Chris Dixon, the founder and managing partner of a16z crypto, explained it this way:

Centralized platforms [in Web 2] follow a predictable life cycle. At first, they do everything they can to recruit users and third-party complements like creators, developers, and businesses.

They do this to strengthen their network effect. As platforms move up the adoption S-curve, their power over users and third parties steadily grows.

When they hit the top of the S-curve, their relationships with network participants change from positive-sum to zero-sum. To continue growing requires extracting data from users and competing with (former) partners. [. . .]

In [W]eb3, [by contrast,] ownership and control is decentralized. Users and builders can own pieces of internet services by owning tokens [. . .]. Tokens give users property rights: the ability to own a piece of the internet. [. . .]

Tokens align network participants to work together toward a common goal—the growth of the network and the appreciation of the token.

This fixes the core problem of centralized networks, where the value is accumulated by one company, and the company ends up fighting its own users and partners.

Dixon highlights a degree of incentive alignment between companies and their consumers that we generally haven't seen in previous products or technology. In the Web3 model, consumers are incentivized to invest deeply in their engagement with the company and its products; conversely, the company has vastly more incentive to create value for the consumer.

Web3 creates this opportunity by in effect making individual consumers part owners of companies' overarching ecosystems—and NFTs are a core enabler of this activity. The symbiotic relationship becomes particularly noticeable when you break down where consumers have fit in each iteration of the internet.

THREE ERAS OF THE DIGITAL SELF

From the perspective of the individual, the three eras of the internet can be summarized as follows:

- **In Web 1, you're the *consumer*:** You travel across the web, ingesting information and participating in e-commerce.

- **In Web 2, you're the *product*:** It's well documented that most social media platforms and phone apps are free because they, at the very least, use your engagement to show you targeted advertising—and some of them even sell access to your information, as well. (As the old phrase goes, if you're not paying for the product, you probably *are* the product!) Even so, because social media is habit-forming, users generate the vast majority of the content for free.

- **In Web3, you're part of the *brand*:** This is the key distinction Web3 brings: Through digital ownership, individuals are simultaneously consumers, active participants, and, to some degree, owners and investors. The same digital assets you use to flex your enthusiasm for your favorite brands also give you a stake in their success (and give the brand a stake in *your* success), because when the brand does better, your brand assets and affiliation can increase in value.

There's a lot of obsession with financial activity and outcomes in the crypto space—possibly a consequence of the fact that the first blockchain application was a form of digital currency. So it's important to pause for a moment and clarify what we mean by "your brand assets and affiliation can increase in value." What people often think of first is resale opportunities, and indeed, that is one way in which this can happen—just like how when a major media franchise like Star Wars or Pokémon breaks out, early collectibles can appreciate in value significantly.

But the trading price is emphatically *not* the only way an NFT's value can increase. Oftentimes, value simply comes from the brand growing and being able to deliver more for its biggest supporters. A lifetime pass to Taylor Swift concerts might not have been that valuable when she was just starting out, but even if such a pass were nontransferable, many people would be very glad to have bought it back then!

Being "part of the brand" can be most valuable for consumers when they help shape the brand's evolution in ways that directly reinforce their engagement. For example, think how cool—and beneficial for everyone—it could be for a restaurant chain's most loyal customers to help design the next incarnation of its menu.

Meanwhile, as a business, it's pretty easy to see how advantageous it is to have your customers see themselves as part of your brand. Once you become part of someone's identity, they're much more likely to stick with your products through thick and thin, and to share their enthusiasm with others. As we'll see, NFTs take this to an all-new level.

The rise of Web3 has also tracked in parallel with conversations about the metaverse, and for the purposes of this book, it's worth explaining what that buzzword means. While many people associate the metaverse with NFTs and Web3, the concept has been around—both in theory and in practice—for decades. A *metaverse* is really just any virtual environment where people can interact with one another. This has manifested itself in games like Roblox and Minecraft and has shown up in pop culture in books and movies like *Snow Crash* and *Ready Player One*. And the metaverse doesn't even have to be 3D—Zoom calls, social media platforms, or even old-school instant messaging/chat rooms and multi-user dungeons (if you happen to be old enough to remember those) are all metaverse spaces, with different affordances and functionalities.

The metaverse has become more real both because we're spending more time in digital spaces (especially since the onset of the Covid-19 pandemic) and because the possibilities of what we can do in those spaces have expanded dramatically.

But the reason many people align the metaverse with Web3 is because digital space is greatly enhanced by the concept of digital ownership. We will discuss that more in the next chapter, but on the surface, it's intuitive to recognize that just like in physical spaces, owning something online gives someone more opportunities than if they are just leasing or borrowing it. Even for digital assets, having an item (a music file, an app, or even a virtual pet) that you fully control and can use anywhere on the internet is better than having that item locked inside of a single platform, especially when there's a threat that the platform could take it away at any given moment.

NFTS AND YOUR BUSINESS

At the time we started writing this book in late 2022, there were significant technological and cost barriers to participating in the world of Web3. But we don't anticipate that will last forever. Indeed, the rollout of any novel technology comes with these sorts of frictions—especially when it's a general-purpose technology that can be used in many different applications but must be adapted for each one.

A quick Google search (there's that Web 1 again) will turn up 1990s-era opinions from experts saying that the internet itself was a fad because it was hard to use and too expensive. Of course, time proved them wrong, and we think Web3 will only continue to expand from here as it becomes easier and more affordable to use. Moreover, as it stands today, many long-established companies are already using Web3 to build a new digital footprint, even though they already have Web 1- and 2-style websites, online stores, and social media feeds.

In the long run, NFTs may become so ubiquitous that we don't even think about them explicitly as "NFTs." You probably don't call your music files "MP3s" anymore, and we doubt you say, "Let me pull up my QR code so we can go into the baseball game." Most people just look at MP3s as "songs" or "music" now. And you talk about your "ticket" to a game; the QR code is just the technology that makes it work. As NFTs become embedded in applications (including digital tickets, incidentally!), it's likely that the term "NFT" will fade into the background in much the same way.* NFTs will just be an underlying core technology to empower consumers and businesses across industries and platforms.

We designed our framework with all of this in mind—to give a model a business can deploy at any time to drive a successful Web3 program, without necessarily having to think about the technical aspects of NFTs, and instead just focusing on how to make use of them. In the chapters ahead, we'll explain each step of the NFT Staircase and share strategic implementation considerations, accompanied throughout with examples of how the technology can be applied.

---

*Indeed, we're already starting to see that, with companies simply referring to NFT assets as *digital collectibles* or keys to *digital experiences*—with no mention of the underlying technology except buried in the documentation somewhere.

PART II

ASCENDING

THE

STAIRCASE

5

Establishing Ownership

Think about your points or status in your favorite loyalty programs, movies you purchased on Apple TV or Amazon Prime, or all the various "Pocket Monsters" you've caught in Pokémon Go. At least at the time of this writing, all of those digital goods existed only inside of the associated platforms. You couldn't take them with you if you wanted to move to a different platform or server. Moreover, if the hosting platforms went out of business, or even just changed their terms and conditions, all of those assets—and the time, effort, and money you had put into acquiring them—could disappear instantaneously. (This is often true even of digital goods we might think of as somewhat essential; for example, Scott for years couldn't get an electronic copy of his undergraduate course record because he lost access to the relevant web platform.)

NFTs aren't like that. They're actually yours.

What does that mean?

As we've already described, each NFT is a digital record, which can be linked to other digital assets like imagery, videos, or data; to physical assets like a car; or even to abstract assets like intellectual property.

When you hold an NFT, it resides in a software application that you control—often called a *wallet.** The key word here is *control*. This may not sound like a big shift; however, historically, digital goods have typically been controlled by the platforms on which they were created. Amazon provided a particularly ironic demonstration of this soon after launching its Kindle e-reader by clawing back unauthorized digital copies of George Orwell's famous novel *1984*.

Owning a physical asset typically comes with the right to use whatever features it has, as well as the ability to bring it with you as you move from place to place. Digital ownership with NFTs is the same way—you have direct access to the asset, can bring it with you to any platform, and can use it however you want within the constraints of its design.

If you own a skateboard, you can take it to the skatepark, use it at home, or just skate down the street. In the same manner, if you own a digital cat in Petaverse (an NFT company started by 2K Games founder Susan Cummings), you can bring your cat with you throughout the metaverse. And with the integration of augmented reality, you

---

*To avoid confusion with physical wallets, we'll refer to these digital asset wallets as "digital wallets" throughout the text; people also often call them "crypto wallets." Fun fact, though: Scott's very first Harvard Business School case study was about how to sell *physical* wallets on the internet.

actually can import your digital cat into the physical world as well. Compare this to the over eighty million Tamagotchi holders whose digital pets lived inside their keychains, or even the over twenty million Nintendog owners whose pets were confined to the Nintendo DS. Petaverse cats are cross-platform and can take on new functionality as the technologies and opportunities for interacting with them expand.

Some people manage their own digital wallets directly; this is kind of like storing a photo of your partner or children in the physical wallet you carry around in your pocket. Other digital wallets are managed by third parties. Those are more like online banking applications: They hold your assets for you, but they take your instructions on what to do with them, and you can generally withdraw your assets and move them elsewhere.* In either case, you're the *owner* of the asset in the sense that you can determine how and where it is stored and used.

So, owning an NFT is about controlling it. In that sense, while NFTs are a new technology, their concept of ownership isn't really any different from the way we've owned physical property for millennia. But in the digital world, NFTs entail a big shift in power and control from the platform to the user.

---

*Yes, many banks are closed on weekends; and yes, you can't necessarily withdraw when everyone else is trying to withdraw at the same time; and yes, these are things people point out when arguing in favor of crypto as financial technology. But no, this is not what we're focused on here. In the sense of ownership, holding digital assets in a digital wallet is more akin to holding money in a bank than it is to having your data on a Web 2 platform.

CREATING AND OWNING DIGITAL GOODS

For the purpose of market design, we're mostly not just interested in owning abstract digital tokens, but rather other assets associated with them—those Ape images, perhaps, or copies of songs, or tickets that get you into a Broadway show. This is the same sense in which you're interested in owning the house itself, rather than just the piece of paper with the deed printed on it.

NFTs can be associated to such assets in a variety of ways. Some are connected directly through source code—an indelible link that's part of the NFT itself. Others, like with property deeds, are managed through institutions and contracts. That's how most NFTs for physical property currently work, like for that tungsten cube we mentioned. Similarly, the intellectual property rights associated with Bored Apes and various other NFTs are managed through terms of service (although nowadays sometimes even those terms of service are encoded on the blockchain in order to make them both easy to reference and immutable). Still other NFTs are just linked to assets by social convention—i.e., a bunch of people have agreed together that a given NFT represents ownership. Whatever the mechanism, ownership of the NFT extends to the associated assets. If you own an NFT associated to a digital media file, for example, you can carry that file with you from platform to platform, so long as the platforms can parse and interpret the NFT.

Can I sell it?

Sometimes! Ownership also often grants the right to transfer or sell an asset to someone else. When you own a house, computer chair, or a trumpet, you can sell it—and the same is true of many NFTs, especially those for digital goods like imagery or music files.

Other assets, such as your education, aren't actually transferable. (Even if you give your diploma to someone else, all the knowledge you've built up about mathematics, marketing, or the Mesozoic era stays with you.)

In the same way, some NFTs may grant ownership over a record of an accomplishment, a charitable donation, or other activity that's personally attached to you. You possess the record and can control its use, but there is no way to transfer it to someone else—and in this case, nontransferability is enforced through software rules. These tokens are programmatically coded to ensure you cannot sell them or even transfer them elsewhere—and as a result, they are sometimes referred to as *soul-bound* tokens. (It's an intuitive name for them, because you can't transfer your soul to someone else.*) We will discuss these different types of NFTs further in later chapters, but first, let's think through some key distinctions from past digital goods technologies.

---

*Unless you're Bart Simpson in season 7, episode 4 of *The Simpsons* (and thankfully his sister Lisa bought it back for him).

DIGITAL GOODS IN WEB 2 VS. WEB3

Part of illustrating why NFT technology matters is understanding how it improves upon existing products we use all the time. You might already get a daily dose of community through your favorite social networks, in which case you could be thinking, *Who needs NFTs? I can follow what's going on with my favorite athletes and celebrities on social media!* But these platforms lack the sense of personal ownership and investment that Web3 provides.

Top Web 2 companies like Meta, the tech conglomerate that owns Facebook and Instagram, are *extremely* profitable—and not only do they *not* give their users ownership over platform assets, but they do what they can to take ownership of all the content that users create. In turn, they use that content, data, and the engagement it generates to drive revenue, commonly through targeted advertising. (Meta made $113 billion in advertising revenue in 2022.)

So why give away even a sliver of ownership when you could keep everything for yourself?

Think about the internet platforms people use every day. It's likely that you use an email program like Gmail or Outlook and that you're one of the three billion people who have a Facebook account. You might use these services tens or even hundreds of times a day. But do you identify as a card-carrying Gmail or Facebook user? Most likely not.

Most people aren't personally invested in these platforms because at a fundamental level, you're a renter. You use them because you have to—for example, to communicate with people and keep up to date on

what's going on in the world. But at any given moment, product features or terms of service can change in ways you really dislike, and
there's not much you can do about it.

Web3 changes that by giving people personal ownership over their
data and other digital assets—and sometimes even a direct stake in
the platform's governance or output. This better aligns platforms' and
users' incentives, and moreover gives users the ability to vote with
their feet. In Web3, if you're mistreated by a platform, or even just
prefer a competing platform's features, you can move your digital assets over. (Compared to the locked-in experience of Web 2 platforms,
that degree of frictionlessness can be hard to imagine—but in Web3,
it's true. To use any given NFT trading platform, for example, you just
log in with your digital wallet, and the NFTs you hold are populated
and available for trading immediately.)

But again, why share ownership in this way? The bet in Web3 is
that when users become personally invested in the success of a platform, they'll engage in ways that make the long-term value greater
for everyone. This isn't a new concept; similar reasoning explains why
some companies give employees an equity stake, for example. The
Web3 model extends this idea to include consumers: platforms and
brands share ownership with consumers in order to incentivize them
to engage in ways that help grow the overall pie—for example, contributing ideas, creating content, or recruiting other users. Meanwhile, when the platform's incentives are more closely aligned with
the users', those users might actually be more willing to join in the
first place.

THE INCENTIVE EFFECT

That's all fine to say in theory, but especially for digital images like primate pictures (versus important personal soul-bound documents), it might still seem like *ownership* is just a semantic distinction. Why would you care if you *own* a picture or not? Sure, maybe you can sell it to someone, but who's actually going to want to *buy* it from you when they can just download their own copy?

Ownership of an NFT—in the form of control—entitles holders to the utility aspects we're going to discuss in the next chapter. If you download an image of a Bored Ape, then sure, you can show it to people. But if you aren't the real owner—i.e., the token holder—then you don't get invited to ApeFest to see top-tier artists perform. (And this is enforced by leveraging the digital token itself as an access pass.) To this end, downloading a picture of a Bored Ape and claiming you own it is no different from Steve downloading a picture of the famous basketball player Shaquille O'Neal, making it his profile picture on Instagram and Twitter, and claiming to be Shaq. Steve could do it, but once it comes time to claim the functional benefits of being Shaq, such as endorsement deals or entry to high-end Miami nightclubs, Steve would be out of luck.* Authorities could check Steve's identification, or simply use their eyes, and realize pretty quickly that he's not a 7'1" NBA Hall-of-Famer.

Our friend Adam Hollander, a serial entrepreneur and cofounder of multiple NFT projects, breaks down this intuition as follows:

---

*Although as a side note, if anyone *does* want to give Steve endorsement deals or VIP nightclub access, he's totally up for that!

Imagine walking into a museum and you see a beautiful piece of art on the wall. You could take a picture of that painting, but it wouldn't be worth very much. You could go to the gift shop and buy a print of it, but again, it wouldn't hold anywhere close to the original's value. The reason that the painting that's up on the wall is worth what it is, is because it's the original—and you can prove that it's the original. Now, with digital assets, whether that be a photo, an image, a video, a music file—up until recently—it's been very difficult to discern the original compared to the copy. That's because when you copy a digital file, the copy is identical to the original. But an NFT allows you to prove ownership of a digital asset, and that has major implications for a variety of markets.

Moreover, codifying ownership is powerful because of the incentives it creates: As we mentioned earlier, if you own your house, then not only do you enjoy any improvements you make while you're living there, but you also get to collect whatever share of that value remains when you sell. That means you might be far more willing to invest in putting in a new, updated kitchen (perhaps with a large, elephant-sized refrigerator) than if you were only renting, where the value of the kitchen would mostly accrue to the landlord.

When "you're the brand" as in Web3, you don't just own your digital dongle—you own a piece of the brand that made it. The owner of a Bored Ape NFT doesn't just own the image and the rights that come with it; they have a stake in the BAYC. (To be clear, owning an NFT doesn't give you equity in the company that created it—but you are still very much invested in the success of the brand in a unique way.)

That means you're incentivized to cheer the brand on—and when possible, help build it up. That's what's going on with members of the Bored Ape community when they launch Bored Ape–themed restaurants or make music videos featuring their pricey primates. Once people have a true stake in a brand, they will "update the kitchen," so to speak, if given the opportunity. Likewise, the fact that you own the education you've received—your *human capital*, in economese—is essential for incentivizing you to acquire that education in the first place.

What do those opportunities look like in practice? Let's work through a couple of example case studies—or "Staircase studies," if you will.*

OWNING YOUR LOYALTY

Some of the top loyalty programs in the world belong to companies in the travel industry. Hotels and airlines reward consistent usage with disproportionate benefits, seeking to make their customers fully invested in their ecosystem, rather than their competitors'. These programs share a simple model: You use hotel and airline services as you gallivant around the world, receive rewards via a points system, and can redeem those points for free flights and stays. Accruing points levels you up to a higher-status tier (silver, diamond, opalized ammonite, etc.), which includes better perks along the way. As a result, if you're anchored in the Marriott rewards program, for example,

---

*Okay, that's a truly terrible pun. Thanks for bearing with us—we promise not to repeat it in all the upcoming chapters.

you probably do your best to stay at hotels in the Marriott family when you travel.* Both of these industries could enhance their loyalty programs with Web3, creating more passionate customers and new streams of income.

In a Web3 world, instead of having one's membership on file with the company, a consumer can own it. Imagine all the status and reward points you've built up residing in your personal digital wallet, which you can leverage directly across a range of service platforms. This would unlock opportunities for benefits outside the travel industry. For example, restaurants might start offering discounts for high-status members, in hopes of attracting business from well-heeled travelers. That's a feature some restaurants might already want to implement, but there's generally too much friction in verifying status for them to do so.

We might moreover dream that status itself could become freely transferable to other users or points programs, although realistically the hotels and airlines probably wouldn't allow that.† But they already allow people to gift or exchange reward points—and moving that activity to a public blockchain would greatly expand the types of exchanges that would be possible. An ordinary merchant could decide to start accepting airline miles in exchange for service without having to interact with the airline at all. And while this would mean the airlines would have less control of how, precisely, miles might be used, it would

---

*Did you know that Marriott apparently has a semisecret top loyalty level named after the twenty-seventh element in the periodic table, cobalt?

†Your Web3 airline status would be soul-bound. Neat.

also provide many new opportunities to their consumers, which at least in principle could drive more demand.

Furthermore, most travel and leisure companies have a credit card that gets you miles or points within their reward system. They could apply this same approach to people who hold certain NFTs. By giving Bored Ape or fine art NFT owners a leg up in their ecosystem, travel brands can attract high-net worth customers. Or, in a more cunning execution, they could try to poach competitors' loyal customers by offering special benefits to holders of those competitors' NFTs—a novel version of the competitive strategy that already exists called *status match*. Imagine if you were the top tier in Marriott, and Hilton could directly offer you the right to transfer your status over to them!

In our experience, brands often have some trepidation about the potential Web3 creates for these sorts of competitive customer-recruitment tactics—colloquially referred to as *vampire attacks* because of the way in which they try to suck away one's loyal customers.[*] And it's true that making loyalty status transparent and easily transferable may lead to increased competition. (Scott has written multiple academic papers about that.)

But these same forces create a significant opportunity, as well. As we discuss further in Chapter 7, in Web3, network effects accrue to digital assets. This means that third-party rewards can reinforce an NFT's value even when those rewards are provided by competitors.

---

[*] While we're not aware of vampire attacks having happened in the context of Web3 loyalty programs—at least as of 2023—they have occurred with some frequency in other Web3 industries.

When Forum3, the agency consulting on Starbucks's NFT-based loyalty program, spoke in Scott's Harvard Business School class in January 2023, one student asked whether it was a problem that Dunkin' Donuts could potentially offer coupons to people holding Starbucks NFTs. The Forum3 team responded that in their view, this could actually increase the value of the Starbucks NFTs—and hence, the value of engaging in the Starbucks ecosystem—because Dunkin' would in effect be providing utility to members of Starbucks's loyalty program.

And we could of course extend this to other types of perks and rewards: An airline could spin up a digital shop with generic pricing on items like free flights, drink tickets, and passes to the airline lounge. In this example, Steve might use his miles to buy a day's lounge access; upon redeeming this benefit, the airline could drop an NFT in his digital wallet, giving him the ability to use the token to access a lounge or transfer it to someone else. (They could even, in principle, allow the token to be sold and take a royalty on secondary transactions.)

This type of ownership in loyalty, empowered by NFTs, can be higher-value for both the company and the consumer.

BLOWING UP THE TRADITIONAL FASHION BRAND MODEL

A well-known streetwear brand called The Hundreds sold a series of NFTs based on their mascot, the Adam Bomb. Holding one of these Adam Bomb Squad NFTs was at first mostly about having a way to represent your enthusiasm for The Hundreds in digital spaces and to connect with like-minded people online and at holders-only events. (Holders also got early access to product releases, so they never missed out on getting the newest hoodies.)

Then one day, The Hundreds went further. Writing on its official blog, The Hundreds explained that they were using the NFTs to experiment with slightly decentralizing the brand itself: they had decided that even though the Adam Bombs represented in the NFTs were intellectual property The Hundreds had created, the brand would in effect license Adam Bombs back from holders when it used their images in a new clothing collection.

Thanks to NFT ownership, they explained, "For the first time in our 18-year-history as a fashion label, our Community has a stake in the notoriety and well-being of our most recognizable design and mascot, Adam Bomb." When specific Adam Bomb images "pulled directly" from the NFTs were used in its winter seasonal line, the company would offer the associated holders a "typical license fee," paid in the form of store credit. This move made sense, in their view, because of the actions and efforts holders were taking to promote the brand by sharing and engaging around their NFTs. Indeed, they explained to holders, "your possession and promotion of those NFTs directly contributed to the success of [the associated clothing] pieces."

The Hundreds followed up by entrusting further aspects of the brand identity to NFT holders. For example, some holders created their own custom "Bombs" in the Adam Bomb Squad style and released associated NFTs as a reward for top Adam Bomb Squad NFT collectors—and all of this activity was recognized and encouraged by the brand's cofounder and chief creative officer, Bobby Hundreds.

These were early experiments—and even at the time, The Hundreds expected they weren't perfect, and would require significant iteration en route to a stable and sustainable model.*

Nevertheless, the community was elated. While the holders of these NFTs were fans of The Hundreds beforehand, this ingrained them within the very fabric of the brand (pun intended). They shared their excitement all over social media (and most likely many of them bought more The Hundreds products). These people weren't doing that because they were paid to—they were promoting the brand because they were truly a part of it.

And while you may not be familiar with The Hundreds, you've likely heard of luxury fashion brands like Louis Vuitton and multinational apparel brands like Adidas, both of whom have made conceptually similar moves with their entries into the high-end NFT market, as we discuss in later chapters.

WHY DOES THIS NEED CRYPTO?

A question we get all the time is "Why do you need NFTs to do this?" Our friends and colleagues often appreciate the value of giving fans of a brand like The Hundreds a stake, but suggest that the better way to do this is just for The Hundreds to maintain a rewards program or other centralized database where it records who the most enthusiastic

---

*The post that made the Bomb-licensing announcement noted, "This could be the first and last time we try this, depending on feedback from the Community. But, it's a START, and we're excited to progress as the technology, logistics, and legalities of Web3 advance."

customers are, and then give those customers early product access, discounts, and such on whatever schedule they want. The company could even potentially make those reward points transferable to other people, just like airlines do with flight miles.

To be clear, a model like that is much closer to what we're advocating than the way most brands work today—which is great!

But like we've already described, there's a big difference for users between a ledger entry on a centralized platform controlled by the brand and a digital asset that's stored on a blockchain and held in your digital wallet: control. With a physical good, it's virtually automatic that the person who owns the good gets to control its function. But blockchains are the only technology we know of that enables that same sort of user control and synchrony of assets across digital space. (Plus blockchains also enable digital goods' creators to commit to those goods having specific features and functionalities by embedding them in source code that can't be changed.)

After Amazon pulled Kindle copies of *1984*, a customer interviewed by *The New York Times* remarked, "It illustrates how few rights you have when you buy an e-book from Amazon. [. . .] I can't lend people books and I can't sell books that I've already read, and now it turns out that I can't even count on still having my books tomorrow." Another customer—a student—lost all of his summer reading annotations because he had made them on the digital copy.

By contrast, as the *Times* put it, "Retailers of physical goods cannot, of course, force their way into a customer's home to take back a purchase, no matter how bootlegged it turns out to be."

Utility features of NFTs—like whether they do in fact guarantee special product access—are platform-provided services and may be subject to change. But on a blockchain, ownership of the underlying NFT asset isn't. Just like Amazon can't claw back a physical book, The Hundreds can't recall or erase holders' Adam Bomb Squad NFTs. And it can't stop people from giving or lending them to others.

In addition to changing the direct incentives around investing in an asset and brand, the degree of control NFTs provide gives holders a greater sense of psychological ownership. Research shows that people are more likely to form attachments to things they feel like they actually own and control. The sense of ownership people get from NFTs is both psychological and functional, and these build on and reinforce each other. And that again feeds back into holders' willingness to invest time and energy into the brand.

Scott wrote with Jad Esber, the founder of koodos labs (not to mention a former student and frequent co-author of Scott's), about how "one's [digital] wallet [can] function as a sort of profile, similar to Facebook or LinkedIn. But unlike [Web 2] profiles, decentralized identities are backed by hard evidence: a permanent, timestamped record of a person's accomplishments, contributions, interests, and activities to date." Furthermore, a digital wallet is a single, unified identity—there isn't cross-platform siloing like there is in Web 2, where, for example, one's LinkedIn identity and reputation are fundamentally separate from Facebook. Thus Web3 has the potential to enable people "to carry their full selves with them as they traverse cyberspace: their affinities and experiences reflected by what they've created, contributed to, earned, and owned online, no matter the specific platform."

Indeed, one of the simplest yet surprisingly valuable applications of NFTs is to use them to record and memorialize events and experiences. In this context, NFTs become like digital badges or stickers—they signify "I was here" or "I did this." People collect them in their digital wallets in scrapbook-like logs, and can both review them for their own reference and share them with others.

At the time of this writing, the leading way to do this was through the Proof of Attendance Protocol (POAP), which provides a lightweight way to create these digital stickers and give them out for free. Both of us have collected plenty of them—Scott's first was a souvenir from a fireside chat with activist music group Pussy Riot; Steve's was from a mindfulness event.* And we've distributed them, too—for purposes ranging from commemorating lectures or attendance at live radio shows, to creating scavenger hunt items for people to collect at a conference. People also use them a bit like digital business cards—NFT artist Bryan Brinkman gives them out when he meets people, and quite appropriately, so does POAP's founder, Patricio Worthalter.†

And, most crucially, POAPs don't have to just serve as mementos! Digital diplomas are themselves a type of POAP, and similar NFTs are already being used as rewards for various activities such as winning a trivia night, meeting a celebrity, or participating in community service—which means they are becoming part of people's online reputation.

Again, NFTs are critical here—this time because of their ease of

---

*Scott and Steve are not sure what the contrast here reveals about them.

†These two examples were respectively suggested to us by penn and 0xBryant, two Writers Room NFT holders, through a community crowdsourcing activity on the platform Avenue.

portability and verifiability. Digital badges for attending events existed for at least a decade prior, but they never caught on. Why? First off, there was no standardized way to collect them—they existed in siloed platforms, or sometimes just as images in email. This meant it was difficult to keep track of one's collection; moreover, if you wanted to show off a badge, you had to figure out a way to port it across platforms, which required nontrivial effort and often disconnected the badge from explanatory text or links.

Verifiability of digital ownership matters here as well—before badges could be manifested as NFTs, there wasn't really any way to be sure whether a badge being displayed as an uploaded image was "real," which meant there was much less incentive to acquire the real thing in the first place. What good is a digital badge saying you climbed Mount Washington if anyone else can just copy the image and make the same claim? But if the proof comes in the form of a nontransferable NFT that you get when you actually reach the top, then anyone you show it to will know you really made it there.*

The blockchain is borderless

And while we'll mostly focus on the business implications of Web3 in this book, it's worth noting that provably owned digital assets also have significant societal functions at scale. When people are fleeing a

---

*This is a bit of an extreme example, but you get the idea. And yes, there is the possibility that people might hire other people to climb Mount Washington and collect the POAP for them. But luckily we already thought of that, and the guy who hands out the Mount Washington Summit POAP checks ID.

country due to fear or unrest, they pack whatever they can—money, belongings, and so forth—and leave as quickly as possible.

When you enter a new country, the contents of your digital wallet come along with you. And that means that with digital ownership, things like money, academic degrees, and work accreditations can travel with a refugee anywhere. It's like digital assets exist everywhere and nowhere all at once, empowering you to bring them with you seamlessly anywhere in the digital and physical world. And this isn't just a theoretical possibility: we have friends who fled Ukraine in March 2022 at the outset of the Russian invasion and brought their crypto assets with them.

The blockchain is forever

Blockchain-based assets are stored on a server architecture that transcends any individual company. NFTs typically don't live inside of a specific platform, or even in a specific server room—they're usually stored on massive decentralized computer networks that operate independently of the software platforms that create them. And while those networks aren't completely immune to destruction, they're designed to be much more robust than any individual company.*

This means that NFTs can quite literally outlast their creators. If you receive an NFT of a collectible, game asset, or diploma, the NFT

---

*In approximately five billion years, the sun is going to turn into a red giant, at which point it may envelop the Earth; if/when that happens, all blockchains are probably toast unless humans have already moved to some other galaxy or developed some pretty incredible fire shielding. But that's a while from now.

still exists even if the creator, developer studio, or university that made it shuts down.

That's much more like our experience with physical assets—if your university goes bankrupt, your paper diploma doesn't spontaneously combust. And it's very different from most of our digital experience of the 2000s and 2010s: If your favorite fitness tracker goes out of business, for example, you're likely to lose all your workout, sleep, and health data because it's stored on a centralized server. (This happened, for example, when Under Armour ditched its fitness tracker and the associated app.) Similarly, if Epic Games, the company that makes Fortnite, were to go bankrupt, you'd lose all the skins, gliders, and emotes you've purchased in the game. (And don't even get us started about digital articles disappearing when an online media platform shuts down—Scott is still trying to locate copies of some articles from the 1990s and early 2000s.)

The blockchain is interoperable

Equally crucially, most NFTs are designed to *interoperate*, which means they can be used with many different platforms—rather than just the one that created them. If you buy a bunch of physical trading cards, you can trade them for other types of cards, or even other assets like cool sunglasses or a xylophone. You can make up your own games with them and teach your friends. And if you want to sell them, you can typically do that in any store. All of this can happen without the creator's *knowledge*, much less their permission.

Most NFTs work the same way. They can be used flexibly across platforms—you can use an NFT you own to display an associated image on Twitter and in a virtual gallery, and if you wanted to, someone could even develop a video game based around it.* All of this can happen without permission—unlike with Web 2 digital assets, which tend to be heavily restricted by platform policies and APIs.

THE DIGITAL AND THE PHYSICAL

Digital ownership isn't just about digital goods! NFTs can provide a powerful way to record and exchange ownership of physical assets, as well. That tungsten cube we mentioned earlier was a one-off, but the same concept applies in many more standard product categories.

Companies have started issuing so-called *physical-backed NFTs*—digital assets that can be redeemed for physical merchandise. This technology gives people a claim on a physical product, which can be held or exchanged digitally, enabling people to gift or resell the associated products without the need for back-and-forth shipping.

This can make sense for primary-market product sales—and indeed, brands like Puma, Tiffany's, and Azuki have sold these sorts of NFTs. But it's an especially powerful technology for product cate-

---

*An important caveat is that while an NFT gives the owner control, the NFT's creator can still moderate use to some degree through terms of service. For example: controlling a digital asset may make it possible to develop a game around it, but in order to distribute or sell that game, you would still need to be granted the appropriate license. (This, too, is the same as with trading cards—the manufacturer can't stop an individual from making up a game using the cards at home, but might still block attempts to commercialize it.)

gories with highly active resale markets and/or complex storage requirements.

For example, the collectibles-resale platform StockX noticed that many of their customers were buying high-end sneakers and other collectibles on the platform, holding them for a while, and then later reselling them again. But that involved a lot of costly steps—numerous shipping charges and having to authenticate the sneakers twice, not to mention the risk associated with the buyer having to store the sneakers safely in the interim. So the platform simplified the problem by issuing a series of NFTs matched to specific collectibles, which it authenticated and held in a climate-controlled vault. Instead of trading the physical assets back and forth, buyers could trade the NFTs; if a holder actually wanted to take possession, all they had to do was turn in the NFT, pay shipping costs and a small processing fee, and StockX would mail them the physical good. Companies like BAXUS and Block-Bar introduced a similar service for fine liquor, and Courtyard.io has done the same for trading cards.

And while the physical-backed NFT applications we've seen thus far are mostly in various collectibles markets, there are many other contexts where having digitally verifiable, tradable property claims could be useful. You can imagine, for example, building a business like this around NFTs for parking spaces.

Meanwhile, leveraging a different type of linkage between digital and physical assets, an NFT brand called Pudgy Penguins recently created a series of physical toys that come with associated NFTs. When someone buys one of the toys, they can scan an associated QR code that gives them access to digital assets and other opportunities in the brand's online platform, Pudgy World. As the company's CEO, Luca Netz, explained, these additional functionalities meant that "[y]ou get more out of your $20 Pudgy Penguin than you do the toy next to it"—both because of the digital assets' use value, and because they are able to be resold, which might sometimes make it possible to earn back a portion of the initial purchase cost. These sorts of product activations—sometimes called *phygital*—expand the surface area of a physical product experience to include the digital world, and vice versa. And there are companies creating solutions to help any product firm do this at scale—IYK, for example, makes digital chips that can link pretty much any product to an associated NFT. With this design, a physical asset can have a digital "twin" that's bound to it. For example, a physical book can be attached to an NFT copy that's accessible to whoever scans an IYK chip embedded in the book's spine; if the physical book is transferred to a new owner, they can scan the chip to take ownership of the ebook as well.

THE DEED TO OUR DIGITAL FUTURE

One of the themes you've likely picked up on in this section, and you'll see throughout as we ascend the NFT Staircase, is that NFTs and blockchain technology have the potential to both transform existing markets and create completely novel forms of interaction and experience.

Like the Industrial Revolution or the advent of the internet, NFTs and Web3 have the power to improve our everyday lives in ways we can't even imagine yet. In the case of ownership, they provide new ways to grant provable possession, offer a new type of data portability, and lead to powerful incentives.

All of this would be impressive—and quite valuable—if it were the only use of the NFT technology. But actually, it's just the beginning.

6

Enhancing Ownership with Utility

When you ascend the NFT Staircase from ownership to utility, the real magic starts to happen. While provable ownership is what defines an NFT, functional features that bring tangible value are often what give people a reason to want to own the token in the first place.

Of course, you may simply want to own Beeple's "Everydays" or a digital trading card of your favorite athlete, no further utility required. But for the purposes of this book, and most businesses, we're focusing on forms of utility beyond the claim to ownership as a driver of NFT value. In fact, we would argue that pretty much any NFT—yes, even just a token associated to an image—can add utility to help move its way up the NFT Staircase. While some industries require a bit more creativity, oftentimes it's easy to think of ways to build in value. It can be as simple as a holder rewards program or as complex as a multifaceted governance and profit-sharing model, but there's almost always a way to use NFTs to engage customers in a meaningful way and keep them in your business's ecosystem.

In many of the instances of utility we describe in this chapter, it's theoretically possible to grant users similar benefits through some cocktail of current technologies. However, NFTs provide a simpler and more seamless solution.

It's akin to how we used to be able to listen to our favorite music with CDs and cassette tapes, but the advent of digital music marketplaces, and then streaming services, made music easier to access and the associated markets easier to create and manage. Likewise, it's in principle possible to use old technology to at least try to give a special gift of appreciation to everyone who has purchased a given product, but this would require, for example, hoping the customer opens and responds to a survey email (an average email open rate is 10% to 15%), ensuring that customers aren't gaming the system with multiple accounts, and authenticating each free gift code individually. With NFTs, pretty much all of those intermediate steps are unnecessary—the company can simply use NFT ownership records to identify who has purchased the product in the first place and send the reward directly to those users' digital wallets.

NFTs can similarly uplevel many other complex marketing, CRM, and customer engagement activities. They can help businesses better reward their most loyal customers; provide access to online and real-world experiences; cut down on scammers and people who look for loopholes; and much, much more.

EVERYTHING CAN BE UTILITY,
AND UTILITY CAN BE *EVERYTHING*

Utility is any functional benefit that comes from owning a given NFT. Abstracting and oversimplifying tremendously, utility means:

- NFTs can do things themselves;

- they can enable you to do things; and/or

- they can give you things.

Moreover, at least with NFTs on public blockchains, these sorts of benefits can come from many different sources: An NFT's creator can develop and provide them, but so can third parties—and holders themselves.

Utility might be as simple as the opportunity to buy exclusive merchandise, or as complex as multilayered IP licensing rights. And while some utility is digital or conceptual, it is also increasingly becoming physical. Think back to the NFT that gives holders the right to touch a giant tungsten cube once a year—although admittedly, we might be stretching the definition of "functional" a bit in that case.

As of this writing, NFTs often offered benefits in a few recurring categories:

- *experiences,* such as admission to exclusive concerts featuring legendary artists (Bored Ape Yacht Club) and high-end conferences with top-tier speakers and media personalities (VeeFriends);

- *opportunities*, such as the chance to vote on the allocation of charitable donations (OnChainMonkey), influence characters and key plot points in a Neil Strauss novel (Jenkins the Valet), and even receive special access to driving tracks (Porsche);

- *intellectual property*, such as the right to use NFT imagery in one's own commercial ventures and to license them for use in everything from pinball machines to feature films (Bored Ape Yacht Club, Azuki, and SupDucks), and use various audio samples in one's own music compositions (Arpeggi);

- *discounts*, such as free or reduced-rate access to paywalled media (Knights of Degen), or across-the-board price reductions on company products (Bugatti Group);

- *digital goods*, such as add-on NFTs to wear in the metaverse (Adidas), and avatars to use in online games (The Sandbox);

- *physical goods*, such as the chance to acquire exclusive apparel (Nike/RTFKT and Tiffany & Co.), figurines (the littles, Thingdoms), and tumblers (Starbucks).

All of these are real benefits. People might attribute different degrees of value to them, of course—not everyone wants more T-shirts (much less ones they can only wear in the metaverse), or cares what happens in Neil Strauss's books. But each of these benefits turns the associated NFT into more than just ownership of a specific digital asset. And any such feature is a new potential source of purpose and demand for the NFT itself—especially when it's well mapped to the NFT's existing audience and holder community.

Default versus additive utility

When it comes to direct and singular functional utility from using a given digital asset, NFTs aren't that different from other types of assets. Lawn mowers, for example, have *default utility*: You can use them to mow your lawn (and that's a big part of the value of owning a lawn mower!*).

Additive utility builds *on top of* core assets, and NFTs have a special advantage because they make it easy to identify and verify who owns them. To give free mulch to anyone who owns a John Deere lawn mower, one would have to verify ownership through a cumbersome process—most likely by examining purchase records (and who knows, maybe the owner misfiled the original receipt, or threw it out). By contrast, if every John Deere lawn mower had an NFT associated with it, the machinery monolith—or any other company for that matter—could reward those owners with a bag of mulch whenever they wanted. (Technically, they'd be rewarding those customers with an NFT that can be redeemed for a bag of mulch. But the key point is that the company can send these rewards directly and know that the right people are receiving them.)

This example illustrates a core concept that drives home a way in which NFTs are a fundamentally better software for businesses. They allow companies to create additive utility for their customers in ways

---

*Unless you're one of those rare people who collects antique or vintage lawn mowers. (Seriously, this is a thing. There are a number of them on display at Picton Castle Gardens in Wales, for example.)

that previously weren't possible, or at least were prohibitively cumbersome to execute. Just as NFTs make it easier to deliver a bag of mulch to John Deere customers, they can make it easier for Trek to offer a helmet to owners of their bicycles or for a football team to offer discounted apparel to people who attended their games. And NFTs can also make it easy for third parties to provide this sort of utility—for example, a restaurant can give discounts to holders of a game ticket NFT, as we discuss later in this section.

As we'll highlight in the following examples, often it's additive utilities that give NFTs the greatest power in terms of ongoing engagement and brand-building.

Airdrops

One particularly common mechanism used to deliver NFT utility is what's referred to colloquially as an *airdrop*, in which new NFTs or other assets are delivered to the holders of a given NFT through a process kind of like email or direct deposit. By looking at blockchain records, it's possible to see who (or rather, which account) owns a given NFT, and send them something additional.

(There's also a lighter-weight version where instead of direct-depositing the new digital asset, you give holders the right to claim it through a software process the user themselves have to trigger. For all intents and purposes, that's the same—except that using a claim system selects for the holders who are paying attention to what's going on.)

While the concept of an airdrop (or claim) is simple enough, there are highly varied applications, providing businesses with an opportunity to bring different types of value to people who hold their NFTs.

Perhaps the easiest approach is to airdrop more NFTs, or possibly fungible tokens like cryptocurrency. Holders of Goblintown NFTs might receive a virtual car for their digital goblins to ride around in. People who buy NFT avatars for use in digital games often receive airdrops of items, entry tickets to special contests or competitions, or in-game currency. But also a digital sports card brand might airdrop a new season's LeBron James cards to everyone who held LeBron cards the entire previous season. Likewise, one might airdrop coupons or even a catalog. There are also opportunities for digital-physical integration here: In one particularly creative example, Web3 streetwear brand Endstate released a shoe NFT in partnership with Philadelphia Eagles wide receiver DeVonta Smith and then airdropped coupons for a free cheesesteak every time Smith made a play longer than 41 yards.

It's easy to imagine how a megabrand like Ralph Lauren or Old Navy might airdrop a limited-edition digital shirt to their fans for the holidays, or a token that can be redeemed for a special physical item. And NFTs make targeting such promotions simple, because you can find exactly who your current supporters are by indexing all the digital wallets that hold your NFTs.

Plus, NFTs don't just serve to identify your top supporters. They can also help make these sorts of perks more meaningful by keeping non-holders *out*, which helps minimize potential gaming of the system. If Old Navy just spontaneously announced that they were giving out free T-shirts to their long-time customers, you'd presumably see a lot of people lining up to declare how "old" their "Navy" fandom is (or even worse, if the giveaway were online, the same people would probably fill out the web form hundreds if not thousands of times).* With NFTs, by contrast, Old Navy can say, "You're only eligible for the free T-shirt if you have at least one of our rewards program NFTs in your digital wallet and have held it for at least six months."

Could Old Navy potentially implement this sort of system through its own purchasing records? Sure! But using a blockchain means that Old Navy doesn't have to build any of the infrastructure itself. Plus, NFTs introduce the completely novel possibility that some other company could directly gift rewards to Old Navy aficionados.

Access

The NFTs you hold in your digital wallet can impact where you can go and what you can see by way of a mechanism referred to as *token-gating*. In essence, the digital assets you own can provide you with entry to exclusive areas or activities, both online and offline. It's a lot like with the online newspaper paywalls, or supporters-only areas on platforms like Patreon. Except here, instead of creating an account with the platform and signing up for a subscription, your NFT unlocks entry just like a key unlocks a door.

---

*Qdoba once gave out free burrito coupons to anyone who played a menu exploration game on their website (technically, it was a free burrito with purchase of a roughly $1.00 drink). Scott sheepishly admits that back when he was in grad school, he and one of his friends played through the game so many times that they were eating at Qdoba multiple times per day for the better part of a month.

Private members-only messaging servers provide NFT holders from around the world a place to meet, chat, and sometimes even launch businesses together. Gated websites give select NFT holders access to ebooks, games, and shops. NFTs can even be used to provide access to real-world goods and events.

In 2021, Shopify introduced a feature that lets its sellers make items available only to holders of a given NFT. As of May 2023, Ticketmaster is experimenting with token-gated sales, allowing holders of a specific performer's NFTs to receive special ticket access ahead of the public. This sort of mechanism helps get products into the hands of dedicated fans, rather than rolling the dice on a first-come-first-served mechanic.

IP rights

Some NFTs grant their holders intellectual property rights to associated images or other media assets. This means that in addition to being able to display the images, NFT holders can potentially profit from their use. Someone can start a business with NFT imagery as the logo, license it into a book or television show, or create and sell clothing based around it. People have done all of this already: For example, Steve uses his Bored Ape as his business logo, and members of a niche NFT community called The Alien Boy have sold whiskey and hot sauce with their Aliens' commercial rights. (We discuss further examples of third-party products based on NFT holder IP in Chapter 8.)

Rewards

Sometimes, you can receive utility almost passively by simply holding an NFT and choosing not to sell it.* For example, Moonbirds, an NFT brand created by entrepreneur Kevin Rose, introduced a mechanism called *nesting* whereby owners of their digital owl NFTs would receive escalating rewards based on how long they "stayed in the nest." At various predetermined time frames, Moonbird holders received bronze, silver, gold, and diamond nest rewards ranging from digital art to physical merchandise. (Although admittedly an extreme case, some of the people who participated received artwork that later sold for thousands of dollars on the secondary market.) It doesn't take much dot-connecting to realize how this sort of model can correlate to more standard brand loyalty programs. (More on that in Chapter 10.)

Stacking utility

The different types of utility we've described are neither exhaustive nor mutually exclusive—and often the greatest value is achieved by mixing and matching them. While there's current technology that implements each of these examples of utility individually, NFTs combine all of them. A single NFT can grant special token-gated access, provide a source of rewards, and be monetized for associated IP rights.

---

*This process is sometimes referred to as *staking* the NFT, and often requires an explicit action such as locking transfer of the NFT for a certain period of time.

And because the token is portable anywhere online, NFTs provide an elegant user experience which simply requires connecting one's digital wallet to a website.

VERIFIED MEMBER BENEFITS

It's important to note that while utility is often introduced by an NFT's original creator, it can also be provided by third parties. (This ties in with the ideas of NFT community and evolution that we're going to discuss in later chapters.) And again, this isn't completely novel to NFTs: Lots of museums offer discounted access to holders of certain credit cards, and some restaurants near where Scott lives offer freebies to people wearing Boston Celtics attire whenever the team wins a major championship. That's third-party utility for Celtics merchandise!*

When it comes to third-party utility, NFTs are especially powerful. Businesses can assess the culture of an NFT holder base—and if it aligns with their target market, they can likely get qualified customers at a higher rate than other marketing efforts. It's a concept we're calling *verified member benefits*, and it's something the blockchain is uniquely well equipped to do. An NFT owner can connect their digital wallet to a company's site, and that company can provide utility without even necessarily getting permission from the creator of the NFT.

For example, the utility of holding a Knights of Degen NFT comes in the form of benefits centered around sports, entertainment, and

---

*Steve, who is a die-hard Cleveland Cavaliers fan, insists on asking: Is it really utility if it requires the Celtics to win a championship? Go Cavs!

gambling, which means the NFT collection attracts holders who fit that profile. In 2022, each Knights of Degen NFT holder was given the opportunity to claim a free one-year membership to Action Network, a paywalled sports betting resource that provides expert picks and other gambling content. Given the interest profile of Knights of Degen holders, they're natural targets for the Action Network product—and there's a high likelihood in particular that the people who claim the free membership may convert into long-term subscribers. Thus the integration provides a form of functional value to the NFT holder, and also drives value to Action Network by giving them an opportunity to attract and potentially retain or even upsell the NFT's holders.

The example highlights a key distinction between giving discounts for wearing Boston sports gear versus giving discounts for holding specific NFTs. A Boston-based brewery might want to provide discounts to big-time Celtics fans—but, like with our Old Navy example, how can it verify whether someone is really a serious fan, much less locate all of the serious fans to make them aware of the offer?

If Celtics season tickets were associated to NFTs, then the brewery could just airdrop coupons to holders—guaranteeing that only true fans receive the benefits. Or if targeting season-ticket holders is too narrow, they could instead airdrop coupons to anyone who holds at least a certain number of NFTs commemorating game attendance. (This isn't too far-fetched because the Celtics have already experimented with NFTs, with a limited-edition Heritage Collection released in June 2021.)

Verified member benefits have widespread business implications, especially as people come to own more NFTs that reveal information about their product preferences and personal identity.

Hot Pockets, for example, has numerous gaming sponsorships because their core demographic contains a lot of gamers. It could appeal to that demographic further by adding a plug-in on its site to give discounts or other benefits to any person who holds a particular gaming NFT. This eliminates friction like needing to show proof of purchase of the game. Instead, the person with the NFT could just connect their digital wallet, enjoy the benefits, and immediately have a positive interaction with Hot Pockets. Meanwhile, Hot Pockets wins because they can market to consumers in a cheaper, more efficient, and more targeted way than with traditional advertising—it's very likely that someone who owns a gaming NFT actually plays the game (and thus is part of the target audience), whereas someone who fits a set of demographic characteristics associated with gamers might not play video games at all.

This is the same dynamic that made targeted advertising through platforms like Facebook so effective in the 2010s. Relative to traditional TV or newspaper ads, these platforms had more granular user data, which led to more targeted and efficient ads. NFTs have a big leg up here, though: They allow brands to bypass the platform intermediary. With NFTs, Hot Pockets can give targeted benefits through its own website, rather than through hit-or-miss social media ads. Moreover, whereas an intermediary like Facebook often had to infer who the Hot Pockets fans were through a mixture of data aggregation and machine learning–driven sleuthing, with NFTs, customers are in effect self-identifying as brand enthusiasts (more on that in the next chapter).

Plus, NFTs incentivize owners to spread the word. If an owner of a Pirate Nation game NFT gets free Hot Pockets, they'll likely brag about it. This helps Pirate Nation of course, and it helps Hot Pockets as well, because they can lower their advertising spending, knowing that unofficial ambassadors will share the information to help out their fellow snack-loving gamers. In addition to the social currency of sharing information with their friends, the more an NFT holder talks about these benefits publicly, the more desirable their NFT becomes for others. This increases value, once again highlighting the new incentive model within Web3. Consumers are no longer just customers; they now can share in the success of their favorite NFT companies. Hot Pockets, the NFT game companies they partner with, and the NFT holders all stand to gain from these sorts of interactions.

While the Hot Pockets example just described is a one-off promotion, it doesn't have to stop there. Indeed, verified member benefits can also be used to build ongoing incentive programs, potentially spanning verticals. When Steve worked at the insurance company Progressive, one of his employee perks was access to a special check-in line at the local airport. But this required him to present his Progressive employee badge, which was easy to forget to bring when traveling. In informal discussions with his co-workers, Steve learned he wasn't alone in this gaffe; many of his work friends would tell tales of traveling for a vacation, forgetting about the perk till they got to the airport, and ending up in the longer line. And this wasn't just an issue at the airport—plenty of local restaurants and businesses gave Progressive employee discounts, but who carries their company badge on nights and weekends? In a world with employee badges recorded as NFTs, this all becomes as easy as connecting your digital wallet to an app—much like using Apple Pay.

And while membership benefits have existed for as long as there have been clubs, NFTs mean that they can be executed far more efficiently and intuitively, with more micro-level mixing and matching than ever before. You can imagine a CrossFit gym giving discounts to anyone who holds another fitness-related NFT, and a further discount if they also hold an NFT showing that they bought a ticket to the CrossFit Games.* Alternatively, Marriott Hotels might offer a free room upgrade to everyone who has Delta or United status NFTs. Piggybacking might even be as simple as creating a special chat channel or event for holders of specific third-party NFT projects.

All of this leverages existing digital assets—NFTs that are already in people's digital wallets. As a business, you can take advantage of these opportunities in both ways, seeing the value of your NFTs increase as other companies offer perks to your NFT holders and providing benefits to holders of other NFTs that fit your ideal customer.

NFTICKETS

As we already talked about, a particularly natural form of utility for NFTs is gating access to events or experiences. This means that NFTs can quite literally function as entry tickets. And conversely, implementing tickets through NFTs can solve a major market-design problem.

Think about the last time you bought a ticket to a concert, movie, or museum. When you bought your ticket, you might've received a

---

*CrossFit is a franchise, so an individual CrossFit gym wouldn't necessarily have easy access to records of who attended the Games.

slip of paper that someone tore in half when you entered the venue—but these days it's likely that what you got was a barcode or other digital reference that somebody scanned.

Those digital references aren't particularly special—you probably wouldn't post a boring-looking email confirmation on your wall. But there's a deeper problem, which has to do with uniqueness: When a ticket is just a barcode, what's to stop someone from sharing it with many different people?

Okay, sure, maybe they scan the barcode at the entrance to the Usher concert, and if it's already been used then an usher will usher you out the door. But that doesn't change the fact that multiple people can hold the ticket and, potentially, think they are the unique owner.

This creates a big problem for secondary-market ticket sales. If you're buying a digital ticket from a reseller, you have to trust that they haven't sold the same ticket to five other people when only one of you can actually get into the venue.

Ticketmaster and other retailers have made a significant effort to build a more secure secondary ticket market through their platforms. Yet people are still scammed through online ticket sales every day—roughly eleven million per year, according to a CNBC study. One reason for this is that the more secure options typically charge higher fees, so people go to peer-to-peer marketplaces, which carry higher risk.

Let's think through how NFTs can address these issues in the secondary ticket market, and even build in more value through the use of the blockchain.

Remember, part of the purpose of NFTs is that it's possible to infallibly verify the history of ownership, from the original owner to the current one. Additionally, because each NFTicket is a unique item (you know . . . non-fungible) there is only one digital, verifiable copy of each ticket that was issued.

This means that when an NFTicket is resold, the buyer can be confident they're buying the only copy. Meanwhile, the software managing the NFTicket can potentially be configured to share secondary sales revenue with the artist and/or venue. These two features together mean that the secondary market can become a core part of the business model around tickets—rather than something artists and venues have to try to shut down.

On top of that, because NFTs make tickets once again unique and persistent assets, they can be kept as mementos, or even resold as memorabilia after the fact. By issuing tickets as NFTs, performers and presenters can potentially share a bit of the long-term value of used tickets being sold to collectors through transaction royalties.

NFTs can also make ticket purchasing a more consumer-friendly process, as we've already hinted. As of May 2023, multiple companies were testing out NFT-based ticket sales, including Ticketmaster, mentioned earlier, and Web3 native YellowHeart. These systems enable true fans to purchase tickets at face value, stress-free, before they go to the public market. And because it's an NFT that gates the drop, if NFT owners decide they're not a fan anymore, they can simply sell the NFT to someone else who wants special access.

This model has applications across industries that deal with high-demand products, such as limited-edition apparel. Adidas, for example, implemented this mechanic successfully with a special drop on their Indigo Herz apparel series—the brand partnered with Web3 startup tokenproof to verify that the people who bought the exclusive Herz items were holders of Adidas NFTs. Instead of a rush to buy the apparel, holders of the required NFT were able to purchase the items over a multiday period, with the tokenproof technology plugging seamlessly into the Adidas app. The NFT became the ticket for true fans to buy the items.

Moreover, NFTs make it possible to add additional utility to tickets. Since we've made a close analogy between NFT holders and sports fans, let's keep running down that field.

If someone buys season tickets for an NFL team, they often get special perks like preseason meet-and-greets with the players. However, in the current model, if you can't make the meet-and-greet, you're simply out of luck. In an NFT world, teams could airdrop a special meet-and-greet ticket NFT into your digital wallet. If you can't attend, you could sell it or transfer it to a friend. The team could even use verifiable randomization tactics, all transparent on the blockchain, to add special benefits to tickets before a game. Imagine a world where you had a ticket in the upper deck for a football game and suddenly it had an added perk of field access, or the opportunity to redeem a game-worn jersey. You now would have the choice to sell that ticket to someone who wants it more or attend the game and get those benefits. It's the first two steps of the NFT Staircase—ownership and utility—come to life.

And that's not all—with people and teams engaging with one another more directly through ticket NFTs, it wouldn't be surprising to see ticket holders begin to have a stronger overall affinity toward the team. Digital tickets wouldn't be something you just use and forget about; rather, they'd become a way to build ongoing and lasting connection—with real, tangible benefits beyond just attending the games. And that might make people more likely to talk about the team on social media, rebuy tickets in future seasons, and, over time, build and reinforce their identity as fans. (Again, more on that in the next chapter!) Similarly, imagine if Lin-Manuel Miranda airdropped a free ticket to his next show to anyone holding *Hamilton* tickets from multiple cities—or if comedian Nate Bargatze opened up a special section of his website that could only be accessed by past ticket holders.

In the Web 2 digital ticketing model, a ticket is just data in an email, and once you use it, its utility is complete. Yet tickets to concerts, sporting events, and commemorations—the physical versions of tickets, that is—have long been collectibles, and there are even established collector communities. And of course, ticket holders and collectors tend to be fans. NFTs bring emotional significance and collectability to digital tickets—and they create the potential for so much more.

NFTs enable artists and teams to transform tickets into the foundations of a digital brand.

But wait, you may be thinking, *wasn't that possible to do before*? Well, let's think through how it might work. Platforms like Ticketmaster have contact information for all of their ticket purchasers, but they're unlikely to share it with artists directly—both to protect customers' privacy and to protect their own position as a platform. Thus, if an artist wants to deliver rewards or other benefits to ticket holders, they have to work through the intermediary platform, which both adds friction and limits the set of potential offerings they can provide. And don't forget, as we touched on earlier, many tickets are resold on the secondary market—the platform doesn't necessarily have records of those sales, and artists don't want to be giving a bunch of rewards to scalpers.

In short, while digital brand-building around tickets may be plausible in Web 2, it isn't particularly efficient or effective. And indeed, we haven't seen much of it in practice. But Web3 makes it easy.

MULTI-THREADED SUBSCRIPTIONS

A few years ago, Scott was working with a platform called NewsBreak to try and better understand the dynamics of local news businesses and readership. And you probably won't be surprised to learn that many newspaper editors he talked with said that one of their top subscriber draws was access to news on local sports.

But these editors also pointed out a funny problem: For pretty much every local sports team, roughly half the games were away, which meant that half their news was in *other newspapers*. Die-hard fans wanted access to this content, of course, but there wasn't really a way to give it to them.

The different papers ran on their own independent web platforms, which were often homegrown. There was no clear way for the *Tampa Bay Times* to let *The Atlanta Journal-Constitution* know that a given person was a subscriber, much less a way for the *Journal-Constitution* to then give that person access to just the article about the Buccaneers versus Falcons game. And even if they could create the proper access structure, it's not clear who would pay for it, and how—would it just be a reciprocity agreement? Or would *The Atlanta Journal-Constitution* have to somehow tally the number of *Tampa Bay Times* subscribers who showed up and bill the *Times* something like five cents per reader?

Plus, remember all of this would have to happen across many different sites at once—the Buccaneers only play the Falcons twice per season; meanwhile, they also play the Saints and Panthers twice per year, which are covered by *The Times-Picayune* and *The Charlotte Observer*, respectively.

The upshot is that Buccaneers fans don't get to know how their opponents cover their team's games. That's a loss especially because many fans want as much content on their teams as they can get their hands on, and sharing access to that content across papers would create value without requiring more effort from staff. This would also benefit the reporters and publications themselves by putting their work in front of readers who might not otherwise visit their websites. Sadly, in the Web 2 platform model it's generally difficult to build cross-platform linkages, so the information ends up siloed behind different paywalls.

Web3 changes all of that: Imagine if a *Tampa Bay Times* subscription were an NFT, and to get past a paywall, holders just had to connect their digital wallets to verify ownership of a subscription. In this world, a third-party website like *The Atlanta Journal-Constitution* doesn't have to be able to interface with the *Tampa Bay Times*'s own database to check whether a given person is a subscriber; they just have to be able to recognize and interpret a *Tampa Bay Times* subscription NFT when someone shows up with one in their digital wallet, and unlock Buccaneers articles for the holder of any such NFT. From a practical perspective, this is much easier (in particular, it doesn't require coordinating with the *Times* at all), especially if all the newspapers agree on a technology standard for how a subscription NFT should be encoded. Micropayments could potentially be embedded as well. The full user flow would then be that a *Tampa Bay Times* subscriber visits *The Atlanta Journal-Constitution* site and connects their digital wallet; the *Journal-Constitution* recognizes the presence of a *Tampa Bay Times* subscription NFT and unlocks content on Tampa Bay–area sports teams; and each time the user reads one of those articles, a software process triggers an automatic micropayment from the *Times* to the *Journal-Constitution*.*

Of course, this approach doesn't just work for local news and sports teams. You could build multi-threaded subscriptions for pretty much any topic of interest—maybe subscribing to *Science* also gets you access to all the microbiology articles in various other journals. Or imagine if you could buy an all-access pass to Star Wars news across newspapers and magazines worldwide. It's possible that these sorts of customized content products would be so valuable to many buyers relative to subscriptions to individual publications that they would raise total readership and revenue overall.

And of course, with people building deeply personalized internet content flows that better reflect their interests and identity, there are opportunities for communities to form around the associated digital assets—but we're getting ahead of ourselves.

---

*In practice, the micropayments might be batched, rather than issued in real time with each article read.

HOW EVERYONE WINS

Utility works best when it reinforces existing consumer and/or community dynamics. Most local news readers like to follow their local sports teams, so adding access to cross-platform team news is a natural form of utility for a local news subscription NFT. Same with The Hundreds offering their NFT holders early access to product releases and exclusive access to the company founders, since fans of The Hundreds love the brand's products, and love the founders even more. In this way, NFT utility becomes a way to foster repeat high-quality interactions that grow the value of participating in the brand.

NFTs enable all the different stakeholders—creators, fans, and even adjacent third parties—to win together. Let's look at NFTickets again as an example: Teams and artists can leverage those NFTs to engage with their fans, and to connect those fans with one another. And as we mentioned before, even third parties like the local restaurants can leverage that same opportunity—for example, by dropping discount coupons to ticket holders when the home team wins the game. Crucially, this creates value for everyone—even the firms that produce the NFTickets benefit from secondary engagement, since it adds value to the tickets themselves.

And all of this comes together to turn the NFTs into far more than just digital ownership records. And importantly, it reinforces the value and experience of owning the NFT for holders.

7

Building and Reinforcing Identity

B y now, we've seen that NFTs are digital assets you can own and make use of. But the value NFTs can create goes even deeper. *NFTs enable uniquely strong affinities and can strengthen people's connections to the things they already love.*

Owning an NFT is a performative act. Especially to the extent that who owns what is visible on a blockchain, as well as in NFT holders' various profiles across the web—more on that in a moment— acquiring a given NFT is to some degree an expression of connection or affiliation. If you own NFTs from Nike, Adidas, and Puma, your digital footprint is signaling that you're a sneakerhead. If you buy a Porsche NFT for $1,000, you're emphatically declaring, "I am a serious Porsche enthusiast." In this sense, each NFT you own becomes one of the many facets of your identity, at least in digital space. It's like the way you might personally identify with a favorite hoodie, music album, or childhood stuffed animal.

If you're a company or creator, you want people to feel that way about your products. In this chapter, we'll discuss why NFTs are by nature ideal for fostering this sort of devoted brand loyalty, and what that means for businesses.

DIGITALLY IDENTIFYING WITH A BRAND

United Airlines wants its customers to think of themselves as people who "fly United"—both because it hopefully means they'll keep buying flights from United instead of from competitors, and because it enhances the experiential value they get from what might otherwise feel like being crammed in a giant metal box. Or speaking of big metal boxes, how about all those people who are personally proud to drive a Jeep (or not even just any Jeep—a Wrangler)? That sense of brand attachment is a powerful force for consumer value creation and retention. But it has to come from somewhere.

With products, someone's much more likely to attach their identity to something they own, or at least have locus of control over. Think back to our discussion about why ownership matters in Chapter 2. Just like with building a new kitchen, it's often easier—or at least less risky—to become attached to a house that's yours than to one you're renting, where a landlord could always decide not to renew your lease. And conversely, identity feeds into a desire for ownership: fans of sports teams, for example, often collect associated apparel, posters, and other memorabilia.

NFTs enable the same ownership–identity loop in digital space.

Plus, they have the potential to speedrun the identity formation step because simply owning an NFT is an act of affiliation with the brand. And utility reinforces these connections because the more value you get from something—and especially, the more frequently and deeply you engage with it—the more likely you are to become personally attached to it and whatever it represents.

It's not an accident that many early NFT successes weren't just about selling random digital assets, but specifically digital assets we might think of as *virtual fashion*: funky profile pictures, rare patterning on digital racehorses (equestrian fashion at its finest), virtual backpacks, and the like. Fashion has always been part of how people express their personal identity, and NFTs made it possible to seamlessly bring that self-expression online.

But of course, a person's identity isn't just about fashion—most people have a range of products and franchises they love, organizations they're affiliated with, and causes they care about. We've already argued that owning an NFT can be a digitally souped-up equivalent of owning a hat or T-shirt repping your favorite team. Likewise, we're already seeing everything from luxury car brands (Lamborghini, Porsche) to nonprofits (Saisei Foundation, Disabled American Veterans) leveraging NFTs for brand-building among their supporters and enthusiasts.

And more broadly, this source of value for NFTs extends to anything one might want to be part of their digital identity—academic and employment credentials, for example, or even personal data like health records (with the appropriate privacy controls in place).

But to really understand why and how NFTs are going to be transformative for digital identity, we have to zigzag for a moment and look at what previous solutions were lacking.

IDENTITY IN WEB 2 VERSUS WEB3

If you're online today, you probably have plenty of profiles, pages, and feeds. You might have a LinkedIn profile you use professionally, as well as Facebook, Instagram, Snapchat, or whatever else is trendy these days for sharing updates with your friends.*

And what you post on those platforms reflects your identity in different ways. You might describe your education and work history on LinkedIn, and share photos of your weekend activities on Instagram. And that's not the only way we store identity information online—Amazon and other online shopping sites are full of our product preferences and past addresses; online newspapers and blogs, meanwhile, are probably recording or inferring our reading preferences.

But you know what? Users don't really "own" that identity information. Web 2 platforms have much more control than users do. Content users add or create often ceases to be "theirs," and might be changed or eliminated (or used by the platform) without notice. Even privacy settings might adjust suddenly, surfacing information to a wider audience than intended. Moreover, users often can't cross-connect their

---

*We're afraid to even conjecture at what the social media app *du jour* is here because we figure that reference will become totally outdated in minutes.

information across the different sites, much less take it with them if they want to switch platforms entirely. That means the different facets of their online identity are trapped in separate places.

Jad Esber, founder of koodos labs, describes Web 2 platforms as letting you create a wall with your favorite photos, posters, or whatnot, but requiring you to leave that wall behind when you go elsewhere on the internet (or God forbid, shut down your account). It's as if you were leasing a room somewhere and were forced to leave your decorations and other possessions behind whenever you move out.

Conceptually, such a setup is baffling: Given that digital goods don't have any weight and are mostly in standardized file formats, shouldn't you be able to take them with you? If you want to show the same image on Twitter and Instagram, why should you have to upload it twice? And for that matter, why should you have to enter your preferred clothing sizes and color preferences into each online shopping site separately?

To be fair, there are technical challenges inherent in making information easily interoperable across platforms. But mostly, it's about incentives.

Web 2 platforms work hard to lock in users and their content in large part because of the incentives built into their business models. As we noted in Chapter 4, these platforms leverage network effects to gather information they use to target products and sell ad space—and the more data they have relative to others, the more that reinforces their competitive advantage in the market. As a result, a small handful of companies own most of the Web 2 iteration of the internet, and they silo their ecosystems because their business incentivizes them to do so. And while that's good for those platforms, it's bad for our digital selves.

Users can't bring their full identities with them from platform to platform. This means we have to create and populate many different profiles. Moreover, to the extent that parts of our digital identities are aspects of our platform-specific reputation—accolades like badges, likes, and upvotes—there's often no way to move that information at all, which leaves our digital selves siloed and disjoined. Scott has plenty of business school professor colleagues who are "Twitter-famous" but effectively unknown on LinkedIn, or vice versa. Even from a raw economic perspective that's inefficient—presumably, if lots of people on Twitter want to hear what you have to say about consumer marketing, then people on LinkedIn will want to hear about it, too. But there's no way to share content and reputation across the two platforms, and it's time-consuming and difficult to build up an audience on both.

But all of that's changing. As we've already discussed, Web3 introduces a new design paradigm under which users have a central repository of digital assets—their digital wallet—which they can connect to whichever platforms they want. And moreover, the underlying blockchain architecture is interoperable by design, with standardized architecture and file formats that make it easy for different platforms to read and work with the same data.

Esber extends his photo-wall metaphor by explaining that while in Web 2 everyone has to leave their photos and other information behind when they switch platforms, in Web3 people have the option of bringing their data with them as they travel around the internet.

Instead of having a copy of an image on Twitter and another copy on Instagram, a person can have a master copy of that image—associated with an NFT in their digital wallet—which Twitter, Instagram, and any other site can read and display.

This is likely to lead to more competition among tech platforms, both because it makes it harder to lock in users and because it means new entrants can bootstrap off of existing content and information networks. And indeed, even in the early days of Web3, we've already seen significant entry and experimentation by new platforms like Bluesky, Farcaster, and Lens creating interoperable social media protocols and providing ways for users to leverage their data that's already stored publicly on blockchains.

But even more importantly, the shift means that users will mostly be building a *core digital identity*—reflected in their digital wallet— rather than individual, platform-specific identity shards. These new core identities will enable people to establish more complete digital representations of themselves than before. And with a greater degree of both psychological and literal control over how their digital identities are used, it's also likely people will invest more effort in building them.

If someone knew they were going to have to throw away their posters when they moved out of their apartment, they might not bother putting them up in the first place. On the other hand, if they knew they could keep their posters with them forever, they might think really carefully about which ones to get—and maybe even splurge on a special signed lithograph that really speaks to them.

NFTs let people collect and curate digital assets in the same way that we're used to collecting and curating physical collectibles. If a person has a basement filled with Ohio State football posters, signed memorabilia, and framed game tickets, it's safe to assume they're a big Buckeyes fan. The same is true if their digital wallet is full of Ohio State NFTs. Moreover, because NFTs are software, it's easy for platforms to verify, reference, and display these holdings across the web.

And again, while we have been talking about images and posters because those make the metaphors particularly sharp, that's *not* all people will have in their digital wallets. People will have NFTs of everything from favorite music recordings to education and work records, and all of that will contribute to their personal identities in digital space. Likewise, people might hold digital assets representing their history and reputation as an online gamer, marathon runner, or academic advisor. Nearly anything that can be represented digitally can be represented as an NFT as opposed to data on a closed platform.

NFTs allow the creation of a single seamless digital identity, while also making the curation and upkeep of that identity much more valuable than in the walled gardens of Web 2. For consumers, the NFT-mediated experience of Web3 will simply be better. When you connect to a platform like LinkedIn, it will read your digital diploma—with your permission—to confirm and populate your education information. When you connect to the website of your new gym, it will import your workout history automatically. A newspaper's website can load your reading and content preferences straight out of your digital wallet— so the second you land at *The Atlanta Journal-Constitution*'s website, you'll see an article about the Buccaneers versus Falcons game.

COMPETING FOR (DIGITAL) WALLET SHARE

All of this means that even the type of firm that doesn't normally think of itself as digitally native is going to have to think about NFTs. Why? Because they want to be part of their customers' digital identities.

In a Web 1 world, you competed to have consumers sign up for your email list.

In a Web 2 world, you drove them to your social media sites to engage with your brand.

In a Web3 world, you have to be part of your customers' digital wallets. If you're not, someone else is probably going to crowd you out. And conversely, if you do become part of your customers' digital identities, they'll become more attached to your brand, and evangelize it all over the web.

You might naturally think of customers' digital wallets as having infinite space—after all, one of the oft-touted advantages of digital advances like ebooks and streaming music was the fact that they gave us unlimited shelf capacity. And it's true that many people's digital profiles are full of what we may think of as *cruft*—photos, posts, and old connections they don't think about much anymore. But at the same time, consumer attention is limited, and in many ways, Web3 will mean intensified competition for consumers' digital identity share.

Whereas in Web 2 a consumer might form one identity on a platform like Facebook and a different one on LinkedIn, in Web3 all of those identities can be interlinked and based on the same core assets stored in the consumer's digital wallet. That doesn't mean that consumers will present themselves in exactly the same way every-where they go on the internet. But it does mean that they'll showcase the digital assets they care the most about more frequently—and the more consumers anchor around one part of their digital identity, the less space there is for others.*

Think about the limited number of brands someone can represent in their day-to-day life. They might be wearing Mizuno shoes and a Gucci T-shirt. But unless they start wearing sneakers on their hands or tying an extra shirt around their waist, they're not likely to be show-ing off any other shoe or T-shirt brands at the same time.

The Web3 world is much the same way. Everyone's digital wallets will hold a multitude of different assets, but there will be a much more limited set of credentials, brands, products, and organizational affin-ities people choose to showcase and engage with regularly. And in many cases, they'll be returning to the same assets again and again, instead of adding new ones on each platform.

A person might use the same profile picture and banner image across all social media platforms, and play the same two or three mo-bile games each day. People typically shop online at a few select retail-ers, and thus even NFTs that provide discounts and memberships are also competing for digital wallet share.

---

*Of course, it's not completely zero-sum, especially since all of this activity will cre-ate new forms of digital interaction that have never existed before. But still, the over-all dynamic is likely to be one of increasingly intense attachment to a smaller set of digital assets.

NETWORK EFFECTS IN WEB3

As we've already mentioned, the most successful businesses in Web 2 are built on powerful network effects—they have massive user bases and data repositories, so the value proposition for each new user grows as a function of how large the platform already is.

There's a network effect in Web3, too, but instead of accruing to the *platform*, it accrues to the *assets*. An NFT community gets more valuable the more people are in it and the more deeply those people engage. In a world where people bring their assets from platform to platform, it matters less which platforms they are active on, and more which assets they like to use.

To make an analogy, a former video game executive who goes by the pseudonym BORED has argued that we may be seeing the final iterations of hardware for video game systems because the communities that can be built around game software are far more powerful. Steve sees this regularly when his son plays Fortnite with his friends. They each play on a different console—one on an Xbox, one on a Nintendo Switch, and one on a PC—and it doesn't matter which. The game itself is what matters, and it can be distributed and used interoperably across multiple devices. Put differently, the player communities—and all the purchases they make—are operating system–agnostic. What matters is not which gameplay device people have, but how many of them show up to play the game each day.

Web3 is the same way. Network effects center on *community cohesion*: the more value a group of people sees in a given digital asset—and the more value that community itself creates—the more other people want to own the asset, growing the community further. That's what happened with Bored Apes, and it has happened with many other NFT brands, including Azuki, Doodles, and VeeFriends. And it matters all across the spectrum of NFTs. In the case of digital certification NFTs, for example, if a given coding class is the one all the businesses are hiring out of, then more people will want that certification, specifically. Or if a company makes the most interoperable digital avatar, then that's likely to be the one people want to use.

And once more, just to drive it home: This isn't just about brands and consumer products—it's about everything people do as reflected in data and digital space. As we've already mentioned a couple times, your identity as expressed in credentials, records, and even government documents can also be leveled up by NFTs. If you're simply trying to ensure cross-platform verifiability of a record like a driver's license or marriage certificate, a blockchain ledger is an ideal solution that works better than a piece of paper or a plastic card. That goes for employment history, organization membership, and charitable contributions, too.* Having these sorts of records in a digital wallet is just as efficient as having a driver's license in your physical wallet—any site you connect with can securely verify the credential. (And indeed, the California DMV has already experimented with putting car registrations on the blockchain.)

---

*Typically, these sorts of records are stored as nontransferable NFTs, which are fixed to a specific digital wallet. (Technically, they're often implemented so that the issuing agency can move or re-instantiate them in the event of digital wallet compromise or loss of access.)

While we're not expecting the DMV to introduce branded utility around driver's licenses (although an airdrop of a special-edition holo-foil New Year's "Drive Safely" collectible might be kind of cool), we very much do see utility and identity reinforcement around other forms of records. Nonprofits can use NFTs to manage and publicize contributor campaigns. As we discuss further in Chapter 10, alumni associations can use NFTs to manage token-gated online communities or events. The "I Voted" sticker can become a verified, public badge of honor. Or those Presidential Fitness certificates you get in elementary school, once NFT-ified, might get you a free ice cream, the ultimate utility for an eight-year-old.

MEDICAL RECORDS GO TO THE METAVERSE

Even when it comes to just using the blockchain to store and codify digital records, giving people control of that data can empower them in new ways. First off, just like with online platforms, there's a convenience factor that may also help drive market competition. We don't know about you, but we've both at times resisted changing doctors and/or dentists simply because of the hassle of calling up the office, explaining that you're moving to a new practice (unpleasant!) and politely trying to extract copies of our medical records.

But if individuals' health records were codified as NFTs, patients would control access, and when a person did transfer, that process would be almost instantaneous. Of course this would need to be implemented carefully to preserve patient data privacy, but in principle, NFT healthcare records could include any notes from your previous healthcare provider, giving your new doctor everything they need to provide the best possible care. And then each new piece of information about your medical history, from diagnoses to medications and surgeries, can be easily added, and then accessed interoperably, with your permission.

On top of that, there's an opportunity for third-party software development on top of users' medical data. There are already a battery of companies that make use of consumer health data to provide customized care, but currently, users often have to build up their medical histories and identities on such platforms from scratch. If—when—medical record data becomes user-controlled, we can imagine numerous plug-and-play services for health information, personalized medicine, and risk screening.

Giving users control of how their data is used also provides them with an opportunity to share it for use in research, or even potentially monetize it in pharmaceutical studies. And conversely, control means that if you don't want your data to be used in a given way, you are empowered to opt out.

ONLINE PERSONALIZATION

As more people acquire digital wallets and start forming digital identities in them, as we've already discussed, there'll be new opportunities for firms to build around that information. Having a collection of Chicago Bulls ticket NFTs conveys the precise message that a person is a Bulls fan; thus, a newspaper that sees those digital assets in a reader's digital wallet might serve that reader more Bulls basketball news. Similarly, the digital souvenirs we collect on our travels might be used by airlines and hotels to offer special deals.

This is akin to the way web platforms have used cookies in the past, but again with a big difference: In Web3, the user is in control. Instead of various websites in effect spying on everyone to try and learn who they are and what types of content they want to see—and jealously guarding that information—now people have an opportunity to form affirmative identities for themselves online, which platforms can curate around. It's a less adversarial model of the web, which has the potential to create more value for everyone involved.

You might be thinking: *Steve and Scott are claiming this is a feature!? The last thing people want is for online platforms to have more information about them!*

It's true that many people have come to feel that online platforms have too much of their data, but to a large extent, that's because of the way Web 2 business models work. In Web 2, remember, users are the product—and the platform is typically trying to aggregate as much data as it can about them in order to sell better-targeted advertisements and extend its lead over competitors. But in the Web3 model, by contrast, the user controls their digital assets, and in particular chooses which platforms access them and how.

Thus Web3 can enable people to build far more expansive digital identities than they've had before, while at the same time giving them more control over how those identities are reflected in their various online activities. It's early days, but we hope and expect this to lead to a more positive online experience overall. (All of that said, when we were writing this, at least, digital wallets still had a ways to go before users could fully control digital asset privacy—but several promising solutions were being developed.)

In sum, we've said that in Web3 you are part of the brand, and NFT-driven digital identity enables this paradigm shift. And of course, to identify with something is one thing, but as we've teased in this section, identity can be kicked into higher gear when it becomes a source of community—shared passion for a brand, product, or creator. That's the next step of the Staircase.

8

Connecting the Community

What value would you place on your friends from grade school, or the people at work who help you get through the day? If you attended college, how would you value the classmates and teachers you met during your time there? Or, especially, how about the people you know from your neighborhood, favorite online community, or—if you're religious—place of worship? Forming community around shared identity is a powerful thing.

We've repeatedly used the example of being a fan of a sports team. If you see someone wearing your favorite team's apparel, you instantly know that you have something in common with them. Sometimes, you'll even approach them based only on that common ground. University of Alabama fans will yell, "Roll Tide!" at a complete stranger in the airport if they happen to be wearing a team jersey. To them, the shared connection of the University of Alabama (and its wildly successful football program) is strong enough to lead them to interact with someone they may never have met before. NFTs can lead to similarly powerful community affinity and shared connection.

In this chapter, we'll explain what community means in the context of NFTs, talk about why it's important, and show you how it can unlock a new level of enthusiasm for your brand. We can't promise your customers will be cheering for one another in an airport, but nevertheless, NFT-enabled communities are intensely bonded—and we'll show you why and how that happens.

NFTS' NETWORK SUPERPOWER

NFTs don't just shape people's identities and the way they portray themselves in digital spaces—they almost automatically begin to connect those people into communities. And for a business, cultivating community is an especially effective form of marketing because there's almost no limit to the enthusiasm and persuasive power of someone who genuinely believes in your brand.

There's an old phrase in the public relations industry, "Advertising you pay for, PR you pray for." Some brands pay people hundreds of dollars per month or more to wrap their cars with an advertisement. By contrast, if done well, a successful NFT program can create an entire community of holders who choose to represent the brand in their digital presence, without geographical limits. Moreover, because all that activity is organic, people are more likely to find affinity with others doing the same.

Community formation around shared interests has been happening forever, of course. But NFTs turn it up to eleven because of what we call their *embedded network superpower*: As we've said, becoming the owner of an NFT is to some degree an act of affiliation with the brand. Yet NFT ownership doesn't just connect you with the brand itself, but also with the entire network of individuals who are similarly affiliated.

Remember that with NFTs, the network effect accrues to the asset. The quasi-converse is that the network is embedded in the asset itself. *The holders of a given NFT comprise a network of brand enthusiasts just waiting to be activated.* And pretty much anyone can start the community activation process.

While all of this sounds great, it often leads to the question: Why would a community be motivated to coalesce around a brand in the first place? Do NFTs really make people more likely to band together? This brings us back to the shared incentive that comes with ownership.

SHARED INCENTIVES

Disney fans don't see financial value when they wear a Mickey Mouse shirt to the office, even if wearing that shirt reminds their co-worker they've been meaning to sign up for Disney+. By contrast, there are many ways for holders to derive value directly from participating in a company's NFT ecosystem—everything from simply raising awareness of the brand in ways that increase the value of the NFT to building businesses around the core NFT offering. Members of the Bored Ape, Azuki, and Women and Weapons NFT communities, for example, have leveraged their holder IP rights to build a range of products and personal brands around the NFT imagery. This borrows some of the value and recognition the NFT brand has already achieved, while at the same time growing the NFT brand's overall footprint.

A few examples are pictured on the next page: Ape Water, a spring water brand, both leveraged and reinforced the BAYC's notoriety by using Bored Ape NFT imagery on its products. (The company was founded by BAYC NFT holders, and also received early investments from fellow Bored Apes.) AppliedPrimate, a Web3 game and puzzle brand, produced a card series featuring many of the rarest Mutant Ape Yacht Club characters—the "Mega Mutants"—as well as associated comics and other products that expanded the scope of Bored Ape IP and exposed many new people to it. Toymaker and Azuki NFT holder Zookit, meanwhile, built a business designing custom mini skate decks for other Azuki holders, featuring their respective NFT images. And finally, Girl in the Verse uses her Women and Weapons NFT image—which bears a striking resemblance to the content creator herself—as a public-facing business logo that creates instant recognition across social channels. Her short-form videos drive further awareness for Women and Weapons, and in turn the NFT project's founder and community support her and her work.

This is a model we haven't seen systematized before, with shared incentives for the consumers of a product and the company that created it. The relationship in the standard model is much more transactional. Disney's great park experience might drive a person to buy souvenirs that memorialize their trip, but the value exchange ends there. You're not going to increase the value of your Disney shirt by wearing it to the office.

Likewise, in the example above of wrapping one's car, a person

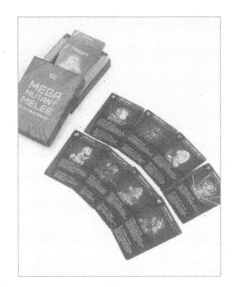

HAND
CRAFTED
COLLECTIBLES

GIRL IN THE VERSE

does it because they're being paid to. There's no community reinforcement because there's no reason for others to expect that the car wrapper indicates true brand enthusiasm. With a well-run NFT program, by contrast, people are actively choosing to represent the brand, and are excited to connect with others who are doing the same.

Meanwhile, the brand is incentivized to increase the utility and underlying brand value for NFT holders, not just to sell more products, but to drive the pride of ownership and a sense of identity. The community is incentivized to be active participants in the brand because their efforts also may raise the value of the NFTs they own. It's a system where everyone wins together.

Taken to the limit, this is leading to entirely new models of brand-building, which borrow conceptually from the open-source software movement. A number of NFT brands have been launched under Creative Commons Zero (CC0) licensing, which means that their core brand assets are available for anyone to build and innovate on—no rights reserved. As Scott explained in an article with the pseudonymous NFT collector Flashrekt, this "jumpstarts 'meme-ability' by actively, not just passively, inviting the creation of derivative works. And as new derivatives are created and shared, attention can flow back toward the original, strengthening its place in the collective consciousness. This in turn may inspire even more interpretations, resulting in a flywheel effect whereby each additional derivative can add to the original's value—akin to platform network effects, whereby platforms become more valuable to users as more users join them."

This strategy for NFT brand-building was pioneered by crypto artist Stellabelle and toy creators David Horvath and Sun-Min Kim (previously well known for creating the Uglydolls brand), and then popularized by an NFT collection called Nouns, whose signature brand asset is a set of square glasses called *noggles*. With both holders and third parties licensed to create around the Nouns assets, those glasses quickly started showing up all over the internet, and even in the physical world. (Multiple companies produced physical glasses in the Nouns shape; meanwhile, the glasses were used in a Bud Light Super Bowl commercial.) There aren't yet good publicly available metrics on the impact of all this activity—but it's driven significant media attention, and at least as of June 2023, new Nouns NFTs were selling for roughly $45,000 each day.

Community-based brand-building can go many layers deep: the Chain Runners NFT project founders were enthusiastic about a CC0 NFT brand called Blitmap, so they included the Blitmap logo on some of their characters' hats. And because Chain Runners themselves were CC0, one of their community members was able to produce and sell his own Chain Runners merchandise, including the hat. Other community members—Scott among them—launched an entire NFT series, 1337 Skulls, inspired by some of the Chain Runners characters, again including variations on the Blitmap logo. Plenty of people who had never heard of Blitmap before learned about it by seeing their logo featured on a third-party digital or physical hat!*

Similar digital brands have been built around CC0 game assets. For example, the Loot ecosystem comprises a series of fantasy games and storytelling tools built around a simple NFT primitive representing

---

*Note that the 1337 Skull pictured is also wearing Nouns-style noggles.

just a bag of adventure game items that others could innovate on top of however they want.

Again, NFTs are critical to making this style of brand-building work because shared ownership of core brand assets gives NFT holders an incentive to invest in building new products around them. And at the same time, CC0 gives holders—and everyone else—a simple and complete license to build on top of the NFT brand IP, which can supercharge brand proliferation and community growth. Both of us still remember the rapid online spread of goblin imagery in the weeks after the CC0 Goblintown NFT project launched: People loved the goblin characters, and started slapping them on stickers and apparel, and borrowing the aesthetic for NFTs of everything from adventurous halflings to grumpy owls, and even anthropomorphized ice cream sandwiches. A year later, the goblins were still popping up in various places—a third-party video game developer even included them in a

3D exploration game that briefly made it to the top ten for streaming on Twitch, drawing yet more attention to the Goblintown brand. The CC0 license allowed this sort of activity, and the NFT nature of the original goblins helped incentivize it.

Of course, the CC0 strategy isn't right for everyone. Like with open-source software, CC0 brand-building works best when the underlying brand assets are composable, in the sense that many distinct extensions can be built on top of them. Nouns and Blitmap benefit from their communities of enthusiasts showcasing their core brand assets—noggle glasses and the Blitmap logo, respectively—in many different contexts.

Meanwhile, although some—especially established brands and media properties—may want to maintain far tighter control of their brand intellectual property, they can still benefit from the same sort of community-driven brand proliferation. Even if holders are not licensed to directly build upon brand IP, NFTs still provide an incentive and a mechanism to share the brand and connect with others around it.

COLLABORATIVE CREATION

Tally Labs built an entire NFT-based content publishing operation based on the IP rights that Bored Ape Yacht Club gave its holders. Two childhood friends built a backstory around an Ape they acquired, naming him Jenkins the Valet, and then created content in a variety of media that told the story of Jenkins's adventures working at the Yacht Club. Eventually, Jenkins became the flagship character of a novel by ten-time *New York Times* bestselling author Neil Strauss. The other characters in the book were fellow Bored Apes, but in addition to the brand's inclusion in the story, the company released NFTs that enabled holders to vote on various plot points of the novel. Even more, the NFTs had varying rarities that allowed their owners to put their Apes into the story in different ways. Holders of a "yacht" NFT—the rarest in the collection—had their Apes added as fully fledged characters. Holders of a "valet stand" NFT, meanwhile, had their Apes included in illustrations. The model has many tiers, and in addition to the level of participation in the Jenkins universe, the tiers correspond to voting power, with rarer NFTs holding higher voting power on key plot points. The concept garnered so much interest that Tally Labs signed with Creative Artists Agency (CAA), one of the world's largest and most influential talent agencies, in 2021, and closed a $12 million fundraising round in 2022.

It's also worth noting that with a dedicated community of "book people" who had contributed to the Jenkins the Valet novel, Tally was able to sell a large number of copies at premium prices right off the bat—the book NFT (which also has other utility in their NFT ecosystem) raised almost $1.9 million between primary and secondary sales. And those who had licensed characters received royalties on the order of $87.46 per NFT. That may not sound like much at first glance, but holders could license multiple NFTs, and the ten largest licensors each made more than $2,100.

While crowdsourcing like what Tally Labs did isn't new, the use of verifiable digital assets provides more secure and efficient practices for making it work well. It proves the owner is "supposed to be there," to combat manipulative voting practices. (If all voting systems were blockchain-based, tying votes to individual identity NFTs could potentially create a provably fair process, all transparently auditable by anyone.*)

To that end, many Web3 companies have community funds which they call DAOs—*decentralized autonomous organizations.* DAOs come in a variety of formats, but the key idea is that members can issue proposals, and then the community of token holders decides which proposals to execute. (Nouns, discussed earlier, operates via such a DAO, and their various activities and asset sales have led to a roughly $22 million treasury as of this writing.)

And at the same time, NFTs create numerous mechanisms for people to engage with one another around the process, rather than just casting their votes into a vacuum. When executed well, the process itself can drive community collaboration and camaraderie. A DAO is almost like a decentralized country. You have a democratic process to pass initiatives, but instead of voting being based on where a person lives, everyone chooses their "country" (and countrymates) by opting in through NFT ownership. And then the eventual product

---

*A common misconception about blockchains is that because they allow user anonymity, they cannot be used for voting or similar applications where you want to limit the number of times a given person can participate. But in fact they can—NFTs solve this problem through what's called a *proof of unique personhood*, whereby a trusted certification authority creates special NFTs, perhaps based on biometrics or a government ID, that uniquely represent a given individual.

the DAO creates has a special meaning to the NFT holders who helped shape it.

Community mechanics like crowdsourcing and DAOs give passionate fans an outlet to feel more connected to a brand and contribute to its growth. This might not be right for every business, but the co-creation model doesn't have to be overly complicated in order to compound.

A local mom-and-pop cookie shop with a loyalty program on the blockchain could let holders conduct a quarterly vote on the next seasonal cookie flavor. They could also solicit cookie name submissions to add an extra layer of pride of ownership. To incentivize participation, all the people who voted for the winning flavor could get one for free, and everyone who participated but did not get their cookie picked could get the special cookie 50% off. The shop could even hold a token-gated event the day that the new cookie is launched and invite holders to bring their friends. Taken together, the program lets the cookie business extend their reach beyond just when customers are in the store, and it can turn an otherwise disconnected set of customers into a community—built on shared experience—that looks forward to a cookie party each quarter.

This example also brings to light how NFTs can enhance a business's operations by simplifying workstreams. Could you hold a vote via email address, email the event tickets, and send individual coupons to each participant? Sure, but the blockchain can do all three of these things with a single NFT—and more securely. During the flavor-selection process, each NFT owner can be limited to a single token-gated vote, helping ensure people don't—pardon the pun—cook the books.* The NFT can also be programmed to link the discount to the user's vote, so that those who vote for the cookie that ends up winning get a 100% discount, and others get 50% off. There is no need to create a redeemable coupon that people may forget to bring, or even counterfeit. Likewise, the NFT can serve as an entry pass to the cookie party itself. Ultimately, the blockchain saves this company time and effort, and provides a more secure system for engaging the community. And that's all before cookie NFT holders start interacting with one another independent of the store.

FINDING YOUR TRIBE EVERYWHERE

Remember: NFTs don't just give someone an image or other media or data file they can use and show off on various platforms. The tokens themselves can serve as access passes to digital and physical spaces where holders can meet one another, hang out, and potentially plot world domination.

When a person goes to a sporting event, pop concert, or Broadway musical, they are surrounded by people who are like them, at least on a core dimension or two. And they *know it* because those people took time out of their days and paid money to attend the same event. But

---

*Just like with email addresses, it's possible to create multiple digital wallets. But in order to game the cookie vote we've described here, users would need to have *earned the relevant loyalty NFTs* in multiple digital wallets—which is difficult if those loyalty NFTs are tied to purchasing behavior.

when you walk out of a venue, most of those otherwise similar people completely disappear, and you have no way to find them again, unless you happen to come across a fandom signifier like a 'Bama or Taylor Swift T-shirt in the airport.

We're not saying that all one hundred thousand people in the stadium should become your best friends—heck, even if you just managed to shake hands with them in less than the three-hour duration of the game, that would probably be some sort of world record.* But still, it would be nice to be able to—if you were so inclined—track down a few of those people and celebrate when your team wins a big upset game—or commiserate when they lose in a heartbreak.

And from the team's perspective, enabling those sorts of connections among people is valuable because it increases the enjoyment of the experience, makes them realize that they're part of something bigger, and perhaps most crucially, increases the probability they will buy more tickets in the future.

NFTs make it possible for people to find their tribes everywhere.

That point is so important that we're going to say it again: *NFTs make it possible for people to find their tribes everywhere.* That's because they give people ways to show their affinities and affiliations publicly, whether by way of profile pictures or branded hoodies. But it's mostly because of the way that NFTs are embedded in software.

Seriously—it may not sound glamorous, but this feature of NFTs is really about the software. Because NFTs are digital tokens that individuals can use across platforms, it's possible to build all manner of

---

*As of this writing, the world record for handshaking was on the order of 48,000.

spaces and activities around them. We gave three illustrations in the cookie example, showing ways that community brand activations can be streamlined through a single NFT. And because the blockchain infrastructure layer that hosts most NFTs is publicly accessible, anyone can do this. No community member has to be granted permission to convene fellow enthusiasts. This means an NFT's holders have tremendous latitude to shape how and where they engage with one another.

If someone's a massive Michael Bublé fan, and they are looking for another Michael Bublé superfan to hang out with, they can just drop into the Bublé NFT holders' chat channel. (You'll find another member of Bungalow-B at any hour of the day.) And if there isn't an established hangout for holders of a particular NFT, anyone who wants to can create their own and empower anyone with the appropriate token to join. This supports bottom-up community development—the most engaged holders will draw other people in and amplify their enthusiasm.

When someone buys season tickets to their local ballet, they know that other people who attend regularly each month must have similar tastes, but they don't have a way to reach those people—they're more in the background. Web 2 community engagement mechanisms don't do a great job of solving this problem. They're siloed in individual platforms, which both makes it hard to figure out where a given community is based (a Facebook group? A specific subreddit?) and limits the form of activity once there.

With NFTs, the other holders are front and center. The NFT serves multiple roles at once—it can be both the entry ticket to a ballet performance and a cross-platform community anchor. At minimum, at least for NFTs on public blockchains, you can look up other holders' digital wallet addresses and see what else they're into. And if you want to team up with some of the more engaged community members, for example, to co-sponsor some new Forsythe choreography, NFTs can help you track them down.

(If you read that and were concerned about unsolicited contact or receiving unwanted NFTs, there are already solutions in place, which will continue to improve over time. Direct contact through an NFT-gated chat channel would require a person to opt in and connect, just like any other current chat medium. Meanwhile, if a person or company wants to send you an unsolicited NFT, there are hidden folders where they land, much like with email spam filters. So, chances are, if someone manages to contact you via NFT, it's a person or entity you'd actually like to hear from.)

And again, this isn't just about supercharging existing superfans; NFTs can drive more community engagement and commitment up and down the spectrum. Micro-communities can even emerge around POAPs, the free NFTs you might collect commemorating various events. Scott gave out a POAP the first time he taught about NFTs in his MBA class, and that turned into a shared memento linking together everyone who was there that day. In another instance, entrepreneur Gmoney handed out POAPs to people who consumed his content or met him at events. Those collectors were then given the chance to mint his Admit One NFT, granting them entry into an exclusive fashion club. The mint was free, and at one point, Admit One NFTs were selling for almost $25,000 on the secondary market.

COMMUNITY IS VALUE

Once an NFT community achieves scale, the community itself—and the opportunities that come with it—can be a principal source of value for holders. Oftentimes, if an NFT creator fosters the right environment, community can far surpass the value created through direct utility. Holders from all walks of life become friends, advisors, or potentially even business partners.

Joe O'Rourke can attest to this firsthand. In the summer of 2021, he accepted an invitation to a gathering at venture capitalist Drew Austin's house. O'Rourke had never met Austin in person, but the two had connected because of their shared engagement in the NBA Top Shot and Zed Run NFT communities. While at the event, O'Rourke connected with another of Austin's friends who was interested in NFTs, Adam Brotman. Within a year, O'Rourke and Brotman, alongside Brotman's longtime friend Andy Sack, co-founded Forum3, a digital transformation company that boasts clients like Starbucks, Anheuser-Busch, and bestselling author Ben Mezrich.

Similarly, Mike Chavez was an active community member in OnChainMonkey, an NFT brand which is considered tech-forward even compared to many of its Web3 counterparts. The team loved Chavez's passion, and ultimately hired him away from Amazon Web Services to work for the brand. Since then, Chavez's role has continued to expand, from software engineer to company evangelist, a role where he represents OnChainMonkey across an array of digital media and real-world events.

O'Rourke's and Chavez's stories aren't particularly unique, either.

People within NFT communities often find ways to help one another—
again, just like with an alumni club. Some particularly elite NFT
communities have evolved to give holders access to a network of individuals across a variety of industries worldwide. Others focus on
holders with specific skills or interests—leading to everything from
fiction writer groups to elite hacker collectives. Many NFT projects
actively encourage community engagement through public social rewards. For example, both DeGods and y00ts, two digital brands created
by the company Dust Labs, support their NFT holders by signal-
boosting them via the brands' popular social media channels. Many
community members follow the company's example and signal-boost
as well, and this creates a strong network effect that reinforces the
visibility of community content creators.

Before NFTs, connecting people with a passion for your brand
was complicated because of all the various places those fans could
congregate, from Reddit to Facebook to traditional fan clubs. Now,
they can all assemble around a single digital asset.

There was also previously less incentive for communities to coalesce in the first place because finding other fans was more difficult,
and there was less they could achieve. Someone who loves your ramen
restaurant might not have a way to find another fan across town, let
alone across the country. But if you both share an NFT that serves as
a digital connection and access point, it's entirely more likely, and stories like O'Rourke's and Chavez's can happen much more easily.

There can be an NFT community for anything—no matter how
small. For example, there are many NFTs centered around comic series with high-quality storytelling. And at the time of this writing, a

couple thousand people were playing—and helping build—a particularly complex NFT-based fantasy game. Content creators host token-gated communities for fans of their work, creating a space where those fans can connect and get the latest updates on new releases. In all of these instances, the community forms around their love of what's being made, and community members can then contribute to that process.

In many ways, NFTs can be an *especially* effective tool for these niche interests. They increase the scale, reach, and accessibility of clubs for any topic. They level the playing field for businesses and creators of all sizes, allowing them to connect with fans in ways that previously weren't possible. And as a company, it lets you offer an entirely new service to your customers, bringing together a formidable network. Whereas in Web 2, you typically can't monetize a community until you achieve large scale, NFTs allow you to create linkages much more easily and deeply, so that a smaller Web3 community can be as strong and lucrative as a larger Web 2 one. (We will discuss this further in Part III!)

NON-*FUNGIBLE*

There is one other intangible element of community which we shouldn't undervalue—it's fun! Think about the feeling you get at a game when your team scores and you high-five the stranger next to you. Or the joy you get when the dealer busts in blackjack and the whole table wins the hand. We've talked about how digital ownership leads to shared goals and incentives—people co-create to drive value back to the

NFT that represents their brand affiliation. But in many cases, the experiences one has with fellow NFT holders in the network can be the key source of value, whether it occurs via online banter or at real-life events.

THE CHICKEN OR THE EGG?

One could make a compelling argument that community often precedes identity. You might join a golf club because it's nearby, and only then develop a love of the game and begin to identify as a golfer. Likewise, you might buy an NFT of a Cool Cat because you think it looks, well, cool, and not start to identify as a "Cool Cat" yourself until you start engaging with other holders of the NFT.

Community and identity complement each other tremendously: Not only does participating in the community around an NFT reinforce the extent to which the NFT becomes part of one's identity, but an enthusiastic community can explicitly encourage that. You'll see NFT projects issue "community announcements" and organize "community meetups." Established community members will often recruit new holders and try to get current ones to become more actively engaged.

But before there can be an active community, someone has to start trying to build it. Often, those are people for whom the identity aspect is already in place. And in our experience, particularly in the NFT space, people often first acquire an asset for the functional benefits and then get excited about those—and that's precisely what leads them to seek out community through conscious participation.

THE FUTURE OF DIGITAL BRAND-BUILDING

Regardless of the chicken/egg order, businesses issuing NFTs can foster a sense of community to drive genuine loyalty to their brand. Community is so important that in the NFT landscape of 2023, a chief community officer is often as fundamental a role as a CEO, CFO, or CTO. Even the venture capital firm Scott works with has a social & community lead; Nicholas Corso serves as the community success lead at VeeFriends; and other companies have community experts with more exotic titles like *director of vibes*. And while those titles may sound odd to someone hearing them at the outset of Web3, it's quite possible that businesses will be hiring for these roles in droves as they look to extend their brands into the Web3 world. In the early Web 2 days, the title *social media manager* sounded ridiculous, but now many companies have entire departments full of social media professionals. Adam Brotman, the former chief digital officer (CDO) at Starbucks who helped architect the coffee giant's mobile payments plan—also Joe O'Rourke's co-founder mentioned earlier—tells a story about how he was somewhat embarrassed about the CDO title when he first got it. Now it's a source of pride, and nobody would blink an eye at a company hiring for that position.

If you read that last paragraph and thought to yourself, *What does a community manager or director of vibes even do?*, it may shock you even more to hear that these people regularly interface with the company executives. Their input is considered invaluable to the success of the brand. Much like social media created a new audience in Web 2, a community in Web3 brings a new group of stakeholders to manage and understand. Community managers interface with NFT holders, field questions, and conduct social listening. They effectively serve as the day-to-day voice of the brand to the customers. But beyond that role, which itself is akin to being a company spokesperson, people in these jobs often provide actionable information and analytics regarding community sentiment.

In one NFT community we know that asked to remain anonymous, the community lead used analytics to identify the most engaged holders and invited them to join a community council. This council was primarily intended as a way of sourcing ideas for utility that the brand might not have previously considered—and it did that quite successfully. But there was an unexpected outcome, too: The positive reinforcement of being on the community council motivated those members to be more active, and their engagement increased by over 60% in the following month. These superfans, who were already the brand's biggest boosters, stepped up even more as unofficial community leaders.*

And beyond direct engagement activities, there are various ways people in community positions can look across analytics and anecdotal feedback to help shape the company's direction. Sentiment analysis around a specific keyword might change how you're describing a product or service. Reactions to an announcement in a community mes-

---

*This outcome—whereby giving people a degree of leadership or ownership in an organization increases their engagement—has long been documented in research on organizational behavior. It again comes back to the idea of psychological ownership, which, as we already discussed, NFTs can facilitate.

saging channel could lead a company to pivot its comms approach. An NFT community is a living laboratory for brand engagement in addition to a core source of customer value.

In short: an NFT community, and the insights it provides, can shape the brand's evolution.

9

Driving Brand Evolution

When NFT ownership, utility, and identity come together to create a community of megafans, there's no telling what might happen. An NFT community can be the world's most perfect idea lab, incubator, or writer's room—members are big-time enthusiasts, and they are constantly connected to the brand and to one another. And because they are owners, NFT holders are incentivized to try to create value wherever they can.

That leads us to the final step of the NFT Staircase: evolution. NFT holders are often perfectly positioned to help guide the brand forward and potentially even develop their own products and services that extend the brand's reach. Naturally, we're going to explain this "evolution" with a biology metaphor—but it might not be quite the one you're expecting.*

---

*In particular, it's not about primates.

THE SEMIPERMEABLE MEMBRANE

Remember cell biology? Cells have semipermeable membranes that allow certain particles through and not others. Nutrients and water are absorbed, while contaminants are kept out.

With NFT brands, there's a semipermeable membrane between the company and the community. Everyone's in effect part of the same organism, with bidirectional communication and shared goals.

That means an NFT community can be a constant source of feedback and innovation. And when someone in the community has a great idea, it's easy for the brand to absorb it—and reward the innovator.

It was early days for this as we were writing, but it was already starting to happen.

Many NFT projects have hired their most enthusiastic community members to fill various roles. An NFT social media meme-master pseudonymously named ThreadGuy created a series of Twitter threads explaining Tally Labs's NFT universe to the uninitiated, and then was hired to manage their community initiatives. A community member suggested a new type of art for OnChainMonkey, and then became the brand's art director and designed a new collection. And as we mentioned in Chapter 5, The Hundreds's Adam Bomb Squad NFT holders have created their own Adam Bomb designs and logos, some of which have been absorbed into the company's own brand iconography. A SupDucks community member got really good at designing digital costumes for SupDucks characters, and so he was given a "tailor shop" in the brand's virtual boardwalk.

This becomes even more powerful when NFT projects give holders the right to develop their own IP and/or products around their NFT assets. An NFT fantasy series called Forgotten Runes Wizards Cult, for example, invited its holders to develop stories about the characters represented in their NFTs, and the most compelling ones are being integrated into cartoon and comic series produced by the brand. Being included is a major reward for community members that can also make the underlying NFT assets more valuable—and as a result, it incentivizes people to create the most interesting characters they can.[*]

On the flip side, when holders are upset about something, the brand can learn that immediately through its community channels and quickly gather suggestions for how to respond. In October 2022, Tally Labs released a profile picture character series for a fictional world it created called Azurbala. The art was so poorly received that it turned into memes among NFT enthusiasts. But thanks to holders who were invested in Tally Labs's success, the team also received real-time, useful feedback that cut through the mean-spirited posts. Within a few days, they had an action plan which included an art council, a community council, new artists, and a web portal that served as a central location for discussion. The result was new artwork that was received extremely well—with a community that felt heard, and that had become even more deeply integrated into the brand.

---

[*]More broadly, community-based storytelling is often a core component of NFT brands' IP development. Like Forgotten Runes, many NFT projects have started with a series of characters and a framing universe, and then worked with the community to build out the associated franchise. Scott has, for example, written "community lore" for anime NFT worlds such as Divine Anarchy and Inkugami. And infrastructure providers like Story Protocol are developing the tools to help creators do this at scale.

This all works because the energy flowing through an NFT community supercharges experimentation and iteration. NFT communities are a constant source of ideas—and sometimes even build out the brand ecosystem themselves. And again, because holders truly own their NFTs, they're both empowered and incentivized to help guide the brand forward in a way that's valuable for all involved.

Serial entrepreneur Jana Bobosikova explained the intuition this way in the context of KIKI, the Web3 beauty brand she co-founded: "If you think about how the beauty industry works now, brands develop products on long, expensive nine to 36 month-long cycles, then they need to figure out how to sell them to customers through KOLs and third-party platforms[.] It just makes more sense to involve the customer in what they want early on and reward them for their attention and voice/vote and give them a stake and reward for when it gets built—that's how we're building KIKI." Co-creating with consumers can lead to a tighter value loop, both by linking what's produced directly to demand, and by giving consumers a stake in the product's success.

This sort of activity reinforces community cohesion and drives further engagement—and the brand can take advantage of it to understand what its holders truly want, and then integrate the best innovations into its products and services.* *Companies born in Web3 are being built collaboratively and in public for everyone to see.*

---

*We could make some sort of primordial soup reference here, with the cells absorbing nutrients and gradually evolving into primates and then primate pictures or something, but you probably get the idea.

BACK TO THE FUTURE?

Of course, the idea of consumers shaping brands isn't new. Activist customers have pushed companies to change their labor practices and to implement better environmental standards, for example. And firms have been receiving customer feedback more or less since time immemorial.*

It's a recurrent theme of this book that NFTs enable transactions in ways that are better and more efficient than before, and that includes the "transaction" of a consumer engaging with one of their favorite brands.† But like with all the other steps of the Staircase, NFTs don't just stand to improve the existing mechanisms of brand evolution— they create entirely new ones.

NFTs foster close-knit, easily identifiable communities of individuals who have a personal connection with the brand. And crucially, that connection is bidirectional—after all, *in Web3, you're part of the brand*. Holders are fundamentally contributing to the company's ecosystem, rather than just receiving updates about new product offerings from the top down.

There really isn't much of a precedent for customers having the opportunity—and incentives—to deliver feedback in this manner. People who hold NFTs feel ownership because they quite literally own a

---

*A 3,750-year-old cuneiform tablet records what might be the oldest surviving customer complaint.

†Ironically, as Harvard Business School Web3 Research Fellow Liang Wu pointed out to us, by facilitating these sorts of "transactions," NFTs enable the underlying relationship between consumers and brands to become less transactional.

piece of the brand's ecosystem. And the value of what they own is determined by the evolution of the parent company and brand. With the addition of identity and community, owners are empowered and encouraged to enter into a feedback loop in a way that's deeper and more personal than the ways in which firms have historically sought consumer market data, such as email surveys and focus groups.

For comparison, let's briefly think about how focus groups work. Scott attended one for a local Whole Foods during his PhD. He met with store management and a handful of other customers to answer questions about the store and its social media presence. It didn't go particularly well.

First off, Scott wasn't really the right person for them to be talking to—he pretty much never shopped at Whole Foods. (As a graduate student, he mostly subsisted on miso soup and boxed pasta, which could be ordered in bulk online.)

By contrast, as we've underscored already, the NFT brand knows who its community is and can identify the most engaged members through their public activity. As we mentioned earlier, many NFT-native companies have even organized their most engaged members into official community councils that give regular feedback and advice.

Moreover, the set of questions Whole Foods asked Scott was bizarre—Scott still remembers them inquiring which people in the focus group were aware of a particular Whole Foods–branded ravioli product. (To the team's dismay, many of the attendees didn't even know that Whole Foods had its own branded products in the first place!) Their questions about social media, meanwhile, were so baffling that at the end, Scott told the team that he was studying market design and digital transformation, and asked whether they might want him to help develop their social media strategy. He got some quizzical looks, and unsurprisingly, they never followed up.

An NFT-connected community is empowered to shape the questions that are asked—and oftentimes, it provides insights the creators didn't even know to look for.

And while there was a reward for participating in the focus group—a gift card and a tote bag—it didn't align incentives in any meaningful way. There was no promise of ongoing engagement, for example, if people gave particularly thoughtful answers. Plus a gift card is itself short-lived—once you spend it down (or lose it somewhere), you might not even care whether the store remains open, much less whether they figure out where to put the ravioli for maximum visibility.

NFT holders have a vested interest and an ongoing incentive to contribute to the brand and its community.

With NFTs, we're talking about a fundamentally new way to build companies that fully leverages customers' relationship with the brand. If you're starting a company, you can find product-market fit among a core community of enthusiasts, and they can then collaborate with you to build out the brand and its ecosystem. If you have an already established company, you can use NFTs to find entirely new markets along with your most engaged customers.

And if you're a consumer, you can participate in—and even demand—that type of engagement.

Both Web3 startups and legacy brands have used NFT-driven community feedback loops to iterate, augment, and evolve their direction.

Doodles, a Web3-native brand known for its eclectic community and bright pastel artwork, ran its first experiential activation at South by Southwest in 2022. The over-the-top immersive environment transported participants to a colorful, interactive world that was unlike anything they had seen inside or outside of Web3. Doodles had previously planned to focus on creating cartoons, memes, and music around its intellectual property. But after the rave reviews at South by Southwest, the brand began to ramp up its experiential efforts. In addition to continued events at tent-pole Web3 moments like NFT.NYC and Art Basel, Doodles signed a partnership deal with upscale shop-and-play retailer CAMP in 2023 to launch a semipermanent 6,000-square-foot immersive experience. In doing so, Doodles became part of CAMP's rotation, alongside household names like Nike, Disney, and Teletubbies. While Doodles is still creating cartoons and music, they leaned into community response and evolved to make real-world experiences a major pillar of how their brand will scale.

As mentioned earlier, constructive feedback can also lead to operational and business model evolution. NBA Top Shot, a platform where consumers trade digital basketball videos called *moments*, heard its community was upset about there being too much supply in the market. It adjusted by reducing the frequency in which they released new moments and adding "burn challenges" with which collectors had the opportunity to trade in multiple moments to earn a single rare one. (The traded-in moments were removed from circulation forever, reducing total market supply.) Previously, NBA Top Shot's structure had only encouraged collecting more moments; while this was good for the company's revenue, it was an inflationary mechanic that left the holder community unhappy. Hearing feedback about oversupply in-spired the platform to create an entirely new mechanism, which they've since carried over to their football NFT platform, NFL All Day.

And again, this isn't confined to scrappy tech startups. Having a direct line into the voice of the customer can help established brands become newly flexible, giving them a better way to adapt to their con-sumers' wants and needs.

Starbucks Odyssey did just that in the first few months of its NFT rewards program, evolving its approach with the help of community feedback. During a limited-edition NFT release, the site was overrun with traffic, crashing for many Starbucks Odyssey participants, while others were able to purchase the high-demand NFT without issue. Headlines outside of the community positioned the drop positively, talking about how the NFTs had sold out in eighteen minutes, carried a hefty price tag on the resale market, and immediately did six figures of secondary-sales volume. And while all of that was true, the com-munity wasn't happy, with many lamenting having missed the chance to get this limited-edition collectible. They relayed the feedback in the Starbucks Odyssey Discord server, where engaged community mem-bers convened. The community response surfaced two key themes: a desire for a token-gated presale for the most loyal members of the program and an increased supply of the collectibles. Starbucks imple-mented both suggestions for the next limited-edition drop, resulting in a much more positive user experience.

In a traditional model without the instant community feedback loop, the Starbucks team might have read the positive headlines, seen the quick sellout, and simply adjusted the site to be more crash-proof for the next sale. The sale was exclusive to Starbucks Odyssey members, so it was already token-gated, and the Starbucks Odyssey team might not have seen any reason to layer in additional mechanics like early drop waves for the most active program participants. It was, after all, a very quick sellout, and royalties from robust secondary sales actually put money in Starbucks's pocket. But the Starbucks team recognized that the community is a big part of the brand. The feedback wasn't random people rage-tweeting about the company—it was coming from their biggest advocates and customers, a contingent of people who, when they felt heard, would only further increase their affinity for Starbucks.

The speed and quality of the feedback also demonstrates the difference between having people invested in your company's success versus a traditional model. If this were a normal small beta program at a Fortune 500 company, the issues probably would have been mentioned to decision-makers on a single slide in a larger quarterly business review. That would be months later, and it's unclear whether the feedback would even be acted upon. But the community feedback from the top supporters was loud and consistent, and Starbucks understood that these community members had a vested interest in the brand. The information wasn't just heard—it made it to the leadership level immediately and drove significant changes to the program.

Now, imagine another scenario in which Target launches an NFT series blending benefits from its current loyalty and subscription programs. Community engagement might not be a primary purpose initially, but the company might nevertheless open up a forum for NFT holders just like Starbucks did for theirs.

And when you think about it, many top Target fans have similarities to one another—for example, quite a few of them have school-age children. It's quite possible that the Target NFT holders' chat would become a source for community commentary about products, or possibly even advice on various aspects of child-rearing. ("Any recommendations for summer camps in the Northeast?" "What do I need for my kid's first dorm room?")

Target already has a simple "Parenting Guide" series on their website, but this could lead to a much more dynamic, personalized, and powerful version of that product. Suddenly Target would have a community of experts it can cultivate, enabling it to become a source of not just products but real-time, highly relevant information for its customer base. Disney does something similar with its planDisney program, in which Disney Parks superfans provide personalized advice to prospective theme park visitors—but NFTs create a way for this sort of community architecture to arise organically, and can also help formalize and streamline it.

More broadly, NFT products can leverage their holder communities for everything from design feedback to full-on co-creation. Steve's two favorite video game series, Fallout and Skyrim, are both open-world games created by the gaming studio Bethesda; we could imagine assorted NFT holders first being invited to help playtest new games, and then eventually co-designing an entirely new game world alongside the company. In this sense, holders would quite literally help the company build the world their community wanted to experience.

You rarely see this type of community-driven evolution in the traditional business world. Yet it occurs all the time with NFTs. Again, that's because shared ownership gives people incentive and license to contribute to the brand, and the NFT community architecture often creates a way for them to actually do so.

Of course, NFT brands lean into community-driven evolution to different degrees, and in different ways. But across the board, NFTs provide a way to leverage your fans to build your future.

10

The Staircase in Action

We've seen how the different parts of the NFT Staircase work individually and described how they can build upon one another to level up the value of an NFT project. However, even with the framework in hand and a solid understanding of how NFT technology works, it can still be challenging to picture how all the different elements might come together in practice. So, to really bring our Staircase climb to the next level, we're going to walk through several extended case studies using both real and hypothetical examples to illustrate how the ownership, utility, identity, community, and evolution dynamics we've described can be combined together in different applications.

We'll start by talking in more detail about what the world's coffeehouse is brewing up in the world of NFTs.

STARBUCKS ODYSSEY:
CONTINUALLY PERCOLATING

Earlier we mentioned that Starbucks, one of the world's most admired brands, has jumped into Web3 by creating an interactive NFT-based loyalty program. The program, called Starbucks Odyssey, gives participants the opportunity to complete "Journeys," which are quests that combine online and real-world activities—including things like visiting stores and buying coffee (of course), but also Starbucks trivia challenges and virtual tours of coffee farms. By finishing these tasks, members can earn digital NFT "Stamps" that boost their Starbucks Odyssey collector's score. A higher collector's score comes with special benefits and perks.

All of these features on their own create a fun new game dynamic for Starbucks customers, whereby they are rewarded for deepening their relationship with the brand. However, because Starbucks Odyssey is an NFT program, the ownership element kicks it up a notch, creating a whole new coffee collectible economy.

Each stamp can be bought and sold on a native marketplace within the Starbucks Odyssey web app or migrated off the app to be sold on third-party sites. In most cases, the only way to buy a stamp is to acquire it from a Starbucks Odyssey member who has completed the associated Journey. It provides a choose-your-own-adventure game of sorts because you can decide if you want to complete the tasks and grow your stamp empire, buy your way to a higher collector's score, or be on the sell-side and profit from your brand loyalty.

There are already micro-communities coalescing around Odyssey. In addition to the larger community that Starbucks itself is fostering, members of the program have started to form their own factions in a way Starbucks never anticipated. When the program launched, users were given three options for their in-game profile pictures—a bear, a hummingbird, or a tiger. People in the Starbucks Odyssey alpha test group immediately began engaging in friendly, yet competitive, banter surrounding Team Bear, Team Hummingbird, and Team Tiger.* While ownership and utility were apparent in the program design, and one could even argue identity was covered with people's love of Starbucks, the community aspect around the three animals is something that happened organically. And of course, the community members are also finding friends who share a passion for Starbucks—an outcome that Starbucks Chief Marketing Officer Brady Brewer intended when they launched the program.

As Brewer put it, "Starbucks has always served as the Third Place, a place between home and work where you feel the warmth of connection over coffee, community and belonging. The Starbucks Odyssey experience will extend the Third Place connection to the digital world. For the first time we are connecting our Starbucks Rewards loyalty program members not just to Starbucks, but to each other."

There's a meta-question about Odyssey, which one of Scott's students raised in a classroom discussion: *Why would Starbucks need a gamified loyalty program at all? Isn't Starbucks a coffee company?* Ironically, the question itself embeds the answer: Starbucks is one of

---

*Steve and Scott are both Team Bear, FYI.

the best-branded coffee companies in the world. They have thirty-five thousand stores in eighty different countries, and each day, millions of people buy coffee there. Almost paradoxically, that makes it difficult for the company to sell more coffee.

Wait what? you're thinking! *If Starbucks is such a well-known coffee company, how can they have trouble selling more coffee?* The issue is that it's kind of like telling a boxer to punch harder. People are already aware of the brand and have already established habits about how frequently they buy coffee from the company (or don't). To drive incremental sales, the company has to find ways of getting people to learn new things about the brand and become excited about it for new reasons—and NFT-based community building is perfect for that.

At the time of this writing, Starbucks Odyssey had just begun, but at least to our vision (biased, of course, since Steve is involved in running it), the program has the potential to significantly level up their legacy loyalty program, bringing in new customers and enhancing the experience for existing ones.

John Darroyo, a participant in Starbucks Odyssey, says he never thought much about the coffee he drank previously. He almost always brewed it at home, and he certainly never read any of the random emails his wife got from the old Starbucks loyalty program. Since joining Starbucks Odyssey, John has watched tons of Starbucks videos and even taken coffee quizzes to earn the associated NFT Stamps. In fact, John was so excited about Starbucks Odyssey that he was eventually brought on as an official community moderator and has since gotten into the world of Starbucks "cold cup" collecting.

For all intents and purposes, John became a totally new customer for Starbucks. That itself is important, but it goes even further, because his sense of identity around the program, and his participation in the community, makes him a brand asset. John went from being completely off Starbucks's radar to being a brand advocate, and eventually, a critical part of managing the community.

Meanwhile, the program also boasts longtime Starbucks fans like Chris Jourdan who have seen their average check increase. For example, Jourdan bought a $16 bag of coffee he would not have purchased otherwise as part of a Journey. Moreover, part of that Journey required him to scan a QR code on the back of the bag which shows the coffee's origin, a feature Jourdan was not previously aware of but he has since told people about. Similar to John, getting the extra purchase is great for Starbucks, but the win gets even bigger once you realize he's now generating unsolicited publicity for the brand.

And, even if Odyssey only achieves the same level of success as the legacy Starbucks loyalty program, it's still great for the company. Why's that? It's not because giving out NFTs proves how cutting-edge the brand is—rather, it's because NFTs change the way rewards are treated on the balance sheet. Reward points that can be redeemed for coffee or other merchandise are a big liability—they're essentially money you're committing to rebate to customers, and you can't control the payout time. Digital assets, by contrast, have low (or often zero) marginal cost. And even to the extent they do convey discounts and rebates as part of the program utility, Starbucks has a higher level of control than it does over reward points.

DIGITAL MUSIC: YOU BELONG WITH NFTS

Archaeologists have uncovered musical instruments from as far back as forty-two thousand years ago, so it's safe to say that music has been a central part of our lives for most of modern human history. But the current *business* of music is relatively new. In recent decades, it has been dominated by intermediaries, especially record labels, which are in effect fancy marketing and production companies that know how to get new music in front of an audience. While this is a valuable service, it can make it difficult for new artists to enter the market. And even when new artists are successful, the labels often take a big cut of their revenue.

Web 2 platforms like Bandcamp and Kickstarter created novel ways for artists to market their music directly to consumers, and even crowd-fund album releases and performances. Social media and streaming platforms like Spotify, SoundCloud, and YouTube—all Web 2 inventions—provided artists with new ways to reach their fans. But the entrenched record labels remained in place, in large part because these platforms didn't provide a way for most artists to build from an initial fan base into a sustainable business. (At the time of this writing, Spotify was estimated to be paying the average artist about $0.005 each time one of their songs was played, so to earn $50,000, an artist needed approximately 10,000,000 streams per year—roughly the equivalent of 2% of Spotify users listening to their music at least once, or 0.4% listening five times.)

NFTs can change all that.

Just like with digital artists and other types of creators, NFTs give musical artists a new way to do business that shifts the model in favor of themselves and their fans. Using NFTs, musicians can remove expensive intermediaries and connect more deeply with their most committed supporters.

If Taylor Swift, for example, were rising to fame today, she could release a series of NFTs for $500 each. Perhaps Swift would have a solid fan base on YouTube (hurray Web 2!) and could sell song NFTs directly to her subscribers. Swift could attach benefits to these NFTs as well—like concert tickets, access to exclusive merchandise, and the opportunity to attend token-gated meet-and-greets with the up-and-coming country singer. (Did you remember that Taylor Swift started as a country singer? We didn't think so!)

Suppose Swift managed to sell ten thousand of those NFTs—the same number as there are Bored Apes. That primary sale would raise $5 million, allowing Swift to hire her own team and create her own cost structure. And it would establish a dedicated community around her work—early fans who would be especially incentivized to share her music with their friends.

It's likely that along the way, many in the Swift NFT community would become friends as they see one another at concerts and other holder events. They are, after all, in a super-exclusive club and share a common passion for Swift's music. This is especially likely if Swift and her team foster this sort of engagement by providing a shared social hub for fans to interact with one another, and perhaps even interact occasionally with Swift herself. Leaders within the community would become known to Swift and her team.

As Swift then became one of the biggest musical acts in the world, the value of the benefits attached to the NFTs would rise exponentially.

(After all, individual Taylor Swift concert tickets are selling in the thousand-dollar range these days.) Some early fans might choose to sell their NFTs and profit; others would continue holding, and appreciate their benefits even more. (Meanwhile, Swift herself might receive royalties on every secondary sale, providing an extra income stream in perpetuity just for giving more value to her earliest supporters.)

Oh, and don't forget that when you do it this way, you know who your fans are! Taylor Swift was one of the first musical artists to use Ticketmaster's Verified Fan system to try to target concert tickets to her biggest fans. As Scott wrote in *Bloomberg Opinion* at the time, this was a great idea because true Taylor Swift fans engage in lots of Swift-related online activities. But in execution, there was a problem: the types of activities the Verified Fan program tracked were easy to game—things like posting about Swift on social media, or watching her music videos over and over again. By contrast, as we've already discussed, NFTs make it very clear who's been a supporter for how long, and how strongly. It's the ultimate way to verify fandom. And so it's not surprising that (as we mentioned way back in Chapter 6) Ticketmaster has decided to test an NFT-gated ticket-sales mechanism.

NFT ownership and utility give fans the opportunity to receive benefits for and form community around supporting their favorite musical artists. Meanwhile, the artists themselves can fund their own careers and interface with their fans directly, rather than through an intermediary like a label. What's more, artists and their fans can evolve, grow, and potentially even profit—together.

Of course, not every artist is Taylor Swift. (She is after all the first person in history to hold all positions on the *Billboard* Top 10 at once.)

But you don't have to be Taylor Swift to implement this strategy. Even a musical artist with just a few fans can leverage NFTs to identify and reward those fans and turn them into a community. And indeed, at the time of this writing, Web3 was already starting to see a few break-out music stars, such as Daniel Allan and Violetta Zironi, who were successfully using versions of this model.

All of this can drive a positive feedback loop on the consumer side, too, by providing a direct incentive to seek out new high-quality music. The Web3 platform Sound.xyz, for example, was launched to help artists put out songs as NFTs in numbered editions. The theory is as follows:

> Each edition of the NFT is numbered uniquely, so listeners can showcase their early support.
> Since early editions are considered more valuable than later editions, backers are incentivized to discover new music early. [...]
> Show off the Sound NFTs you've collected and prove you were a fan from way back in the day. Can you find the next big sound?

NFTs have the potential to decentralize not just music creation but also the discovery of new artists. Sounds awesome!

PIZZA COMMUNITY: IT'S NOT DELIVERY, IT'S AN AIRDROP

Any study or poll of the most popular foods in America will include one special cheesy carb bomb: pizza. But despite its popularity—and despite many global pizza brands—how many pizza *communities* do you know? Outside of the Teenage Mutant Ninja Turtles, who rally around pizza after every crime-fighting victory, there aren't many. But that doesn't mean it can't be done.

At the time of writing this book, the most popular frozen pizza brand in America was DiGiorno. In addition to great sales, the company had a well-established presence in pop culture, with mentions on late night shows, big sports sponsorships, and even placement in popular movies. Thanks to a long-time ad campaign, for many Americans, the entire concept of frozen pizza was synonymous with DiGiorno. Indeed, if we had to bet, we expect most of our friends would at least know the company's catchphrase: "It's not delivery, it's DiGiorno."

Yet most people wouldn't call DiGiorno a part of their identity—it's frozen pizza, for heaven's sake! And people certainly weren't participating in the DiGiorno brand directly.

So how do you get someone to be passionate about frozen pizza? With a not-so-secret ingredient: NFToppings.

DiGiorno has a great social media personality and brand identity, creating a real opportunity to use NFTs for two-way value creation with their customers. So let's play out a delicious hypothetical.*

To start, DiGiorno identifies their most frequent customers, along with anyone who's regularly engaging with them on social media platforms. They gift those people branded NFTs themed around perhaps the most important part of any pizza: the toppings.

---

*As far as we know, DiGiorno wasn't working on this as of 2023—but if anyone there is reading, please call us!

The "NFToppings" come in all shapes, sizes, and flavors. They have slightly different color schemes and patterns, making each one unique. Each recipient gets two of them to start off with, randomly selected from the collection.

You know what comes next: Everyone has a favorite pizza topping, and thanks to the vagaries of randomization, almost nobody receives their preferred topping initially. So they start trading! Some people collect a complete set of all four cheeses, while others try to hoard the mushrooms.

Conversely, others decide they identify with the toppings they have, even if they haven't in the past. Steve may never have considered himself a pineapple pizza person before, but after getting airdropped the "BIG GRIN" golden pineapple, he'd be the first to tell you that tropical fruit absolutely does belong on pizza pies—frozen or otherwise.

Of course, DiGiorno packs the NFTs full of utility, as well. In the spirit of the Ninja Turtles, DiGiorno throws an annual holders-only pizza party.* Plus, there are product discounts: If you collect a set of NFTs corresponding to a given topping set that DiGiorno actually sells, you get 15% off whenever you buy that pie. Acquiring certain NFToppings also gets you access to new product samples; and, leveraging the company's sports partnerships, especially rare NFToppings might even get you tickets to a game.

Over time, the NFToppings series evolves into a full-blown gamified loyalty program, with NFTs for people who buy certain specialty

---

*Cowabunga, dude!

pizzas, product rewards, and even company-sponsored fan-art competitions.

The company might even give holders some degree of intellectual property rights to their NFToppings, inviting them to build characters around them. Popular fan-created topping characters like Tony Pepperoni (neon red, with '80s sunglasses) and Melinda Mushroom are featured on DiGiorno pizza boxes, and their creators are invited to a special factory tour.

The ownership value here is clear, as is the utility. Even more importantly, the entire concept encourages DiGiorno's biggest fans to engage with the company in a (pun intended) brand-new way. And with all that engagement, especially as the utility gets better and bigger, comes identity. If you're building a collection of your favorite DiGiorno toppings and getting rewards like the ones just mentioned, you'll likely be showing them off on social media and telling your friends. Whether you consciously do it or not, you'll start to be a "DiGiorno person," even forming attachments to your NFToppings characters. And since the company advertises regularly on both traditional television and platforms like YouTube, the company might even pay NFToppings holders to license their characters for use in commercials.

And the community is baked in. Once DiGiorno opens a chat server for NFToppings holders to engage with one another, people with various toppings start connecting. Shared taste in food is a unifier, and individual holders start to offer to help out to their "topping crew." DiGiorno creates separate token-gated channels for each topping type; now, holding multiple distinct toppings is a way to gain access to different subcommunities at the same time.

And remember that "Does pineapple belong on pizza?" debate? People have strong views.*

Holders of pineapple NFToppings mount a "YES ON PIZZA" messaging campaign to celebrate International Pineapple Day. Led by Melinda Mushroom, the mushroom holders develop a good-natured rebuttal, and for a week, social media is full of people posting their views on the pineapple-versus-mushroom debate. (And don't even get us started on the epic fantasy-football rivalry between the Pepperoni Posse and the Sausage Squad.)

And of course, that's not the only way community happens. People make friends at the pizza parties, for example—perhaps discovering shared interest not just in mushrooms and peppers, but also in puzzle-solving and long-distance biking. They stay in touch afterward, and maybe even meet up for ice cream or a DiGiorno pie on occasion.

Some particularly active community members might even get tapped by the brand to become local DiGiorno ambassadors. They get special jackets with their favorite toppings embroidered on the sleeve, organize local meetups, and write regularly about how much they love the brand—and their NFToppings crew. Now the pizza giant has perhaps thousands of brand ambassadors spreading the good word about DiGiorno around the web. Whether they're talking about their fun meetups with fellow frozen pizza cognoscenti, flexing the free or discounted products they've consumed, or simply displaying their NFToppings on social media feeds, the passionate online com-

---

*Although Steve and Scott are not sure why this is even a question—obviously pineapple belongs on pizza! Anyone who thinks otherwise is a mushroom.

munity is effectively a marketing and content-creation wing for the brand. And it carries more credibility than traditional advertising because it's coming from fans.

Of course, as we already said, the DiGiorno NFToppings example is hypothetical, at least as of when we were writing—but all the phenomena it illustrates are completely real. In the first six months of Starbucks Odyssey, the coffee company was already seeing participants create videos around free coffee from the program, sharing images of themselves unboxing custom cups, and raving about the rewards they had received in Facebook groups. Nike saw similar forms of engagement when they first launched digital sneakers as part of their .SWOOSH NFT ecosystem. NFTs, when used correctly, can help practically any consumer-facing company boost their brand's public perception in this way.

ACTIVATING ALUMNI: THE NEW COLLEGE TRY

A few times in the book, we've compared NFT communities to those of people who share an alma mater, so let's explore how NFTs could enhance the functionality of a college alumni club. For starters, anyone who has registered for alumni events has likely found that communication and event coordination is scattered across a litany of channels. Sometimes the organizers use platforms like Eventbrite. Alternatively, they might use manual entry through Google Forms. Still other times there are websites built by the alumni club itself. And in each instance, you need to put in your data and registration information line by line, even though the alumni club has reached out to *you* and already knows you're a card-carrying member. (And that's assuming you even hear about the event in the first place—alumni event messaging tends to be spread across email lists, Facebook groups, and even WhatsApp chats.)

Universities could simplify this process by awarding all graduates a nontransferable NFT, giving cross-platform access to the alumni club. This could in turn streamline the registration process for all manner of events, leading to higher participation. Increased participation would likely (hopefully?) result in increased donations, which could again be managed through alumni club members' digital wallets. And closing the loop, donors could be rewarded with further NFTs that provide special benefits and access down the line.

Such NFTs could also be used to anchor a central messaging and communications platform, and to token-gate alumni access to campus event tickets, such as for homecoming games or commencement. And they present a natural opportunity for third parties to offer verified member benefits in the form of alumni discounts, as well.

Meanwhile, the role of alumni status in identity is automatic—as we've already discussed, people frequently share alumni status on their personal and professional digital profiles. And there's a community advantage here as well, as these NFT assets would surface the global alumni network digitally.

As to how things evolve from there . . . ? Well, that's up to the school and its community.

PART III

PUTTING

IT ALL

TOGETHER

11

Finding the Proper
Price and Scale

Hopefully by this point, you have a sense of how NFTs work and how they can create value for businesses and consumers. And maybe you've started to grok two parallel senses in which NFTs can become ubiquitous in our digital lives:

- NFTs can be almost everywhere,

- and they can shift the way we do almost *everything*.

In a Web3 world, each account, activity, or experience can be tied to a digital asset. And every digital asset can take on multilayered significance, up to and including becoming a source of personal identity, a community anchor, and a brand springboard.

As we were writing, there were signs and experiments pointing in this direction: Top brands, platforms, and media franchises like Starbucks, Amazon, and Disney were dipping their toes into the NFT space. Consumers were pouring into the ecosystem as well, drawn in by major NFT releases from the likes of Reddit and Nike—with millions of people buying NFTs in consumer-friendly custodial digital wallets. Meanwhile, government regulators were taking a serious look at how to separate NFTs from other digital asset classes such as cryptocurrency.

If that NFT-filled future comes to be, what does it mean for your company? And while we're at it, how will we know if we're really moving in that direction? In this chapter, we're going to look at some dynamics of the NFT business ecosystem. And then in the next chapter, we'll explore the principles the NFT Staircase implies for leveraging NFTs for existing businesses—as well as for launching a novel NFT-based brand.

THE EARLY NFT MARKET (DIS)EQUILIBRIUM

The very first NFTs were mostly projects simply exploring the technology. But NFTs' potential to serve as collectibles quickly became clear, and in 2017, they got mainstream attention with the popularity of Dapper Labs's CryptoKitties—an NFT collection of cutesy cat images with fur colors and other features of varying rarity. But interest in the category tapered off in the following year, alongside a decline in public interest in crypto and blockchain technology more broadly.

By the time we entered the NFT market in 2021, however, the technology was having a resurgence. NFTs were increasingly used as digital deeds to various artworks, and digital brands were experimenting with the NFT model. Even then, however, the vast majority of

NFT projects focused on scarcity as a principal driver of demand. NFTs would be produced in series of ten thousand, one thousand, or even a few hundred. This was because the total number of participants in the early NFT market was small—there was little overall demand, and producing products in low supply was to some degree the proper response. Yet at the same time, scarcity combined with some degree of speculation about potential future value led to high prices— with some mainstream NFTs, such as the Bored Apes, trading in the tens or hundreds of thousands of dollars or more.

In practice, however, the vast majority of collectibles are sold at relatively accessible prices, at least within their product category— maybe a dollar for a souvenir keychain; $5 to $10 for a pack of trading cards; $20 for a special edition game-day program; or $250 for a fancy pair of sneakers. That doesn't mean they aren't produced in limited editions—but those editions might run in the many thousands or occasionally even millions.

That's the type of scale we expect to see for collectible NFTs in the long run: NFTs priced appropriately for their audience, and with supply large enough to make those prices sensible. Moreover, many of them will be acquired automatically with other purchases, or earned through effort or engagement, rather than being bought outright.

That's what already happens in many virtual game worlds. Roblox is a prime example, boasting over sixty million daily active users at the time of this writing. Players can use an in-game currency called Robux—which costs real money to acquire—to buy various aesthetic upgrades to their characters, as well as to gain access to exclusive virtual experiences (Club Roblox, anyone?). There are also opportunities to earn upgrades and experiences through completion of quests, victories in competitions, or sheer luck through lottery-type mechanics. This system isn't unique to Roblox, either. Fortnite, Minecraft, World of Warcraft, and many other online games have seen millions of users participate in these microeconomies.

Businesses are already selling these sorts of inexpensive digital collectible NFTs, and with that, the range of NFT consumers has already expanded substantially. As of June 2023, Reddit had sold more than ten million of its digital avatar NFTs, bringing in more than $32 million in sales volume. Similarly, programs like Starbucks Odyssey and Nike's .SWOOSH bring new consumers into NFT-world almost every day. Ubiquity of access doesn't mean that future NFTs will have any less pull or power—quite the opposite. Think Pokémon cards or Star Wars figurines, but digital, upgradable, portable across platforms, and easily tradable with anyone in the world. And then imagine using those digital collectibles to bring top fans into direct communication with one another and with the brand itself.

Or think about those souvenir "passports," where people collect stamps from national parks or other major landmarks. Turning those stamps into NFTs makes them permanently maintainable and instantaneously shareable.

TRUE FANS

At the same time, part of what's special about NFTs is that they emphatically *don't* require global scale to get started—an NFT community can form around just a few people and spin outward from there. And just like how the subscription-based television has made it possible to produce niche shows that appeal to fewer people but generate a lot more value for those viewers, NFTs enable even small creators to build communities and cultivate fandom.

Blockchain infrastructure is open-source and broadly accessible, which makes it relatively easy for an individual or small team to launch their own NFTs without support from the likes of a studio, agency, or record label. (Don't worry—there are already well-established platforms to help with the software bits.)

For all the reasons we've already discussed, NFTs can be especially valuable when a creator is just getting started. They give a way for early fans to build their enthusiasm into their digital identity, and to find and interact with the creator and one another. And of course, NFTs also provide fans with some upside in the creator's success because then the ownership value and utility can expand. (This can happen even when the NFT's value simply increases because new fans decide they want to join the community. But for an extreme example, think back to Taylor Swift, or imagine if you had been one of Billy Joel's earliest supporters back in the 1970s, and received a "founders' edition" NFT that entitled you to free concert tickets in perpetuity.)

Kevin Kelly, founder of *Wired* magazine, famously wrote a 2008 essay called "1,000 True Fans," in which he argued:

> To be a successful creator you don't need millions. You don't need millions of dollars or millions of customers, millions of clients or

millions of fans. To make a living as a craftsperson, photographer, musician, designer, author, animator, app maker, entrepreneur, or inventor you need only thousands of true fans. [. . .]

Here's how the math works. You need to meet two criteria. First, you have to create enough each year that you can earn, on average, $100 profit from each true fan. That is easier to do in some arts and businesses than others, but it is a good creative challenge in every area because it is always easier and better to give your existing customers more, than it is to find new fans.

Second, you must have a direct relationship with your fans. That is, they must pay you directly. You get to keep all of their support, unlike the small percent of their fees you might get from a music label, publisher, studio, retailer, or other intermediate. If you keep the full $100 of each true fan, then you need only 1,000 of them to earn $100,000 per year. That's a living for most folks.

Now, $100 per year per fan sounds like a large number at first, but that's really just $8 to $9 per month—roughly the same price as a Netflix subscription, or what you might pay in a couple trips to a favorite coffee shop. Plenty of people pay that much to support their favorite artists, puzzle creators, or video game streamers on platforms like Patreon or Twitch.

And speaking of Patreon and Twitch, NFTs are continuing a trend that those platforms started and extending it to the broader market: tilting the balance of brand attachment toward the thousand true fans, or even the hundred mega-megafans. With NFTs, a brand or creator can find their biggest enthusiasts and supercharge their engagement and connection for mutual gain.* That means a market where firms work harder to convert customers into the megafan category, and cater to those customers more once they get there. And in turn, the firm benefits from those customers becoming longtime, or even lifetime, enthusiasts who actively invest in engaging with and helping build the brand—not to mention buying from it.

Just as we were finishing writing this book in June 2023, the luxury brand Louis Vuitton announced a particularly exceptional approach to megafan cultivation: a €39,000 NFT "Treasure Trunk" that would be nontransferable, i.e., it would become permanently bound to buyers' digital wallets. The Treasure Trunk NFT comes with a physical analog. But a key selling point was the promise of ongoing access to special products and other opportunities—in effect, permanently attaching holders to the evolution of the Louis Vuitton brand. And moreover—get this—prospective buyers could only purchase via application.

But again, NFTs aren't just about big brands with big-bang products. Two of Scott's favorite restaurants in Cambridge, the noodle shops Yume Wo Katare and Yume Ga Arukara, have historically had a program whereby customers can buy a pass—a physical card—granting the holder unlimited noodles for a year. The pass price is far less than

---

*In economese, borrowing an explanation from Scott's friend and co-author Alex Tabarrok: A lot of classical marketing is about appealing to consumers who are "on the margin" in the sense that they are just on the edge of being converted into buying a brand's product. NFTs enable brands to focus on creating more value for—and further activating—existing customers, especially those who already see the most value in the brand.

€39,000, of course, but conceptually the process is similar: prospective holders have to apply, and those who receive the pass even customize it by stating a personal "dream for the year" that hopefully eating massive quantities of ramen and udon will help them focus on and achieve.*

Yume pass holders often become the restaurants' top evangelists. And because they dine at the restaurants so frequently, many of them get to know one another and become friends. But all of this interaction is analog. Scott was a pass holder for several years, and while he self-identified as such, there was never a clear way to interact with the Yume brand digitally, other than periodically replying to the restaurants' Facebook and Instagram posts. And similarly, while he made friends among the pass holders, there was no mechanism to stay connected. NFTs would solve all of that—and they're well within the restaurants' ability to create, even with off-the-shelf technology available as of early 2023.

Similarly, we can easily imagine people collecting digital stamps, say, of all the rotating flavors at a local donut shop, and sharing their enthusiasm for the company online.† (The donut shop could even directly incentivize that: "Connect your donut log to Twitter to receive

---

*The "dream for the year" concept came about because the ramen shop Yume Wo Katare was explicitly created in part as a "dream studio," where people would share their dreams with fellow diners and cheer one another on.

†Scott's local donut shop, Union Square Donuts, has eclectic flavors like Ube Coconut, Peach Melba, and S'mores—all of which he's sampled and would be proud to feature on his digital profiles. Same with the pumpernickel and potato/chive seasonal English muffins at Vinal Bakery.

15% off your next order!") And these sorts of NFTs can also be used to deploy community rewards, like access to after-hours donut parties where regulars can get to know the staff and one another—in turn increasing the quality of the experience those regulars get whenever they visit the store.

It's easy to see how a program like that could lead someone to buy an extra donut and coffee every couple of weeks—and there's the $9 per month required to be one of the thousand true fans already. And of course that's actually more than what Kevin Kelly was imagining because it's incremental relative to what those customers were already spending. Plus, it's before fans become actively invested and try to help build up the brand themselves.

ONE SIZE DOESN'T FIT ALL

So is the optimal NFT project big or small?

Yes. We're a bit wary of sounding like we're claiming that NFTs are perfect for all applications—they're very much not. But they really can be value-creating at both large and small scales.

The examples we've covered thus far illustrate how NFTs can replace (or at least reconstitute) numerous categories of digital assets we already have—music files, electronic tickets, digital identity records, and the like—and also lead to a massive scale-up in the creation of *digital assets as products*, such as NFT Pokémon cards or Star Wars collectibles.

At the same time, NFTs stand to transform the emphasis of brand engagement by enabling companies and creators to build community among their megafans. NFT-based community building can work for Starbucks and Louis Vuitton, and also for your local noodle or donut shop.

Such activity will become more universal and valuable as digital wallet technology becomes more robust and accessible to consumers. In many cases, this will happen through customers acquiring their first few digital assets from some company or brand they already love and engage with frequently—hence why the likes of Nike and Reddit have been so successful in bringing new consumers into the NFT space.

And in parallel, the potential opportunity associated with any given NFT project expands as more platforms can interface with Web3 assets. Twitter was a bellwether for this in 2022, and as we were writing in 2023, many more platforms were beginning to integrate ways of displaying and interacting with NFTs.

Finally, from the perspective of an individual company, we should emphasize once more that there are many ways to win with NFTs. But depending on your goals, how you want to engage, and the scale and composition of your audience and market, your NFT strategy may be very different. That's where we're going next.

12

Designing Your NFT Strategy

In many ways, figuring out how NFTs fit into your organization's business operations isn't terribly different from implementing other new products and software. But since NFTs are a technology with novel functionalities and applications, there are some nuances and pitfalls to avoid. We've seen it all, from massive successes to unfortunate failures, and have compiled a few best practices to ensure your company enters Web3 with the highest chance of success.

SPOTTING MARKET FAILURES— AND THE ASSOCIATED OPPORTUNITIES

In Scott's course on marketplace design, he trains students to identify market failures—places where a market isn't achieving its maximum social potential. Loosely, identifying market failures requires asking,

Where is there an activity or transaction that people would like to engage in, but they aren't? Whenever that happens, there is (almost tautologically) an opportunity for value creation if you can solve whatever the blocker is.

Critically, it's important to focus on the reason why people can't engage or transact in the desired way. It's not enough to say "People would like to buy more used bicycles, but don't"; you have to understand whether the reason these transactions aren't happening is, for example, because of lack of supply, or high search costs, or difficulty executing the transaction itself.

We referenced a simple example very early in this book: Before NFTs, it was much harder to establish and track property rights over digital art, which made it difficult for the market to function. Even though there were lots of digital artists who wanted to be able to sell their work and—as we now know—a large market of potential buyers, many potentially value-creating transactions didn't happen. In this sense, NFTs helped address a fundamental market failure in the digital art market.

Note also that if you observe people going out of their way to use a somewhat inefficient work-around, that's often a hint that a market failure is present. Prior to NFTs, many digital artists had established subscription services through platforms like Patreon, but these weren't robust sales mechanisms because they often didn't make it possible to exclude nonsubscribers from gaining equal access to the product. Indeed, once an artist had shared their new work to their "patrons," it could quickly end up reposted to public platforms such as Reddit. Or, alternatively, they had to hand over the right to their art to third-party solutions like Shutterstock, where they were unable to maximize their earnings potential.

OKAY, BUT WHAT DOES THAT HAVE TO DO WITH LAUNCHING AN NFT PROJECT?

Defining an NFT opportunity is very much about identifying a market failure and its underlying cause (and of course, how NFTs can address the issue).

Here are some of the market failures—and associated opportunities—we described in earlier chapters:

- A theater or concert venue might want to solve the trust problem in the digital ticket resale market to ensure that tickets to sold-out shows don't get wasted.

- A local donut shop (or global coffee chain) might want to establish a loyalty program that rewards customers for repeat purchases and/or exploring the menu.

- An online education platform might want to distribute publicly verifiable credentials to people who have completed its courses, so that those people can verifiably prove their education, and potentially even network as alumni.

- An author might want to invite a number of their readers to co-create a new book or edition.

- A frozen pizza business, soda maker, or other consumer goods company might want to give purchasers an incentive to share their enthusiasm for the product with others, form a community around the brand, and drive it forward.

The solutions draw upon different features of NFTs, which loosely progress from simple ownership all the way to evolution:*

- Just like with digital art sales, solving the trust problem in ticketing is mostly about clearly defining a unique owner of each digital ticket.

- Rewards programs, meanwhile, focus on giving people ownership of their purchase history, and then stacking utility on top of that.

- Online education credentials are mostly about establishing identity records that a user can bring with them across platforms.

- Co-development of a book or other creative work relies on defining the community of contributors, and giving them a mechanism to share and evaluate their ideas—such as through a token-gated platform.

- And of course, as we've emphasized throughout this book, community-driven brand evolution is about . . . *everything*.

The NFT Staircase guides you to think about what NFT holders will *own*, what *utility* those assets will deliver, and how they will shape *identity* and *community* formation. At the same time, it's important

---

*Sorry, we know the Staircase here is reading down the page rather than up, but that's because people typically read from top to bottom. If you want it to look more like a proper staircase, just flip the page over!

to ground the question of what NFT product to build in the context of a true market failure/opportunity for your company.

You have to ask yourself: *What is the brand purpose?* And: *Do NFTs solve a real problem here?*

Scott knows of one NFT creator (name omitted for courtesy) who was a well-established illustration artist, with work regularly appearing in magazines and shows. But few, if any, of his existing customers were engaged in the NFT market. He launched an NFT series of his extremely cool art—but he did it without teaching his existing enthusiasts about Web3, or even clearly defining why this product opportunity could be special. The main utility of the NFT, at least at launch, was just the ability to acquire physical prints of the creator's work—making it unclear why he didn't just sell the prints directly.

On the flip side, the company DraftKings is solving a real problem with its Reignmakers NFT platform. DraftKings's core business model is a concept called *daily fantasy sports*, which allows participants to draft a fantasy sports team for one single game. Reignmakers combines this concept with the traditional fantasy sports model where people draft players for an entire season by allowing people to own player cards, which are issued as NFTs, that can be added to your team lineup each week or sold on the open market. In this instance, using a blockchain enables the player cards to be bought and sold in a frictionless manner, saving DraftKings the need to create a back-end system, which would have been more susceptible to failure, or worse, manipulation if it were hacked. The blockchain establishes ownership of DraftKings's digital cards, solving a problem; moreover, Reignmakers is a logical extension of the company's existing business model.

You can imagine the same sort of NFT system working well in many other contexts with digital assets that people might want to frequently exchange—digital versions of collectible card games, for example, or even trading physical collectibles like in the context of the StockX Vault, which we described in Chapter 5.

Likewise, Starbucks Odyssey has a clear purpose—it's leveling up loyalty rewards, a critical element of Starbucks's company strategy, in an area where Web3 adds value. And token-gating of both product drops and digital tickets ensures true fans can purchase stress-free without being front-run by scalpers, bringing value to the company's most loyal customers.

DEFINING THE ASSET

Understanding your design goal and the ways the different steps of the NFT Staircase factor in makes it possible to start thinking about how to define the NFT asset itself. You might consider, for example:

- **Quantity:** *How many units should be available?* For tickets, natu-rally, there should generally be one per seat. For digital collectibles where there is no physical constraint on supply, you might never-theless want to impose limits as a way of creating scarcity or rarity. (That said, as we talked about in the previous chapter, you might not want your collectible to be *too* scarce!) For rewards and cre-dentials, meanwhile, supply might instead be uncapped and tied to activities like product purchases or course completion.

- **Transferability:** *Should users be able to exchange the asset among one another?* Enabling trade is often a key part of the reason to adopt NFTs for use with tickets or collectibles. (Although there are exceptions—it would be a real pain if airlines made their tickets transferable, for example, because then speculators might buy up all the seats in advance, making it nigh impossible for ordinary consumers to plan travel.) Digital credentials, meanwhile, are typically nontransferable because they reflect a specific individual's record of activity. And in the case of community co-creation, transferability might in essence be partial—one might be able to transfer their NFT to someone else, but still keep whatever rights or responsibilities they acquired while holding it.

- **Metadata:** *What information will the NFT actually embed?* An online education credential, for example, might encode information about the course, its instructor, and the date of completion—just like in a school transcript. A ticket would encode information about the show you're seeing, seat number, and any benefits it might come with, such as an included food item.

- **Acquisition process:** *How will people obtain the NFT?* Maybe people collect rewards NFTs by scanning a QR code at the time of purchase. Tickets, meanwhile, might be distributed in a single primary sale or airdrop. At the same time, game assets or brand tokens might be continuously available—perhaps you can always get one at a fixed price by going to the company website, just like you might with a pack of trading cards.

CHARACTERIZING THE HOLDER
AND MAPPING OUT UTILITY

From there, you'll have a better idea of who your target consumers are and what they want, which should help make it clear which forms of utility they'll value. Just as important, you know who your target consumer is *not*, which can provide a critical check on whether the utility you're planning makes sense.

If your NFT gives access to discounts at local businesses around Cleveland, Ohio, for example, then you might naturally partner with businesses in Columbus, Ohio, to offer further verified member benefits. Your NFT holders can take a weekend trip to Columbus with a two-hour drive and receive benefits when they arrive, while the city of Columbus can boost its tourism industry with qualified travelers who are nearby enough that they might make repeat visits. But at the same time, it might not make nearly as much sense for the same Cleveland-based NFT to do cross-promotion for businesses in Tokyo, Japan—how many holders of any given local business NFT are likely to take a $5,000 trip across the world just to leverage NFT-based discounts?

For established businesses, this step might be easier because it's an extension of the existing brand. Starbucks already knows and understands its target consumers deeply, so what the company did with NFTs became a natural next evolution of its existing loyalty program, drawing on many of the same features such as purchasing rewards and fast-play online games. The Hundreds similarly understood its customers and the ways in which they think about style, collectibility, and affiliation with the brand; this made it intuitive for the company to formulate utility such as early access to clothing drops and opportunities to interact with the founders.

FOSTERING IDENTITY
AND COMMUNITY FORMATION

Once you understand your reasons for creating digital ownership and your target market for the desired utility, you're ready to ascend the rest of the Staircase. For many NFT projects, you'll want to think about precisely how holders will integrate the NFTs into their personal and public identities, and how community will coalesce (and what purpose it will serve). You may need to encourage this directly, perhaps by creating the space for it, such as a community message board or chat channel, and even rewarding it ("Anyone who uses one of our NFTs for their profile picture gets a free sweatshirt!"). Even big brands like Adidas and Budweiser have created Discord communities to connect holders with one another.

Identity and community cohesion can provide retention and network effects, but in many cases a bit of activation energy is needed to kick them off. (Although you might get lucky and have the process start itself—the Bored Ape Yacht Club's early success was in part due to many people's immediate sense of personal affinity for the Ape images.)

Community formation, especially, may start prior to launch— successful NFT projects often go out of their way to build a proto-community before minting even begins, or to tap into existing communities and networks. Not only does this serve to confirm that the target holder for your NFT actually exists, but early experimentation along the search for product-based community can help shape what the right product actually is. The Web3 brand Doodles, which we mentioned earlier, is a great example of this. Over a period of weeks, the company identified individuals they felt fit the ethos of their business and invited them to a private Discord chat server, where they engaged in a variety of virtual community events and educated them about the brand Doodles was trying to build. Doodles then gave those initial community members a few referrals to invite their friends, expanding the community outward through people's trusted networks. In the end, the founders allocated a significant share of the NFTs to the people in their Discord, ensuring that most of the assets at least initially went to people who had already been recruited and socialized into the brand's culture.

GOING TO MARKET

More broadly, unless you're just using NFTs as infrastructure for the creation, sale, or trade of a specific digital asset, the process of launching an NFT product is different from other categories. You're often in effect *launching alongside your community*, rather than just *selling a product to customers*. Brands need to clearly communicate the value proposition while recognizing that the product is likely to evolve over time. Moreover, as of 2023, the accessibility of the underlying technology was still an issue, so launching an NFT often came with a need to educate customers about what they were actually buying.

When Adidas launched its Into the Metaverse NFTs in 2021, it partnered with Pixel Vault, a Web3 gaming and comic company; the Bored Ape Yacht Club; and Web3 fashion aficionado Gmoney. This gave them a few major advantages. First, the partnership helped Adidas curate their holder base. Adidas gave mint access to holders of Pixel Vault and Bored Ape Yacht Club NFTs, who were already experienced and active in Web3. And partnering with those high-end NFT brands also helped justify the primary sale price of $765, which was far more than most customers were used to paying for the brand's physical products. The move also gave Adidas access to the NFT-native brands' software developers, which came in handy when there was a bug during the launch. By having top developers at their fingertips, Adidas was able to fix the issue and have the sale live again within a few hours. Without that partnership, it could have been days before they re-launched, which could have killed momentum before they ever got going.

On the other end of the spectrum, when Reddit launched their digital avatar NFTs to their community of forum posters, they were facing an almost entirely non-NFT-native audience. Knowing that the avatars' purpose was to help users further define and reinforce their identities within the Reddit community, the platform launched a series of NFT avatars that sold at fixed costs ranging from $9.99 to $49.99—and, as we noted earlier, with most of the underlying NFT technology obscured.

In short, your go-to-market strategy will differ based on your goals and what you're hoping to accomplish. The examples used in this section alone show that there's more than one way to successfully create an NFT program. Adidas launched to already crypto-attuned communities; Starbucks and DraftKings launched to a mix of current customers and NFT enthusiasts; and Reddit launched to a non-NFT crowd.

BE CREATIVE . . .

In many cases, there are benefits to leveraging multiple steps of the NFT Staircase even when you might naturally think just one or two of them are first-order. For example, although NFTickets seem to mostly be about ownership and a very simple form of utility (i.e., access to an event), there is a real opportunity to transform those tickets into part of a person's digital identity, giving them a way of sharing their fandom. And meanwhile, although an NFT certifying completion of an online course might mostly be about identity, it's also easy to imagine that it could anchor a form of alumni community, increasing user engagement with the platform, and possibly driving people to take more courses.

. . . AND BE RECEPTIVE

As we've already said, a huge part of the opportunity in many NFT applications is to enable others to innovate around the underlying asset. This might be as simple as inviting third parties to offer verified member benefits (like discounted drinks for anyone who's holding an NFTicket to the day's Celtics game). It also often comes from encouraging holders to expand upon the NFT or create derivatives—everything from writing the fictional backstory of your Bored Ape (or

NFTopping) to creating community content independent of but encouraged by the NFT's original issuer.

One of the world's most famous entrepreneurs and content creators, Gary Vaynerchuk, has done the latter well with his NFT project VeeFriends, comprising a series of animal characters Vaynerchuk invented such as Brave Bison, Prudent Polar Bear, and Genuine Giraffe. One of the most supportive VeeFriends holders, Jeremy Jannielli, began creating content around the brand shortly after launch, including educational videos about the company, pack openings of VeeFriends trading cards, and live virtual community gatherings on Twitter's social audio platform, Twitter Spaces. Vaynerchuk saw this, and rather than send Jannielli a cease-and-desist letter, he encouraged it—motivating Jannielli to produce even more. Jannielli then took to organizing unofficial community events and meetups, providing direct value to the VeeFriends brand with no work from the VeeFriends team. (And as perhaps the ultimate symbol of support, Vaynerchuk himself attended some of these events, even though he had no obligation to.)

In short, Gary Vaynerchuk's openness to Jannielli's community innovations has given VeeFriends an extra marketing arm, while Jannielli became a community leader and received recognition and attention from one of his favorite creators. This became an even bigger win-win when, after a couple of years of being a highly engaged community member, Jannielli was actually hired to the official team. Now in addition to the brand publicly supporting its biggest evangelists, community engagement could lead to a particularly aspirational outcome—a job with Vaynerchuk himself.

Vaynerchuk's receptiveness to up-and-coming community content creators isn't anything new; it was part of his ethos before Web3 and is on full display at his annual tech and culture megaconference, VeeCon. The aforementioned VeeFriends NFTs double as access passes to the conference (NFTickets in action!) and Gary pulls out all the stops to put on a must-attend event. The conference has A-list speakers such as Hollywood filmmaker Spike Lee, music and fashion mogul Pharrell Williams, and entrepreneur Daymond John, as well as various leaders and luminaries from Web3. By all accounts, the first year of VeeCon was successful, but one piece of feedback stuck with the VeeFriends team—in addition to the star-studded lineup, holders wanted to find ways to feature more actual VeeFriends community members. Thus, in the conference's second year, Vaynerchuk and team implemented a community stage to spotlight select VeeFriends holders with specific expertise. From compliance and ethics to community building and content creation, the stage has highlighted people the VeeFriends community interacts with each and every day. Attendees raved about it.

The Bored Ape Yacht Club did something similar when a notable holder known as Swickie, along with her husband Peter Fang (who is also heavily involved in the Ape ecosystem), organized an unofficial BAYC community event during Art Basel in Miami. The party, called OtherBlock, featured various artistic interpretations of the Bored Ape images, performances by community members who hold BAYC NFTs, a Bored Ape–themed food truck, and even an Ape-based banana pudding brand (because what else would a community full of Apes eat for dessert?). While there was no official corporate connection to the

Bored Ape Yacht Club, the BAYC founders showed up at the party as a special surprise to the community. Especially since they don't do many public appearances, this served to reinforce the idea that what the community creates is fundamentally part of the brand—which of course encouraged the community to create even more.

Of course, one has to be careful when inviting others to build on top of your brand. Not everyone will be a great fit the way Jeremy Jannielli was for VeeFriends. But remixing like this can be powerful. A rough analogy is product placement. Reese's Pieces increased in popularity significantly after appearing in the movie *ET.* Similarly, the DeLorean gained pop-culture awareness (and a cult following) after being featured in the *Back to the Future* series.* NFTs make this sort of embedding incredibly simple at the software level—one can literally write a piece of software that pulls the media and other information associated to an NFT straight into a new product. And as we've seen in the context of NFTs that grant holders IP rights, NFTs can also ease the process at the level of licensing. For example, if a cartoon wants to include a SupDucks character, they don't need the permission of the company—per the SupDucks terms of service, the cartoon just needs to acquire a SupDucks NFT, or license one from a current holder.

Giving this sort of control to consumers might be a scary proposition for legacy companies that have traditionally held their brand

---

*"Wait a minute. [. . .] Are you telling me that you built a time machine out of a De-Lorean?" "The way I see it, if you're gonna build a time machine into a car, why not do it with some *style*?"

identity close to the chest. And assuredly, most brands will want to put some degree of structure on the form of community engagement, even if it's just baseline constraints like "No hate speech."

But still, the brands that best encourage co-creation through NFTs have an opportunity. The technology reduces friction for official partnerships, unofficial verified member benefits, and third-party innovation. And with the coming influx of NFTs—and most importantly, with shared ownership—everyone in the community has some incentive to help build the brand. You'll likely want to be open to this, and even encourage it.

13

Ongoing Challenges

Of course, the opportunities NFTs create can't be realized automatically. At least as of 2023, there was significant effort needed before NFT technology could achieve its full social potential.

That said, high-value applications drive innovation, and so even then, we could already see those challenges starting to be addressed.

INFRASTRUCTURE

Just as the internet uses a decentralized network of servers to store and propagate information, the blockchain platforms underlying the NFT revolution rely on decentralized networks of computers to process transactions. This protects the blockchain from censorship, expropriation, and other forms of centralized control, but it entails high transaction costs at both the network and user levels.

In early 2022, the dominant blockchain for NFT creation and

exchange—the Ethereum network—was estimated to represent as much as 0.34% of the world's daily energy usage because it used a computationally costly system to securely record transactions. While the Ethereum network's 2022 switch to a new transaction processing architecture called *proof-of-stake* reduced its environmental footprint by more than 99%, throughput remained an issue—transaction costs for something as simple as sending an NFT to a friend could be as high as a dollar or more.

On the one hand, a dollar to ship an asset might sound cheap relative to postage costs (at least in the US, where it costs about $0.50 to mail a folded sheet of paper). But for digital assets that are just bits in a computer network, such costs are exorbitant, and prohibitive for many ordinary types of transactions. (Imagine if you and a friend wanted to trade Magic: The Gathering cards and had to pay a dollar per trade.) Worse still, these costs typically scale with the level of network activity, which means they can be much higher at peak times. (Effectively, a high density of trading at a virtual gaming convention could gum up the network's processing pipeline and raise transaction costs so much that nobody would actually want to trade.)

And all of that's with only the relatively low number of people who were engaging in blockchain transactions at that time. The infrastructure wasn't ready to handle Visa- or Mastercard-level transaction density of up to thousands of transactions per second.

Luckily, even as we were writing, these challenges were starting to be addressed—both through improved blockchain infrastructure design to increase throughput, and through a variety of solutions that process many transactions quickly and then encode them into the blockchain all at once through a single settlement transaction. In both cases, increasing the effective computational power of the blockchain has reduced the marginal cost required to execute a given transaction—much as widespread availability of cloud computing infrastructure eventually led to low-cost processing and storage.

CONSUMER ACCESS AND PROTECTION

In parallel, as we've mentioned a couple times already, there are significant challenges around accessibility and usability of NFT technology. When we were writing this, many consumer digital wallets interacted directly with the blockchain itself, and were "self-custodial" in the sense that the user had absolute control of their digital assets and was personally responsible for their security.

The experience was thus a bit like the very early internet: Navigating crypto transactions required a sophisticated understanding of the technology and could be fraught with error. Even just purchasing an NFT sometimes required a consumer to interact with source code directly. Both digital wallets and transactions needed more intuitive interfaces separating user activity (e.g., minting an NFT, activating its utility, or sending it to a friend) from the technological rails making it happen.

Moreover, crypto transactions' instantaneity and finality have meant that they lack many of the protections people are used to from most other online consumer services. Sending an NFT to someone else is like sending an email—as soon as the computer system has processed the transfer, it's irreversible. This means if you type an address incorrectly, a digital asset could go to the wrong person, or even just be lost in the pipes of the network. Conversely, hacking or account compromise can lead to irreversible loss. (In late 2021, Bored Ape NFT theft was briefly so commonplace that "All my apes are gone" unfortunately achieved meme status.)

And finally, there were challenges around fine-grained data control and privacy. As of mid-2023, while digital wallets gave users control of which platforms could interact with their digital assets in the first place, this access was generally all-or-nothing. Most available solutions did not provide a robust mechanism for users to filter a platform's access to specific digital assets within a wallet. And at the same time, the data underlying users' digital assets was often fully public on the blockchain. This limited the use of NFTs, and crypto more broadly, in privacy-critical applications like healthcare.

But again, solutions were in development—this time by digital wallet service providers, who had a lot to gain from improved accessibility and security, because that could drive broader consumer adoption. Scott's first NFT purchase in mid-2021 had to be done with cryptocurrency and involved multiple failed attempts over the course of the week, even with a close friend helping him navigate the process. By contrast, when Reddit launched its collectible avatars in the fall of 2022, the platform sold more than five million NFTs, many users paid using credit cards, and the process was so simple that many non-Web3-native buyers had no idea they were interacting with a blockchain at all. Meanwhile, numerous Web3 identity- and data-management solutions with greater degrees of privacy and user control were in development.

DIVERSITY, EQUITY, AND INCLUSION

But of course access to NFTs and other digital assets isn't purely a tech problem. Digital divides are pervasive across socioeconomic, racial, and geographic lines; and with crypto technology, especially, the cost and complexity of entry have been barriers to access for many. As we've mentioned, early NFTs during the boom of 2021 often required access to cryptocurrency to purchase—and carried significant price tags. The resulting consumer base skewed affluent, as well as disproportionately white and male. Then the next wave of NFT products by and large catered directly to those consumer demographics, further exacerbating the challenge of diversifying engagement in the space.* Moreover, the tech industry has struggled to mirror the general population in the representativeness of its workforce, in terms of corporate leadership and employment, as well as who receives investment—and Web3 is no different.

Just like the internet, NFTs have the potential to create value for all types of people. And especially given the decentralized and open nature of public blockchains, there is in principle an opportunity for NFT space to become *more* diverse than many technologies that came

---

*Emerging technologies also often struggle with disability access. For example, most early NFT projects based around imagery launched without explanatory text for the visually impaired. That said, as Giselle Mota, founder of NFTY Collective, noted in *Harlem World Magazine*, there are significant opportunities here as well: In metaverse spaces, "[i]ndividuals who are mobility-impaired can explore without limits, while many people who struggle in social environments find it easier to interact digitally. Voice changers and sound boards can also help individuals with speech issues, or those who are nonverbal, to communicate."

before it—both geographically (instead of anchoring just in the few countries that host the dominant Web 2 platforms), and also in terms of who participates. But without broader representation among the creators and consumers of NFT products and infrastructure, the technology could become regressive instead.

These inclusivity challenges are complex to solve, and the business world was continuing to address (and struggle) with them as we were writing this. We don't claim to have a panacea for creating a more diverse and representative environment in Web3. But the first step toward fixing these issues is recognizing that they exist.

And, especially in the context of Web3, we are optimistic—or at least hopeful: Because of Web3's focus on decentralized access and user control, it has the potential to upend traditional hierarchies and power structures. At scale, for example, it's possible that Web3 could improve market access across gender, race, and socioeconomic lines because it enables creators to reach consumers directly.* Likewise, the bottom-up community building NFTs enable can help people from a wide range of backgrounds create spaces to meet and collaborate. We know many NFT creators and collectors from underrepresented groups who share these sentiments, and have personally found success and belonging in Web3.

Companies like House of First are championing diverse NFT creators, and NFT brands like World of Women, People of Crypto, and

---

*There is evidence that direct-to-consumer Web 2 crowdfunding platforms may have achieved this to some degree.

Miss O Cool Girls are providing Web3 education and access to underrepresented groups. And numerous NFT collections have been created by and to support women, nonbinary, and LGBTQIA+ creators; racial minorities; indigenous groups; disabled communities; neurodiverse individuals; and people facing humanitarian crises.

So while in 2023 there was still a long way to go to improve equity of access and opportunity in the NFT space, these projects hint at what NFTs may eventually be able to achieve. As World of Women COO Shannon Snow optimistically remarked, "Pushing forward the next generation of the web won't happen overnight, and there are many challenges to overcome. However, innovations like NFTs [. . .] offer opportunity to reshape the world in the image of fairness and equality[,]" especially by leveling the playing field in terms of access to marketplaces for creative work.

REGULATION

At the same time, as with any novel asset class, NFTs raise questions about regulation. At a basic level, it can be hard to even determine what type of asset an NFT is—and indeed, the answer might vary with the format of the NFT and the specific functionalities it has. Many NFTs, such as those that simply confer ownership of digital artwork or collectibles, have a narrow range of characteristics that make them analogous to commodities or physical property. But some NFTs have a range of characteristics, including features that make them analogous both to commodities and to securities; active secondary markets for this latter category of NFTs raise significant regulatory and policy questions given the different ways commodities and securities markets are regulated.

The challenge of disentangling the various types of NFTs—and how they should be regulated and taxed—was ongoing at the time of this writing. Of course, the fact that NFT assets might evolve and take on new functionalities makes the puzzle especially difficult. If an NFT starts as a simple ownership record, but later starts paying dividends based on the creator's various products, does it morph from commodity into a security—and if so, what sorts of registration, disclosure, and customer identity tracking processes would be needed? The form of the reward matters, too—giving out digital music NFTs as rewards to repeat buyers of concert tickets is very different from paying those ticket holders a share of concert revenues.

Beyond that, there were also regulatory challenges at the level of the broader crypto ecosystem, such as determining what types of consumer protection to mandate and how. Similarly, there was a need to sort out how NFTs should interact with existing rules around ownership and property—especially IP.

DECENTRALIZATION

Most crucially, in some ways, it also remained to be seen how much decentralization Web3 would truly support. There was a possibility that the need to aggregate computational power and data storage could lead to centralization in the infrastructure underlying NFTs and other digital assets. And there were also concerns that even if the infrastructure managed to be highly decentralized, platform centralization and market power could arise at the application layer—just like it had in Web 2.

Some have speculated that the need to develop intuitive, accessible digital wallets and other platforms to support Web3 will drive a new form of centralization, concentrated on the platforms with the best consumer experiences. Plausibly, that movement might even be led by existing Web 2 giants. (Certainly Facebook, with its transformation into Meta, has been attempting to lead the charge.)

There were some instances of this sort of centralization in the early NFT market—for example, at one point, many platforms displayed images and other media associated to NFTs via reference to OpenSea, one of the top NFT trading platforms. When OpenSea removed an NFT collection, perhaps because of copyright violation, the image references elsewhere broke, as entrepreneur and computer security expert Moxie Marlinspike observed in late 2021.

But even so, there were signs that giving individuals control of their digital assets was nevertheless having an impact on the structure of the market. By the end of 2022, OpenSea had several major competitors, all of which had launched by using public blockchain records of users' NFT transaction histories to offer rewards to active traders who chose to switch platforms. The ease of simply connecting one's digital wallet to a different trading site made switching easy—and as a result, it was harder for any individual platform to dominate the market.

Meanwhile, when Web 2 giant Twitter made its first foray into the world of Web3, it had to accept that users would want a different level of data control than they had previously. In particular, Twitter had to open its platform up to the possibility of users connecting and loading data out of their own private digital wallets without handing over control.

WAITING ON THE METAVERSE . . . UNLESS IT'S ALREADY HERE?

On top of all of that, of course, there's also the sometimes-elusive metaverse. We've mentioned the metaverse occasionally throughout this book (for example, in the context of digital wearables). But we haven't discussed it in detail, even though a lot of the excitement around NFTs and crypto comes from imagined metaverse applications.

There are two reasons for that:

1. We believe much of the impact of NFTs will be in the "real world," as the preceding examples hopefully made clear.

2. Our view of the metaverse is different from how many people approach it, which is why we are discussing it here, alongside other challenges that NFTs must grapple with.

The word *metaverse* often calls to mind images of an immersive, fully fleshed out virtual world—possibly owned by a science-fictiony megacorp. But as we mentioned at the outset (back in Chapter 4), we take an expansive view, which Scott first heard phrased by digital artist and futurist Francisco Alarcon (also known as FAR): *to us, the "metaverse" comprises all the various digital spaces people build around themselves.* That means social media platforms, private Zoom rooms, and even 1980s multi-user dungeon games are technically part of the metaverse because they provide digital frameworks for people to engage and create alongside one another.

In that frame, most of the applications of NFTs we've talked about *are* metaverse applications. And when you reflect on it for a moment, that actually seems kind of natural: Plenty of people use Bored Ape or other NFT images as their profile pictures on social media platforms like Twitter, or even on professional networking platforms like LinkedIn. And if there is a place where you identify as a cartoon ape with a spinner hat, how could that *not* be the metaverse?

In that sense, *the metaverse is already here—and NFTs are one of its key enablers.*

Bobby Hundreds put it this way in his essay "The Street Does Not Really Exist":

Not only is our social life already grounded in the metaverse, so is much of our identity. [Early on in the pandemic], we used filters to alter our appearances, posted black squares and blue stripes to declare our political stances, and farmed carrots in Animal Crossing to feel productive and purposeful in a flat and motionless season (all while binging Tiger King, prostrate on the couch in tie-dyed sweatpants by a DTC brand). In the metaverse, we can be whomever we want, unfettered by physical constraints, geography, even race, class, and gender. [. . .]

If you can accept that we're already steeped in the metaverse, that our bodies remain in the physical world while our brains are increasingly minding a digital life (are you having trouble concentrating on your dinner date, anxious to return to a developing conversation or situation on your phone?), then it only follows that there needs to be some type of protocol to establish ownership, goods, and property in cyberspace.

(He's talking about NFTs here, in case that wasn't clear.)

And as we form deeper identities and connections in digital spaces, Hundreds describes how:

Fashion doesn't have to just be dresses and jackets anymore. Fashion can be polka-dotted skin, 37 rabbits circling you like a hula hoop, or a liquid sweater that's 11 miles wide.

Fashion can be a square NFT in your avatar.

Giant, immersive 3D metaverse platforms aren't a prerequisite for NFTs to be adopted widely in existing digital spaces. And again, encoding digital assets as NFTs frees them from the confines of a single platform, meaning their uses can evolve as our digital spaces do. (There are companies building the infrastructure to support this, incidentally—Ready Player Me, for example, produces software that makes an NFT asset from one digital environment realizable in other platforms automatically, without having to directly adapt the asset at the software level.)

The flexibility and cross-platform mobility this provides should ultimately drive more innovation in the underlying platforms themselves. As a result, NFTs mean that there hopefully won't be just a few dominant metaverse environments in the same way that a small number of players have ruled the Web 2 social media landscape (much less a single platform like the OASIS from *Ready Player One*). Rather, there will be many different digital spaces with a variety of purposes and affordances, and people—and their assets—will be flexibly mobile across them.

The metaverse is here, NFTs enable it, and moreover, Web3 will help ensure that it is open and continues to evolve.

14

How NFTs and Web3 Can Shape Us

The evolution of novel technology is hard to predict. We've explained what NFTs are and how they create value, provided a framework to create an effective NFT program, and even laid out actionable steps to start your own journey into the world of Web3. But one wonderful thing about technology is that it always seems to surprise us.

When the internet started to take its current form in the 1990s, few could have predicted that many would be able to work entirely remotely within just three decades. When Facebook launched in the early 2000s, it was pretty hard to imagine the Web 2 revolution that gave us instant news (Twitter), online networking (LinkedIn), a place to discuss pretty much anything (Reddit), and short-form ultra-viral video (TikTok).

Web3 has that same potential to reshape the digital landscape and, in doing so, fundamentally transform our world. We can already see ways that NFTs can enhance existing industries—sometimes behind the scenes or under the hood, like with digital tickets, and sometimes very publicly, like we're seeing with Starbucks and Nike. And, as we've illustrated throughout this book, NFTs are already creating novel industries, with new ways of building companies and brands. But the greatest and most transformative applications most likely haven't even been imagined yet.

What can you build on top of digital ownership? With a tall enough staircase, the sky is the limit.

To close, we want to offer a very personal story about how NFTs, and the NFT Staircase, have changed our lives forever. Just as we were wrapping up this book, our editor—with whom we had talked almost every week for more than a year—learned a fun fact about us that had not come up before: *We've never met in person.* Instead, we've followed our own NFT Staircase, which started us on an extraordinary journey of friendship and collaboration.

We were both drawn to NFTs out of curiosity, and quickly became excited about NFT ownership and the utility that often came with it. But it was identity and community that brought us together. We first met in an audio-only virtual meetup hosted by the SupDucks NFT community. The SupDucks created a shared space where we could meet, and an aesthetic we could bond over.

That community led to friendship, and a couple of years later, two people who never would have met without Web3 have become deeply connected both professionally and personally. From co-authoring the first *Harvard Business Review* article about NFTs together in 2021 to today, we've spoken on livestreams, shared classrooms, helped each other juggle major life challenges, and now, written a book. In that way, our friendship and partnership as collaborators has very much reached the top step of the NFT Staircase, evolving into something we couldn't have imagined the very first time we chatted, much less when we first bought our digital ducks.

And this sort of story is far from unique—we've seen it with numerous friends and colleagues who have met through NFT communities and then launched podcasts, clubs, and even businesses together. NFTs are creating massive changes in how we interact with brands and each other, but by nature, they do so by enabling many, many micro-connections. NFTs stitch together dispersed networks, connecting people with shared interests all across the world. And when strangers with shared interests meet, all manner of wizardry can happen.

Technology is funny like that sometimes. From a practical perspective, we often focus on the software infrastructure and the specific problems it can solve. But if used well, this particular technology can go far beyond software to give us better and more fulfilling lives as humans.

We hope that this book brought you some value, and at the very least, made you more open to the idea of embracing NFTs and everything that comes with this emerging technology. Because if we can help just one company shape their strategy to be more customer-aligned, or inspire even one person to build something in this brave new world of Web3, this book was a success.

ACKNOWLEDGMENTS

We're deeply grateful to all the creators and consumers in NFT-world who are exploring this new technology together. We've learned so much from so many of you.

We also particularly appreciate all the NFT communities we've had an opportunity to be a part of—especially Adam Bomb Squad, Alien Frens, AppliedPrimate, Art Blocks, Azurbala, Bored Ape Yacht Club, Chain Runners, DeGods/y00ts, dGEN Network, Divine Anarchy, Doodles, FINE, Forgotten Runes, Goatz, Gradis, Hungry Wolves, Inkugami, 1337 Skulls, OnChainMonkey, Pirate Nation, Proof/Moonbirds, Pudgy Penguins, ripcache's Squad, SamurAI, Shibuya, Skybrook, Tally Labs/ The Writers Room, The Alien Boy, Thingdoms, Truth/Goblintown, Two Bit Bears, Tycoon Tigers, VeeFriends, World of Women, and most especially SupDucks, which sparked our friendship and collaboration.

We've also taken special inspiration from Erick Calderon (Snowfro), Chris Dixon, Bobby Hundreds, Laura Rodriguez, Gary Vaynerchuk, and of course the BAYC founding leadership team, particularly Gargamel

(Greg Solano), Gordon Goner (Wylie Aronow), and V Strange (Nicole Muniz).

The ideas in this book owe a tremendous debt to those we've worked closely with and/or learned from directly on NFTs and Web3. This includes: Adamtastic, Nate Alex, Cynthia Alexander, Patrick Amadon, Arjun, Cameron Armstrong, Atlaude, Drew Austin, Sari Azout, Lucas Baker, Roy Batty, Bucky Bear, Morgan Beller, Elza Berdnyk, Jonah Blake, Tony Boetto, BORED, Bowman, Brian Brinkman, Robbie Broome, James Brünner (manovermars), Jack Butcher, Vitalik Buterin, John Carl, Chase Chapman, Curvy, DKB, Dos, Julia (Julzy) Dray, Drucritt, Skaff Elias, Valentine Fadie, Kenneth Fernandez Prada, Nicole Fernandez Prada, Nick Fontova, foobar, Hiroto Furuhashi, Darshan Gandhi, GeneralDegener8, Georgie Boy, Girl in the Verse, Gmoney, Gremplin, Fabrice Grinda, James Gutin, James Raymond Hattem, Andrew Hayward, hedgehoghodgepodge, HMDT, Dom Hofmann, Julian Holguin, David Horvath, JackGK, JANK, JrCasas, Kaiba, Vini Kaul, Won Kim, Zeev Klien, Serj Korj, Kyrzel, Toby Lasso, Wil Lee, Loft, Brandon Lovelace, Freddy Lowry, MagnumAPI, Mike Maizels, David Marcus, metabananas, Ben Mezrich, Andrew Miller, MIRZA, Mariale Montenegro, Luca Netz, NiftyPins, Norvo, numo, NYC Punter, Outer Lumen, Ozbot, David Phelps, professorM, Punk 6529, Quit, Miloš Rakčević, Vivek Ravishanker, Ringalls, Brian Roberts, Shwaz, SlabberDan, Shannon Snow, Sniper, Pancho Socci, Sora, Spottie Wifi, Sam Spratt, Eric Sturtevant, Jennifer "Jenny from the Blockchain" Sutto, Steph Sutto, Kyle Swenson, Swickie and Peter Fang, Mark Symkin, Sarah Tavel, Thierry & Prosper, thomas, ThreadGuy, Timshel, Shlomit Azgad Tromer, UncleBimBim, Vel, Estevan Vilar, Amber Vittoria, Vive, Jesse Walden, Wale, Will Weinraub, Sandy Weisz, Udi Wertheimer, Whalesink, Mike Williams, Winny, WIWYA, Amy Wu, XCOPY, XmasBeer, ZachXBT, Zeneca, Zookit, Zooko, and especially Jana Bobosikova, Josh Bobrowsky, James Currier, Jad Esber, Vinnie Hager, Adam Hollander, Li

Jin, ripcache, Gabe Weis, and Luca White-Matthews; the 1337 Skulls, especially the 532s (Flashrekt, 51991, Braindraind, Casey, Dodix [Domenico Distilo], Epikur, Fishboy, hoanh, kam-t, loothero, Maning, monno [Rhys Taylor], 1980k, nwmd, R4cerx, SaintStereo, Snjolfur, and 573v3); Dad Mod, Entropy, GG, King Kong, Mojojojo, Pak Gregg, Ramy Saboungui, Ice Cream Sandwhich, Wirelyss (Alyssa Suro), and many other Goblins; expert puzzlers Justin Tobin (JTobcat), Brett Buerhaus, LorekTemplar, Zarin Pathan, Ziot, and Zoz; Ash, Raymond Cook (LunarRaid), Gonz, Lemon-Boy, VirtualJohn, Haiu-Izado, and all the other Wizards of the Tower Shade; penn, 0xBryant, and many other users of Avenue; and the teams at Adim (especially Melissa Kaspers, Spencer Marell, Rob McElhenney, Kris Paruch, and Chase Rosenblatt), Ape Beverages (especially Gene), AppliedPrimate/Fragment Studios (especially PTM, Mistaken President [Jeff Boison], Alex Segura, VonDoom, Abbott Gibbons, and Avila Pires), BakerHostetler (especially Jerry Ferguson, Oren Warshavsky, and Deborah Wilcox), Chain Runners (especially Dozer, Knav, and Mid), Citizens of Tajigen (especially Dith, Nao, Rob, Vlad, and wkm), Clubhouse Archives (especially James Costa), DeGods/y00ts (especially Frank and Kevin), Divine Anarchy (especially BossyDog, Diversity, Slchld, and 2tone), Euler's Posse (Greg, Justin, Michael, and Stephen), Every (especially Nathan Baschez and Dan Shipper), Exaltation of Larks (Greg Pliska [Daedalus]), Farcaster (especially Dan Romero), FINE Digital (especially FAR and Chelsey Wickmark), Flowcarbon (especially Dana Gibber), Forgotten Runes (especially Bearsnake), Friends of Pooly (especially Kames Geraghty, Ryan McPeck, and Rollin Phillips), Hologram (especially Hongzi Mao), Hunches, Inkugami (especially Eishi, Huntclubhero, niKo, and oneETHman), IYK (especially Christopher Lee and Ryan Ouyang), Korus (Eislyn, Frankie, and Gus), Lighter (especially Vlad Novakovski and Scott Wu), Manifold (especially Wilkins Chung, Eric Diep, and Richerd), Metaverse Publishing (especially Dan and Sol), Miss O Cool

Girls (especially Juliette Brindak Blake), Neuco (especially Anthony Ivy), Nifty Gateway, Nifty Island (especially Charl3s and Cade Walker Green), Optimism (especially Karl Floersch, Liam Horne, Ben Jones, and Jing Wang), Pixel Vault (especially GFunk, VGF, and Chris Wahl), Proof/Moonbirds (especially Amanda [akaStevey], David Huber, Justin Mezzell, NFTStats, Kevin Rose, and Arran Schlosberg), Proof of Play (especially Adam Fern), SaaSyLabs (especially Richy Rich), Shibuya (especially Maciej Kuciara and Emily Yang [plpleasr]), Story Protocol (especially Seung Yoon Lee, Jason Levy, Jason Zhao, Jonny Chang, Leo Chen, Raúl Martínez, Susan Park, Ben Sternberg, Liz Tingue, Spyros Tsiounis, and Weilei Yu), SupDucks (especially Billy, Franky, Jon Pedigo, and Stronk), Surveycaster (especially Ben Adamsky and Colin Johnson), Tally Labs (especially Valet Jones, SAFA, Roebs, Apewood, Jenkins the Mutant, Jenkins the Valet, Juice, Little Fortunes, Mtnman, Mumbles, Emma Needell, Octo, OP, Snapback, and Tuna), Thingdoms (especially Luke Crawford, Eoghan Crowley, and gomgom), Tokenproof (especially Fonz), Transient Labs (especially Chris Ostoich), Truth Labs (especially Alexander Taub, Sydney Brafman, Jon Macapodi, Process Grey, and Bruce Seaton), Two Bit Bears (especially Kodiak, Spirit, Cophi, and MILK), VaynerSports (especially AJ Vaynerchuk), VeeFriends (especially GaryVee, Daniel Donayre, Jeremy Jannielli, Andy Krainak, and Erik Zettersten), Yuga Labs (especially the founders, Randy Chung, Disco, Chris Fortier, PPMan, and Tantrum), and Yume (especially Sara, Tomo, Jake, Claudia, Henry, Jerry, Mike, and Tsuyoshi-san).

Steve is deeply grateful to his colleagues at Progressive Insurance who helped him find his voice in the business world, especially Jeff Charney, Kathleen Farris, Tricia Griffith, Erin "Boss" Hendrick, Kim Hetzel, Linday Karklin, Jo Lawson, Neil Lenane, Amanda Lupica, Lori Niederst, Bruce Perlman, Mari Pumarejo, Jeff Sibel, Erin Vrobel, and Lexy Yurovitsky; his colleagues at Metagood, especially Mike Chavez, MissKeenEye, Owzen,

Bill Tai, Amanda Terry, and Danny Yang; his colleagues at Forum3 and Starbucks Odyssey, including Lindsey Bretz, Adam Brotman, Ryan Butz, John Darroyo, Sydney Flynn, Marissa Garyfer, Sydney Goldsmith, Chris Hodl, Van Lu, Morgan Matoskey, Joe O'Rourke, and Michael Suarez; his colleagues at Nestlé, including John Carmichael, Shannon Harrell, Josh Morton, Dana Stambaugh, and Emily Zurawski; and his colleagues and collaborators at *dGen Network*, including Giorgia Bettio, Dao Jones, Chris Jourdan, Chad Townsley, CryptoPain7, Macki, MrH0use, Kyle Riggins, Jeremy Weber, the *Night Shift* crew (especially Mizzle, JPCaz, Ph0nics, Shane, and TJ), the team at *Alpha Afternoons*, and the changemakers at *Saturday Morning Cartoons*.

Scott is deeply grateful to his colleagues at Harvard Business School and elsewhere in the broader academic world, including Zachary Abel, Maya Ajmera, Mohammad Akbarpour, Teresa Amabile, Tomomichi Amano, Bharat Anand, Lynda Applegate, Maureen Armstrong, Itai Ashlagi, Steve Atlas, Jill Avery, Larry Bacow, Maite Ballestero, Hélène Barcelo, Jennifer Bard, Jordan Barry, Rachel Bayefsky, Gary Becker, David Bell, Dirk Bergemann, Ethan Bernstein, Martin Bichler, Péter Biró, Megan Blewett, Jörn Boehnke, Alain Bonacossa, Christian Borgs, Eric Budish, Ryan Buell, Jeff Bussgang, Frank Cespedes, Jennifer Chayes, Yeon-Koo Che, Justin Chen, Yan Chen, Yiling Chen, Raj Chetty, Pierre-André Chiappori, Hannah Chung, Tony Clark, Jeff Cohen, Lauren Cohen, Mary Lou Corradino, Matthew Cortland, Caroline Costello, Vince Crawford, Angela Crispi, Zoë Cullen, Jean Cunningham, Enit Curry, Eric Deakins, David Delacrétaz, Erik Demaine, Martin Demaine, Mihir Desai, Rohit Deshpande, Marco Di Maggio, Joann DiGennaro, Umut Dur, Steven Durlauf, Federico Echenique, Ben Edelman, David Eisenbud, Noam Elkies, David Ellsworth, Aram Elovic, Kate Epstein, Joline Fan, Michal Feldman, Marta Figlerowicz, Thomas Finan, Ray Fisman, Jason Fleming, Abigail Fradkin, Dan Freed, Richard Freeman, Frances Frei, Ben Friedman, Drew Fudenberg,

Joe Fuller, Theresa Gaignard, Alfred Galichon, Peter Galison, Kiran Gajwani, Ben Ganzfried, Pingyang Gao, Alan Garber, Shantanu Gaur, Claudine Gay, Ani Gevorkian, Shikhar Ghosh, Sarah Glatte, Francesco Goedhuis, Claudia Goldin, Ben Golub, Paul Gompers, Yannai Gonczarowski, Gregg Gonsalves, Alan Goodwin, Daniel Goroff, Helene Granof, Robin Greenwood, Ranjay Gulati, Umit Gurun, Guillaume Haeringer, Hanna Halaburda, Jonathan Hall, Bert Halperin, Lars Hansen, Kelley Harris, Oliver Hart, Jason Hartline, Andrea Hawksley, John Hawksley, Ike Haxton, Scott Haywood, Paul Healy, Jim Heckman, Ann Hiatt, Moshe Hoffman, Richard Holden, Bengt Holmström, Elyse Hope, John Horton, Jeff Huizinga, John Eric Humphries, Minh Huynh-Le, Marco Iansiti, Greg Ihrie, Nicole Immorlica, Ebehi Iyoha, Matthew Jackson, Sonia Jaffe, Sanja Jagesic, Christina Jarymowycz, Emir Kamenica, Michihiro Kandori, Daniel Kane, Miles Kang, Akiko Kanno, Louis Kaplow, Larry Katz, Nicole Tempest Keller, Rakesh Khurana, Olivia Kim, Takuya Kitagawa, Paul Klemperer, Ray Kluender, Carin Knoop, Joe Koerner, Fuhito Kojima, Rem Koning, John Korn, Michael Kremer, Anna Kreslavskaya, Josh Krieger, Sarah LaBauve, David Laibson, Karim Lakhani, Fong Fong Lam, Sam Lazarus, Dianne Le, Changhwa Lee, Robin Lee, Mark Lemley, Josh Lerner, Jacob Leshno, John Lesieutre, Danielle Li, Shengwu Li, Wanyi Dai Li, Jonathan Libgober, Nori Gerardo Lietz, Katrina Ligett, Martha Lincoln, Greg Llacer, Stephanie Lo, Uta Lorenzen, Richard Lowery, Mike Luca, Brendan Lucier, Taylor Lundy, Alex MacKay, Dahlia Malkhi, Michael Malkoff, Markobi, Greg Marsh, Eric Maskin, Jim Matheson, Yasukane Matsumoto, James Mattey, Freda Mazis, Barry Mazur, Janice McCormick, Chris Mihelich, Eva Meyersson Milgrom, Karen Mills, Irene Minder, Ciamac Moallemi, Youngme Moon, Meg Morrison, Xiaosheng Mu, Jen Mucciarone, Rae Mucciarone, Ellen Muir, Sendhil Mullainathan, Kevin Murphy, Rohan Murty, Kyle Myers, Roger Myerson, Tymofiy Mylovanov, Greg Nagy, Nikhil Naik, Ramana Nanda, Abdoulaye Ndiaye,

Tsedal Neeley, Stirling Newberry, Ging Cee Ng, Tom Nicholas, Nitin Nohria, Mike Norton, Max Nova, Felix Oberholzer-Gee, Carol Oja, Ken Ono, Tamar Oostrom, Michael Ostrovsky, John Owens, Mallesh Pai, Lynn Paine, Ariel Pakes, Bobby Pakzad-Hurson, Van Papadopoulos, David Parkes, Monica Pate, Parag Pathak, Christina Pazzanese, Paul Peebles, Chris Peterson, Naomi Pierce, Gary Pisano, Eric Price, Ariel Procaccia, Narun Raman, Matt Readar, Sean Reid, Phil Reny, Marco Reuter, Marion Richter, John Rickert, Natalia Rigol, Jan Rivkin, Assaf Romm, Damari Rosado, Adam Rosenfield, Raffaella Sadun, Bill Sahlman, Akiko Saito, Steffano U. Saldrium, Larry Samuelson, Nobuo Sato, Elaine Scarry, David Scharfstein, Julia Schlozman, Thibault Schrepel, Josh Schwartzstein, Rob Sedgebeer, Margo Seltzer, Amartya Sen, Jenny Sendova, Sven Seuken, Nihar Shah, Varda Shalev, Jesse Shapiro, Kay Kaufman Shelemay, Andrei Shleifer, Ran Shorrer, Harry Shum, Elizabeth Sibert, Ludvig Sinander, Rob Sinnott, David Smith, Noah Smith, Eric Sodomka, Paul Solman, Tayfun Sönmez, Hugo Sonnenschein, Anne Sosin, Bradly Stadie, Stefanie Stantcheva, Chris Stanton, Jeremy Stein, Ariel Stern, Greg Stone, Zak Stone, Andrew Storey, Andy Strominger, Iolanthe Stronger, Tomasz Strzalecki, Adi Sunderam, Ronny Tabeka, Steve Tadelis, Erik Tait, Maria Tatar, Éva Tardos, Avni Patel Thompson, William Thomson, Bill Todd, Grace Tsiang, Utku Ünver, Winnie van Dijk, David Vendler, Helen Vendler, Sergiy Verstyuk, Luc Vincent, Rakesh Vohra, Nicole Volpe, Jenny Wanger, Andy Wasynczuk, Matt Weinberg, Matt Weinzierl, Mitch Weiss, Alexander Westkamp, Andy Wu, Vincent Wu, Daniel Xu, Nur Yalman, Paul Yang, Shing-Tung Yau, Erez Yoeli, Marais Young, Anthony Zhang, Ping Zhang, Yufei Zhao, and Feng Zhu, as well as Anu Atluru, Francisco Barroso, Kevin Chen, Yunseo Choi, Yunus Semih Coşkun, Aditya Dhar, Naveen Durvasula, Jo Ellery, Suat Evren, Brendan Falk, David Freed, Brandon Freiberg, Andrew Garber, Louis Golowich, Natalie Guo, Alexander Haberman, Caetano Hanta-Davis, Jack Hirsch, Zoë Hitzig, George Hou, Helen

Huang, Bryn Huxley-Reicher, Nick Jaeger, Meena Jagadeesan, Simon Jantschgi, Andrew Kahn, Patrick Kim, Andrew Komo, Moran Koren, Daniel Kornbluth, Alan and Simon Lam, Kevin Li, Shira Li, Jimmy Lin, Katherine Lou, Hongyao Ma, Jonathan Ma, Robbie Minton, Faidra Monachou, Eliza Oak, Charlie Pasternak, AnaMaria Perez, Maxi Pethö-Schramm, Duncan and Ross Rheingans-Yoo, Seven Richmond, Suproteem Sarkar, Ben Scharfstein, Matthew Shum, Mirac Suzgun, Neil Thakral, Kentaro Tomoeda, Nathaniel Ver Steeg, Jennifer Walsh, Angela Wang, Franklyn Wang, Alex Wei, Hubert Wu, Gerald Xu, Douglas Yang, Catherine Yeo, Michael Yin, Ryan Yu, Samuel Zwickel, and many other members of the Lab for Economic Design, and particularly Susan Athey, Shai Bernstein, Christian Catalini, Allison Ciechanover, Scott Cook, Âriel de Fauconberg, Piotr Dworczak, Jeanne Eagleton, Tom Eisenmann, Noah Feldman, Joshua Gans, Wally Gilbert, Ed Glaeser, George Gonzalez, Jerry Green, John Hatfield, Kerry Herman, Ravi Jagadeesan, Bill Kerr, Kevin Leyton-Brown, Paul Milgrom, Jeff Miron, Diana Morse, Mary Ann Mroz, Das Narayandas, Alex Nichifor, Canice Prendergast, Al Roth, Ben Roth, Matthew Stein, Alex Tabarrok, Alex Teytelboym, Susan Schwartz Wildstrom, and Liang Wu; his colleagues at Quora, particularly Adam D'Angelo, Chris Luhrs, Ricky Arai-Lopez, Karl Krehbiel, Tracy Lee, Faizan Qureshi, Nick Sher, Ho Chung Siu, Wenwen Tao, George Wang, and Lexie Wu; and especially his colleagues at a16z crypto, including Marc Andreessen, Jeff Amico, Claire Austin, Neveen Bader, Maryam Bahrani, Gaetan Barthelemy, Elena Berger, Dan Boneh, Joseph Bonneau, Jared Bricklin, Sam Broner, Brittney Burrows, Victoria Butcher, Paul Cafiero, Pyrs Carvolth, Noah Citron, Sagar Dhawan, Shari Doherty, Jay Drain, Ian Dutra, Nass Eddequiouaq, Riyaz Faizullabhoy, Adina Fischer, Caroline Friedman, Pranav Garimidi, Angelica Gehr, Samantha Gelt, Matt Gleason, Emily Graff, Andrew Hall, Mason Hall,

Elizabeth Harkavy, Mehdi Hasan, Bill Hinman, Emily Hinsch, Ben Horowitz, Maggie Hsu, Mike Jones, Charlie Keinath, Jen Kha, Michele Korver, Jane Lippencott, Daren Matsuoka, Packy McCormick, Collin McCune, Craig Naylor, Valeria Nikolaenko, Whitney Owens, Daejun Park, Claudia Picanco, Brian Quintenz, Sam Ragsdale, Jai Ramaswamy, Daniel Reynaud, Richard Rosenblatt, April Roth, Eva Sakkas, Anna Semenova, Porter Smith, Mariano Sorgente, Helen Stoddard, David Sverdlov, Andisheh Tahriri, Justin Thaler, Erin Tice, Scott Tyler, Dozie Uche, Ish Verduzco, Danielle Wessler, Carra Wu, Guy Wuollet, Michael Zhu, and particularly Tim Roughgarden, Anthony Albanese, Michael Blau, Joseph Burleson, Kate Dellolio, Chris Dixon, Zachary Gray, Miles Jennings, Sriram Krishnan, Eddy Lazzarin, Chris Lyons, Mike Manning, Kim Milosevich, Jean Reilly, Jason Rosenthal, Justin Simcock, Arianna Simpson, Scott Walker, Ali Yahya, and the editorial team (listed below).*

Scott also thanks Vinal Bakery, Dado Tea, Grace Street Coffee, Nine Bar, Union Square Donuts, the ASAASA, Cafe Sushi, and lime chips. Steve, of course, thanks Starbucks. We would also like to recognize the Team Beans Fund and, more importantly, its namesake, Francesca "Beans" Kaczynski.

Particular shoutouts to the people who first brought us into NFT-world—in Steve's case, education from Josh Ong, Baron Von Hustle, Kevin

---

*Scott also gratefully acknowledges academic research support from the Washington Center for Equitable Growth, the Digital, Data, and Design (D³) Institute at Harvard, and the Ng Fund and the Mathematics in Economics Research Fund of the Harvard Center of Mathematical Sciences and Applications. Part of this work was conducted during the Simons Laufer Mathematical Sciences Institute Fall 2023 program on the Mathematics and Computer Science of Market and Mechanism Design, which was supported by the National Science Foundation under Grant No. DMS-1928930 and by the Alfred P. Sloan Foundation under grant G-2021-16778.

Rose, Snowfro, and Zed Gazette was invaluable; and in Scott's case, the intro was made by Limp, Marklar, D33J4Y, Bread, Kyle Chayka, and especially FAR, Jad Esber, and Flashrekt.

Special thanks to our many editors, past and present, who have helped us shape our thoughts and writing on NFTs and Web3: Tom Stackpole at *Harvard Business Review*; Robert Hackett, Stephanie Zinn, and particularly Sonal Chokshi and Tim Sullivan at a16z crypto; Mark Gongloff, James Greiff, Jessica Karl, Katy Roberts, David Shipley, Lara Williams, and particularly Mike Nizza and Jon Landman at *Bloomberg Opinion*; Ken Murphy at *Project Syndicate*; and Lauren Murrow at *Future*.

Singular mentions to a number of people without whom this book could never have happened: Leila Sandlin and Jane Cavolina; production manager Matthew Boezi, indomitable production editor Brianna Lopez, managing editor Jessica Regione, and numerous copy editors and proofreaders (particularly Dorothy Janick, Lisanne Kaufmann, and Nick Michal); Daniel Lagin for art direction, designer Alissa Theodor, and cover artist Zoe Norvell; as well as our publicist Lauren Monahan, marketer Mary Kate Rogers, and UK editor Jamie Birkett; Scott's movement coach Armin Kappacher, counselor Ray Sherbill, and key grip Tynan Seltzer; and our spectacular book lawyer Paul Mahon.

And of course, to our utterly extraordinary editor at Portfolio, Merry Sun: Thank you for *everything*.

Finally, infinite thanks, as well, to our families—parents, grandparents, siblings, partners, in-laws, aunts/uncles/cousins/etc., and in Steve's case, kids. Special shoutouts to Ellen Dickstein Kominers and Zoe DeStories for reading multiple full drafts of the manuscript 🙏.*

---

*Last, Scott thanks Steve for being awesome. Steve thanks Scott for being awesome, too! And they really appreciate you, the reader, for joining them on this journey.

DISCLOSURE NOTE

None of the preceding is investment, business, legal, or tax advice. Both Kaczynski and Kominers hold digital assets, including fungible and non-fungible tokens from some of the companies mentioned in this book. They also advise companies and serve as experts on marketplace and incentive design, Web3 strategy, NFT brand-building, and other topics. Additionally, Kominers is a research partner at a16z, an investment advisor registered with the US Securities and Exchange Commission. a16z and its affiliates may maintain investments in the companies or tokens discussed in this book.

IMAGE CREDITS

[Here and hereafter, image references refer to the NFT associated to the image where appropriate.]

Pg 3 Bored Ape #9976, from Bored Ape Yacht Club, created by Yuga Labs (NFT owned by Steve Kaczynski as of June 2023): courtesy of Steve Kaczynski

Pg 22 Stoic #3372, from The Stoics by Gabe Weis, created by Gabe Weis (NFT owned by Scott Duke Kominers as of June 2023): courtesy of Gabe Weis

Pg 23 Blockchain sale and transfer records for Stoic #3372, captured from OpenSea: screenshot adapted by the authors in June 2023

Pg 121 (top left) AppliedPrimate Mega Mutant Melee Deck, created by Fragment Studios, featuring Mega Noise, Mega Robot, Mega Radioactive, Mega Electric, Mega Gold, Mega Death Bot, Mega Zombie, and Mega Swamp, all from Mutant Ape Yacht Club, created by Yuga Labs: AppliedPrimate Mega Mutant Melee and logo are TM and © 2023 Fragment Studios

Pg 121 (top right) Ape Water Can, created by Ape Beverages Company, featuring Bored Ape #5382, from Bored Ape Yacht Club, created by Yuga Labs: courtesy of Ape Beverages Company, 2023

Pg 121 (middle) Zookit Customs—Skaters of the Internet, created by Zookit, featuring Azuki #9146, created by Chiru Labs: courtesy of Zookit

Pg 121 (bottom) Girl in the Verse logo, created by Melina Giubilaro, featuring Women and Weapons #7195, art by Sara Baumann: copyright © Melina Giubilaro

Pg 124 (top left) Blitmap Logo, from Blitmap, created by Dom Hofmann/Sup (NFT owned by Dom Hofmann as of June 2023)

Pg 124 (top right) Chain Runner #780, from Chain Runners, created by the Chain Runners Architects, featuring a Blitmap Hat (NFT owned by Knav as of June 2023)

Pg 124 (bottom left) Blitmap Logo Hat (Dad Cap Style), created by NiftyPins

Pg 124 (bottom right) 1337 Skull #1891, from 1337 Skulls, created by the 1337 Skulls 532s, featuring a Blit Beret and Noggles (NFT owned by Paolo Leone as of June 2023)

The Blitmap logo and materials, Chain Runner #780, Blitmap Logo Hat image, and 1337 Skull #1891 have been placed in the public domain by their creators via CC0.

NOTES

1. INTRODUCTION

3 **at $4 billion:** Olga Kharif, "Bored Apes NFT Creator Yuga Raises $450 Million from Andreessen, Animoca," Bloomberg.com, March 22, 2022, https://www.bloomberg.com/news/articles/2022-03-22/bored-apes-creator-yuga-raises-450-million-to-fund-expansion; Lucas Matney, "Bored Apes NFT Startup Yuga Labs Raises Seed Round at Monster $4B Valuation," TechCrunch, March 22, 2022, https://techcrunch.com/2022/03/22/bored-apes-nft-startup-yuga-labs-raises-at-monster-4-billion-valuation.

3 **created by a computer process:** Langston Thomas, "The BAYC Bible: Everything to Know About Bored Ape NFTs," NFT Now, March 18, 2022, https://nftnow.com/guides/bored-ape-yacht-club-guide.

4 **sites like Quora and Reddit:** See, e.g., Alice Conway, "Why are NFT digital monkeys valuable? What is their market appeal?," Quora, https://www.quora.com/Why-are-NFT-digital-monkeys-valuable-What-is-their-market-appeal; Giri Ganapathy, "Why are pictures of monkeys on sale for outrageous prices as NFT?," Quora, https://www.quora.com/Why-are-pictures-of-monkeys-on-sale-for-outrageous-prices-as-NFT; and Yener07, "Why would anyone buy a picture of a monkey drawn by a computer for thousands of dollars?," Reddit, https://www.reddit.com/r/CryptoCurrency/comments/rewygd/why_would_anyone_buy_a_picture_of_a_monkey_drawn.

4 **a different kind of primate:** "About Apes," Center for Great Apes, https://centerforgreatapes.org/about-apes.

4 *never produce any more:* Kerem Atalay (@TomatoBAYC), "The contract owner has now been burned," Twitter, June 7, 2022, 7:08 p.m., https://twitter.com/TomatoBAYC/status/1534311393763241986.

4 **images in the collection:** "Welcome to the Bored Ape Yacht Club," BAYC, https://boredapeyachtclub.com.

4 **network called a *blockchain*:** See "Contract 0xBC4CA0EdA7647A8aB7C2061c2E118A18a936f13D," Etherscan, https://etherscan.io/address/0xBC4CA0EdA7647A8aB7C2061c2E118A18a936f13D.

5 **scratching their heads:** Kai Ryssdal and Andie Corban, "Why Are People Spending So Much Money on NFTs?," Marketplace, March 3, 2021, https://www.marketplace.org/2021/03/03/why-are-people-spending-so-much-money-on-nfts.

5 **form of gluttonous excess:** Nathan J. Robinson, "Are NFTs the Dumbest Thing to Happen in the History of Humanity?," *Current Affairs*, December 16, 2021, https://currentaffairs.org/2021/12/are-nfts-the-dumbest-thing-humans-have-ever-done; Luke Savage, "NFTs Are, Quite Simply, Bullshit," Jacobin, January 26, 2022, https://jacobin.com/2022/01/nfts-fallon-paris-hilton-bored-ape-digital-imagery-commodification.

5 **Bored Ape Yacht Club:** For a general survey, see Scott's Harvard Business School case study on the BAYC: Scott Duke Kominers, Das Narayandas, and Kerry Herman, "Bored Ape Yacht Club: Navigating the NFT World," Harvard Business Publishing, March 14, 2022, https://hbsp.harvard.edu/product/822065-PDF-ENG.

5 **your ticket in:** Kyle Chayka, "Why Bored Ape Avatars Are Taking Over Twitter," *The New Yorker*, July 30, 2021, https://www.newyorker.com/culture/infinite-scroll/why-bored-ape-avatars-are-taking-over-twitter.

6 **in their personal business ventures:** "Terms & Conditions," BAYC, https://boredapeyachtclub.com/#/terms.

6 **annual music festival:** Cam Thompson, "28 Hours in the Sewer: Yuga Labs' Dookey Dash Game Kept Players Running," CoinDesk, February 10, 2023, https://www.coindesk.com/web3/2023/02/10/28-hours-in-the-sewer-yuga-labs-dookey-dash-game-kept-players-running; Kyle Orland, "The First 'Bored Ape' NFT Game Costs $2,300+ for Three Weeks of Play," Ars Technica, January 19, 2023, https://arstechnica.com/gaming/2023/01/the-first-bored-ape-nft-game-costs-2300-for-three-weeks-of-play; "ApeFest 2022," ApeFest, https://apefest.com.

6 **utility and benefits:** See, e.g., Swoosie, "World's 2nd NFT Restaurant | Bored

Ape Yacht Club (BAYC) Members Eat Free," YouTube, https://www.youtube
.com/watch?v=wWLNLGX9LZ4; Kyle Swenson, "This Bored Ape Is Giving
Every BAYC Member A Free Drink At His Ape Themed Convenience Store,"
Bored Ape Gazette, updated October 30, 2022, https://www.theboredapegazette
.com/post/thisty-this-bored-ape-is-giving-every-bayc-member-a-free-drink
-at-his-ape-themed-convenience-store; Truth Labs (@truth), "If you
own a @BoredApeYC you can add yourself to the whitelist now:," Twitter,
December 10, 2021, 10:20 p.m., https://twitter.com/truth/status/14695073
69231126532; Reethu Ravi, "BAYC Trezor Hunt: Will It Be IRL, And
Who Is Applied Primate?," *NFTevening*, updated January 17, 2023, https://
nftevening.com/bayc-trezor-hunt-will-it-be-irl-and-who-is-applied-primate;
מר שיבולת Tech, "Bored Ape ARG Explained | Applied Primate Engineering
(A.P.E)," YouTube, https://www.youtube.com/watch?v=KLQnqYtJEHI; see also
AppliedPrimate, https://www.appliedprimate.com.

7 **just a few months:** Ekin Genç, "Bored Ape Yacht Club Sells $96 Million of
Mutant Ape NFTs in One Hour," Decrypt, August 29, 2021, https://decrypt
.co/79718/bored-ape-yacht-club-sells-96-million-of-nfts-in-hour-for-mutant
-apes-launch.

7 **from in-game microtransactions:** Thompson, "28 Hours in the Sewer."

7 **limited-edition pendant:** Kyle Swenson, "Gucci Sold 3,019 KodaPendants
for $5,719,000 USD in 24 Hours," Bored Ape Gazette, April 7, 2023, https://
www.theboredapegazette.com/post/gucci-sold-3-019-kodapendants-for
-5-719-000-usd-in-24-hours.

7 **roughly $16 million in revenue:** Jamie Redman, "Yuga Labs' Twelvefold
Collection of Ordinal Inscriptions Generates 735 Bitcoin, Worth More than
$16 Million," Bitcoin.com, March 7, 2023, https://news.bitcoin.com/yuga
-labs-twelvefold-collection-of-ordinal-inscriptions-generates-735-bitcoin
-worth-more-than-16-million.

7 **hundreds of millions of dollars:** See, e.g., Eric James Beyer, "Yuga Labs:
The NFT Company Taking Over the Metaverse," NFT Now, May 24, 2022,
https://nftnow.com/guides/yuga-labs-an-overview-of-the-nft-company
-taking-over-the-metaverse; Zeynep Geylan, "Yuga Labs' NFT Royalty Income
Hits $107.8M in 2022," CryptoSlate, January 3, 2023, https://cryptoslate.com
/yuga-labs-nft-royalty-income-hits-107-8m-in-2022.

7 **a part of its magic:** Kyle Swenson, "WELCOME A-BORED: Yuga Labs
Appoints Activision Blizzard's Former COO, Daniel Alegre, as Its New CEO,"
Bored Ape Gazette, December 19, 2022, https://www.theboredapegazette
.com/post/welcome-a-bored-yuga-labs-appoints-activision-blizzard-s
-former-coo-daniel-alegre-as-its-new-ceo; Kyle Swenson, "'NEXT LEVEL':

Yuga Labs Hired Epic Games' EVP of Development, Mike Seavers, as Its Next CTO," April 28, 2023, https://www.theboredapegazette.com/post/next -level-yuga-labs-hired-epic-games-evp-of-development-mike-seavers-as-its -next-cto.

8 **music videos to streetwear:** Kyle Swenson, "Timbaland Released a New Bored Ape Yacht Club Themed Music Video Today," Bored Ape Gazette, June 30, 2022, https://www.theboredapegazette.com/post/timbaland-released-a -new-bored-ape-yacht-club-themed-music-video-today-watch-it-here; Richard Lawler, "Snoop Dogg and Eminem's Bored Ape Music Video Is Here to Try and Sell Us on Tokens," *The Verge*, June 24, 2022, https://www .theverge.com/2022/6/24/23181936/bayc-eminem-snoop-dogg-yuga-labs-nft; Helen Partz, "Post Malone Features BAYC NFTs in New Music Video with The Weeknd," Cointelegraph, November 18, 2021, https://cointelegraph.com /news/post-malone-features-bayc-nfts-in-new-music-video-with-the-weeknd; The Hundreds Staff, "Lookbook: The Hundreds X Bored Ape Yacht Club," The Hundreds, August 20, 2021, https://thehundreds.com/blogs/content /lookbook-the-hundreds-x-bored-ape-yacht-club.

8 **FTX imploded in November 2022:** Matt Levine, "How Not to Play the Game," Bloomberg.com, December 30, 2022, https://www.bloomberg.com /features/2022-the-crypto-story-FTX-collapse-matt-levine.

9 **quickly came crashing down:** See, e.g., David Gura, "2022 Was the Year Crypto Came Crashing Down to Earth," NPR, December 29, 2022, https:// www.npr.org/2022/12/29/1145297807/crypto-crash-ftx-cryptocurrency -bitcoin; Shai Bernstein and Scott Duke Kominers, "Why Decentralized Crypto Platforms Are Weathering the Crash," *Harvard Business Review*, December 7, 2022, https://hbr.org/2022/12/why-decentralized-crypto -platforms-are-weathering-the-crash; Christina Pazzanese, "After the 'Crypto Crash,' What's Next for Digital Currencies?," *Harvard Gazette*, July 18, 2022, https://hbswk.hbs.edu/item/after-the-crypto-crash-whats-next-for-digital -currencies.

9 **get into cars:** Rosabeth Moss Kanter and Daniel Fox, "Uber and Stakeholders: Managing a New Way of Riding," Harvard Business Publishing, June 22, 2015, https://hbsp.harvard.edu/product/315139-PDF-ENG.

9 **stay in complete strangers' houses:** Joseph B. Lassiter and Evan Richardson, "Airbnb," Harvard Business Publishing, September 28, 2011, https://hbsp .harvard.edu/product/812046-PDF-ENG.

10 **these systems remained robust:** See, e.g., the discussion in Bernstein and Kominers, "Why Decentralized Crypto Platforms Are Weathering the Crash."

12 **an unnecessary advancement:** "Bill Gates Explains the Internet to Dave," *Letterman*, video, 7:53, November 27, 1995, available on YouTube at https://www.youtube.com/watch?v=fs-YpQj88ew.

12 **with younger demographics:** Chris Wheat and George Eckerd, "The Dynamics and Demographics of U.S. Household Crypto-Asset Use," JPMorgan Chase, December 2022, https://www.jpmorganchase.com/institute/research/financial-markets/dynamics-demographics-us-household-crypto-asset-cryptocurrency-use; Michelle Faverio and Olivia Sidoti, "Majority of Americans Aren't Confident in the Safety and Reliability of Cryptocurrency," Pew Research Center, April 10, 2023, https://www.pewresearch.org/short-reads/2023/04/10/majority-of-americans-arent-confident-in-the-safety-and-reliability-of-cryptocurrency.

12 **interest in NFTs:** Daren Matsuoka, Eddy Lazzarin, Robert Hackett, and Stephanie Zinn, "2023 State of Crypto Report: Introducing the State of Crypto Index," a16z crypto, April 11, 2023, https://a16zcrypto.com/posts/article/state-of-crypto-report-2023.

12 **more than ever:** See, e.g., "Opportunities in the Metaverse," JPMorgan, https://www.jpmorgan.com/content/dam/jpm/treasury-services/documents/opportunities-in-the-metaverse.pdf and the references therein.

13 **We wrote the first:** Steve Kaczynski and Scott Duke Kominers, "How NFTs Create Value," *Harvard Business Review*, November 10, 2021, https://hbr.org/2021/11/how-nfts-create-value.

13 **navigate the NFT world:** "Steve Kaczynski," LinkedIn, https://www.linkedin.com/in/skaczynski.

13 **Harvard Business School:** Scott Duke Kominers, http://www.scottkom.com; "Scott Duke Kominers," Harvard Business School, https://www.hbs.edu/faculty/Pages/profile.aspx?facId=500905.

13 **design of markets and marketplaces:** Scott Duke Kominers, Alexander Teytelboym, and Vincent P. Crawford, "An Invitation to Market Design," *Oxford Review of Economic Policy* 33, no. 4 (Winter 2017): 541–571, https://academic.oup.com/oxrep/article/33/4/541/4587951; Scott Duke Kominers, "Good Markets (Really Do) Make Good Neighbors," *ACM SIGecom Exchanges* 16, no. 2 (June 2018): 12–26, https://www.sigecom.org/exchanges/volume_16/2/KOMINERS.pdf. For further reading on the field of market design, check out Alvin E. Roth, *Who Gets What—and Why* (New York: Harper Academic, 2015), https://www.harperacademic.com/book/9780544288393/who-gets-what-and-why, and/or Ray Fisman and Tim Sullivan, *The Inner Lives of Markets* (New York: PublicAffairs, 2016), https://www.hachettebookgroup.com/titles/ray-fisman/the-inner-lives-of-markets/9781610394925.

13 **and marketplace builders:** "We Back Bold Entrepreneurs Building the Next
Internet," a16z crypto, https://a16zcrypto.com; Thomas R. Eisenmann and
Scott Duke Kominers, "Making Markets," Harvard Business Publishing,
January 24, 2018, https://hbsp.harvard.edu/product/818096-PDF-ENG; Scott
Duke Kominers, "A Three-Part Framework for Entrepreneurial Marketplace
Design," Harvard Business Publishing, January 4, 2021, https://hbsp.harvard
.edu/product/821065-PDF-ENG.

15 **from the perspective of most:** See, e.g., Paul Tassi, "How to Know If Your
Charizard Pokémon Card Is Rare And Valuable Or Not," *Forbes*, February 7,
2021, https://www.forbes.com/sites/paultassi/2021/02/07/how-to-know-if
-your-charizard-pokmon-card-is-rare-and-valuable-or-not; "Sports Card
Grading 101 Guide," The Cardboard Connection, https://www.cardboard
connection.com/collecting-101/sports-card-grading-101.

15 **people are generally paying:** See, e.g., Devon Thorsby, "Property Deed
vs. Title: Key Differences," *U.S. News & World Report*, April 14, 2023,
https://realestate.usnews.com/real-estate/articles/whats-the-difference
-between-a-deed-and-title.

16 **special Nike releases:** "About .SWOOSH," Nike, https://www.swoosh
.nike.

16 **an annual "Apefest":** "ApeFest," ApeFest, https://apefest
.com; Reethu Ravi, "ApeFest 2022: Everything You Need to Know,"
NFTevening, June 6, 2022, https://nftevening.com/apefest-2022
-everything-you-need-to-know.

16 **historical artifacts and documents:** Emily Neale, "Vatican Library
Embraces the Digital Age with Blockchain and NFTs!," *NFTevening*, April 27,
2023, https://nftevening.com/vatican-library-embraces-the-digital-age-with
-blockchain-and-nfts.

2. DIGITAL OWNERSHIP AND WHY IT MATTERS

18 **There's an old joke:** The original sourcing for this joke is not entirely clear,
although it has been attributed to Andersen Consulting. In any event, it
appeared on Car Talk: see "Thinking Quiz," CarTalk.com, https://www.cartalk
.com/radio/letter/thinking-quiz-0.

20 **record of who owns what:** See, e.g., the discussion in Andrew M. Goldstein,
"Bitforms Gallery's Steven Sacks on How to Collect New Media Art,"
Artspace, March 10, 2014, https://www.artspace.com/magazine/interviews
_features/expert_eye/how_to_collect_new_media_art-51998.

20 **Roblox pet or Fortnite skin:** See, e.g., the discussion in Sander Lutz,

"Roblox Adds Rare, Resellable Digital Items—But They're Not NFTs,"
Decrypt, April 14, 2023, https://decrypt.co/136834/roblox-adds-rare
-resellable-digital-items-theyre-not-nfts.

20 **inside their game environment:** Samuel Heaney, Veerender Singh Jubbal,
and Casey Defreitas, IGN, "How to Trade in Pokemon Go," updated
December 28, 2021, https://www.ign.com/wikis/pokemon-go/How_to_Trade
_in_Pokemon_Go.

20 **hack your GPS:** Simon Crawford, "How to Increase Your Pokemon Go
Trade Distance," LuckLuckGo, March 31, 2023, https://www.luckluckgo.com
/pokemon-go/pokemon-go-trade-distance.html.

21 **declares you the owner:** "Deed," Cornell Law School Legal Information
Institute, https://www.law.cornell.edu/wex/deed.

21 **in case of a dispute:** "Register of Deeds," Cornell Law School Legal
Information Institute, https://www.law.cornell.edu/wex/register_of_deeds.

21 **protect against that possibility:** "What Is Owner's Title Insurance?," Consumer
Financial Protection Bureau, last reviewed September 4, 2020, https://www
.consumerfinance.gov/ask-cfpb/what-is-owners-title-insurance-en-164.

22 **tungsten cube weighing roughly 2,000 pounds:** Sean Murray,
"Midwest Tungsten Service Cube NFT," Midwest Tungsten Service,
https://shop.tungsten.com/blog/midwest-tungsten-service-cube-nft; James
Vincent, "A One-Ton Tungsten Cube Was Just Bought by a Crypto Cabal for
$250,000," *The Verge*, November 3, 2021, https://www.theverge.com/2021/11
/3/22761305/tungsten-cube-meme-nft-crypto-midwest.

22 **applications will expand over time:** Marc Bain, "How Fashion Is Using
NFTs to Sell Exclusive Physical Products," Business of Fashion, August 4,
2022, https://www.businessoffashion.com/articles/technology/how-fashion
-is-using-nfts-to-sell-exclusive-physical-products; Johan Hajji, "Guide to
Using NFTs in Real Estate," *Forbes*, August 4, 2022, https://www.forbes.com
/sites/forbesbusinesscouncil/2022/08/04/guide-to-using-nfts-in-real-estate;
Marco Quiroz-Gutierrez, "Someone Just Bought a Florida Home for $653,000
through an NFT Sale," *Fortune*, February 12, 2022, https://fortune.com/2022
/02/12/nft-florida-home-sale-ether-crypto; Emily Rella, "A House Sold as an
NFT for the First Time in History," *Entrepreneur*, October 19, 2022, https://
www.entrepreneur.com/business-news/the-first-nft-home-just-sold-for
-175000/437522.

22 ***Who owns the digital image:*** "Stoic #3372," OpenSea, https://opensea.io
/assets/ethereum/0x12632d6e11c6bbc0c53f3e281ea675e5899a5df5/3372;
see also "Stoics Token Tracker," Etherscan, https://etherscan.io/token
/0x12632d6e11c6bbc0c53f3e281ea675e5899a5df5?a=3372.

23 **public record on the blockchain:** "Stoic #3372," OpenSea, accessed June 5, 2023, https://opensea.io/assets/ethereum/0x12632d6e11c6bbc0c53f3e 281ea675e5899a5df5/3372.

23 **digital wallet address is 34202F:** Technically, those are just the first characters in Scott's account address on the Ethereum network; the full address goes on for another thirty-four characters.

24 **at astronomical prices:** Sarah Cascone, "Here Are the Top 10 Most Expensive NFTs Sold to Date, from Beeple's Record-Setter to Edward Snowden's Court Transcription," Artnet, June 21, 2022, https://news .artnet.com/market/most-expensive-nfts-june-2022-2130218.

24 **each sold for over $7 million:** XCOPY, "Right-click and Save As guy," SuperRare, https://superrare.com/artwork/right-click-and-save-as-guy-1154; Dmitri Cherniak, "Ringers #109," Art Blocks, https://www.artblocks.io /collections/curated/projects/0xa7d8d9ef8d8ce8992df33d8b8cf4aebabd5bd270 /13/tokens/13000109.

24 **sold for $69 million:** Beeple, "Everydays: The First 5000 Days," Christie's, March 11, 2021, https://onlineonly.christies.com/s/beeple-first-5000-days /beeple-b-1981-1/112924.

25 **The global collectibles industry:** "Collectibles Market Size, Statistics, Growth Trend Analysis and Forecast Report, 2023–2033," Market Decipher, https://www.marketdecipher.com/report/collectibles-market; see also Ryoma Ito, "The Future of Collectibles Is Digital," TechCrunch, March 25, 2020, https://techcrunch.com/2020/03/25/the-future-of-collectibles-is-digital.

25 **ticket sales were estimated to be:** "Event Tickets—Worldwide," Statista, https://www.statista.com/outlook/dmo/eservices/event-tickets/worldwide; see also "Online Event Ticketing Market Size & Share Analysis—Growth Trends & Forecasts (2023–2028)," Mordor Intelligence, https://www.mordorintelligence .com/industry-reports/global-online-event-ticketing-market-industry.

26 **so much easier:** For further discussion, see, e.g., Christian Catalini and Joshua S. Gans, "Some Simple Economics of the Blockchain," *Communications of the ACM* 63, no. 7 (July 2020): 80–90.

27 **associated software programs:** See, e.g., "What Is Blockchain," McKinsey & Company, https://www.mckinsey.com/featured-insights/mckinsey-explainers /what-is-blockchain; "What Is Blockchain Technology?," IBM, https://www .ibm.com/topics/blockchain; Ramana Nanda, Robert F. White, and Alexey Tuzikov, "Blockchain, Cryptocurrencies and Digital Assets," Harvard Business Publishing, November 5, 2017, https://hbsp.harvard.edu/product/818066 -PDF-ENG.

27 **shut the whole thing down:** See, e.g., Jeff Tyson and Chris Pollette, "How

Internet Infrastructure Works," howstuffworks.com, https://computer
.howstuffworks.com/internet/basics/internet-infrastructure.htm; "What Is
BGP? BGP Routing Explained," Cloudflare, https://www.cloudflare.com
/learning/security/glossary/what-is-bgp.

27 **are economically incentivized:** See, e.g., E. Napoletano, "Proof of Work
Explained," *Forbes*, last updated August 25, 2023, https://www.forbes.com
/advisor/investing/cryptocurrency/proof-of-work; @wackerow, "Proof-of-
Work," Ethereum, last updated September 26, 2022, https://ethereum.org/en
/developers/docs/consensus-mechanisms/pow; "What Is Proof of Stake,"
McKinsey & Company, January 3, 2023, https://www.mckinsey.com
/featured-insights/mckinsey-explainers/what-is-proof-of-stake; @bskrksyp9,
"Proof-of-Stake (POS)," Ethereum, last updated May 12, 2023, https://
ethereum.org/en/developers/docs/consensus-mechanisms/pos; Joshua Gans,
*The Economics of Blockchain Consensus: Exploring the Key Tradeoffs in
Blockchain Design* (New York: Palgrave Macmillan, 2023).

27 **tamper with it:** See, e.g., Maryanne Murray, "Blockchain Explained," Reuters,
June 15, 2018, http://fingfx.thomsonreuters.com/gfx/rngs/TECHNOLOGY
-BLOCKCHAIN/010070MF1E7/index.html.

28 **to trace the item's origin:** See, e.g., @MLibre, "Transactions," Ethereum, last
updated July 7, 2023, https://ethereum.org/en/developers/docs/transactions.

28 **real magic of the blockchain:** For more magic of the blockchain, see Michael
Blau, "Secrets, and How to Prove Them: A Magician's Guide to Zero-Knowledge
Proofs," a16z crypto, https://a16zcrypto.com/posts/videos/a-magicians-guide
-to-zero-knowledge-proofs.

28 **that maintain the network:** See, e.g., Benedict George, "What Is a Consensus
Mechanism?," CoinDesk, updated May 11, 2023, https://www.coindesk.com
/learn/what-is-a-consensus-mechanism; @seb1220, "Consensus Mechanisms,"
Ethereum, last updated January 13, 2023, https://ethereum.org/en/developers
/docs/consensus-mechanisms.

28 **approve the various transactions:** Bessie Liu, "Ethereum Hits 500,000
Validator Milestone," Blockworks, January 12, 2023, https://blockworks.co
/news/ethereum-to-reach-500000-validators.

28 **locking up roughly $60,000:** See "Staking with Ethereum," Ethereum,
https://ethereum.org/en/staking.

29 **detected by the network:** "A Staker's Guide to Ethereum Slashing & Other
Penalties," Blocknative, October 1, 2022, https://www.blocknative.com/blog
/an-ethereum-stakers-guide-to-slashing-other-penalties.

29 **the result of a mixture:** For further discussion, see, e.g., Hanna Halaburda,
Miklos Sarvary, and Guillaume Haeringer, *Beyond Bitcoin: Economics of*

Digital Currencies and Blockchain Technologies, 2nd ed. (New York: Palgrave Macmillan, 2022).

31   **web browsers like Google Chrome:** As of 2020, DebugBear counted as many as 137,345 Chrome extensions, covering everything from screen capture to ad blocking. See "Counting Chrome Extensions—Chrome Web Store Statistics," DebugBear, June 29, 2020, https://www.debugbear.com/blog/counting-chrome-extensions.

31   **mods to add:** Ryan Woodrow, "Minecraft Mods: The Best Mods to Transform Your Game," *Sports Illustrated*, July 12, 2023, https://videogames.si.com/guides/minecraft-mods.

31   **World of Women did just that:** "NFT NYC—A Recap," World of Women, July 7, 2022, https://news.worldofwomen.art/nft-nyc-a-recap-b3841b8951a7; Bruce Houghton, "Madonna to Perform Live for World of Women NFT Project," Hypebot, June 15, 2022, https://www.hypebot.com/hypebot/2022/06/madonna-to-perform-live-for-world-of-women-nft-project.html.

3. THE NFT STAIRCASE

33   **people who had done the same:** For example, the BAYC Twitter account retweeted "ape follow ape" tweets as people changed their profile pictures, providing the social reward of a Twitter follow when someone changed their PFP to a Bored Ape.

33   **Bored Ape–themed businesses:** See, e.g., Kyle Swenson, "Ape Spotlight: Check Out Jenkins the Valet's Writers Room NFT Project," Bored Ape Gazette, July 2, 2021, https://www.theboredapegazette.com/post/ape-spotlight-check-out-jenkins-the-valet-s-writers-room-nft-project.

33   **real-world meetups:** Josh Ong (@beijingdou), "Thank you to @boredapeyc for the community grant to organize some real world ape meet ups," Twitter, June 14, 2021, 11:40 p.m., https://twitter.com/beijingdou/status/1404644963778969603.

33   **featured particularly prominent BAYC NFT holders:** BAYC did this through retweeting accounts directly to its large following, and still did so as of the writing of this book. See Bored Ape Yacht Club (@BoredApeYC), Twitter, https://twitter.com/BoredApeYC.

33   **Prominent Ape owners:** Andrew Hayward, "The Biggest Celebrity NFT Owners in the Bored Ape Yacht Club," Decrypt, March 27, 2022, https://decrypt.co/86135/biggest-celebrity-nft-owners-bored-ape-yacht-club; Ryan McNamara, "Celebrities That Own Bored Ape Yacht Club NFTs," Benzinga,

April 23, 2022, https://www.benzinga.com/money/celebrities-that-own
-bored-ape-yacht-club-nfts.

33 **"What the heck":** See, e.g., Kyle Chayka, "Why Bored Ape Avatars Are Taking
Over Twitter," *The New Yorker*, July 30, 2021, https://www.newyorker.com/culture
/infinite-scroll/why-bored-ape-avatars-are-taking-over-twitter; Kevin Roose,
"Crypto Is Cool. Now Get on the Yacht," *The New York Times*, November 5,
2021, https://www.nytimes.com/2021/11/05/technology/nft-nyc-metaverse
.html; Daniel Van Boom, "Bored Ape Yacht Club NFTs Explained," CNET,
August 11, 2022, https://www.cnet.com/culture/internet/bored-ape-yacht
-club-nfts-explained; Matt Borchert, "What the Heck Is the Bored Ape Yacht
Club (BAYC) NFT Project? $150K Apes?!," YouTube, https://www.youtube
.com/watch?v=KXE5-CBCnJk.

34 **putting the images on everything:** Christopher Gonda, "BAYC-Themed
Burger Joint 'Bored & Hungry' Now Open!," V13, April 13, 2022, https://v13
.net/2022/04/bayc-themed-burger-joint-bored-hungry-now-open; Eileen
Cartter, "Old Navy Is Selling a Bored Ape Yacht Club T-Shirt," *GQ*, July 22,
2022, https://www.gq.com/story/old-navy-bored-ape-yacht-club-shirt-nft;
"Ape Water," Ape Beverages, https://apebeverages.com/products/ape-5382
?selling_plan=3811016957; Kyle Swenson, "BORED BAGS: This Luggage
Company Released a Line of BAYC Inspired Suitcases," Bored Ape Gazette,
December 15, 2022, https://www.theboredapegazette.com/post/bored-bags
-this-luggage-company-released-a-line-of-bayc-inspired-suitcases.

34 **for more than $3 million:** "Rare Bored Ape Yacht Club NFT Sells for
Record $3.4 Million USD," Hypebeast, October 26, 2021, https://hypebeast
.com/2021/10/bored-ape-yacht-club-nft-3-4-million-record-sothebys
-metaverse.

34 **cover of *Rolling Stone*:** "Rolling Stone x Bored Ape Yacht Club Limited-
Edition Zine," *Rolling Stone*, https://shop.rollingstone.com/products/rolling
-stone-x-bored-ape-yacht-club-special-collectors-edition-zine; Sander Lutz,
"Rolling Stone Mints First-Ever NFTs with Bored Ape Yacht Club," Decrypt,
November 10, 2021, https://decrypt.co/85765/rolling-stone-mints-first-ever
-nfts-bored-ape-yacht-club.

34 **hundreds of thousands of dollars:** Elizabeth Howcroft, "Set of 'Bored Ape'
NFTs sells for $24.4 mln in Sotheby's Online Auction," Reuters, September 9,
2021, https://www.reuters.com/lifestyle/set-bored-ape-nfts-sell-244-mln
-sothebys-online-auction-2021-09-09; see also the transaction history listed
on OpenSea at https://opensea.io/collection/boredapeyachtclub/activity.

34 **sold-out megaparty:** Tim Hakki, "Snoop Dogg and Eminem Become Bored

Apes in New Music Video," Decrypt, June 24, 2022, https://decrypt.co/103757
/snoop-dogg-and-eminem-become-bored-apes-in-new-music-video; Shanti
Escalante-De Mattei, "Eminem and Snoop Dogg Performed as Their Bored
Ape Yacht Club Avatars at the VMAs," ARTnews, August 29, 2022, https://
www.artnews.com/art-news/news/eminem-snoop-dogg-bored-ape-yacht
-club-vmas-1234637677; "ApeFest," ApeFest, https://apefest.com; Reethu Ravi,
"ApeFest 2022: Everything You Need to Know," *NFTevening*, June 6, 2022,
https://nftevening.com/apefest-2022-everything-you-need-to-know.

36 *Harvard Business Review* **article:** Steve Kaczynski and Scott Duke
Kominers, "How NFTs Create Value," *Harvard Business Review*, November 10,
2021, https://hbr.org/2021/11/how-nfts-create-value.

37 **holders have gotten access:** See, e.g., Bored Ape Yacht Club (@BoredApeYC),
"Merch drop #2 starts Friday 1pm EST," Twitter, August 4, 2021, 1:15 p.m.,
https://twitter.com/BoredApeYC/status/1422969342619226116; Rosie Perper,
"Bored Ape Yacht Club and SUPERPLASTIC Team Up on Vinyl Collectibles,"
Hypebeast, April 14, 2022, https://hypebeast.com/2022/4/bored-ape-yacht
-club-superplastic-vinyl-collectibles-superbored-drop; Andrew Hayward,
"Why 137-Year-Old Brand Bicycle Is Making Bored Ape NFT Playing Cards,"
Decrypt, October 18, 2022, https://decrypt.co/112202/why-137-year-old
-brand-bicycle-is-making-bored-ape-nft-playing-cards; Kyle Swenson, "The
Bored Ape Yacht Club's Apes Vs. Mutants Mobile Game Competition Begins
Tonight," Bored Ape Gazette, January 21, 2022, https://www.theboredapegazette
.com/post/the-bored-ape-yacht-club-s-apes-vs-mutants-mobile-game-
competition-begins-tonight; Ekin Genç, "Bored Ape Yacht Club Sells $96
Million of Mutant Ape NFTs in One Hour," Decrypt, August 29, 2021, https://
decrypt.co/79718/bored-ape-yacht-club-sells-96-million-of-nfts-in-hour-for
-mutant-apes-launch; Kyle Swenson, "Pixel Vault Announced a New Bored
Ape Themed Comic. Here's How to Claim It:," Bored Ape Gazette, updated
July 20, 2022, https://www.theboredapegazette.com/post/pixel-vault-announced
-a-new-bored-ape-themed-comic-here-s-how-to-claim-it.

37 **including performances from:** Jem, "Snoop Dogg and Eminem Drop a
New Track at Apefest," *NFTevening*, June 25, 2022, https://nftevening.com
/snoop-dogg-and-eminem-drop-a-new-track-at-apefest; Kyle Swenson, "APES
FEST: The BAYC Hosted a Star Filled Ware House Party Wednesday Night!,"
Bored Ape Gazette, November 5, 2021, https://www.theboredapegazette.com
/post/apes-fest-the-bayc-hosted-a-star-filled-ware-house-party-wednesday
-night-all-the-details-here.

37 **granted commercial rights:** "Terms & Conditions," BAYC, https://
boredapeyachtclub.com/#/terms.

37 **a "forever Ape":** See, e.g., Daytona the Ape (@JoseColchao), "Found my
forever ape. Welcome home Daytona!," Twitter, May 12, 2022, 10:11 a.m.,
https://twitter.com/JoseColchao/status/1524754065862799360; Jaylissa
(@Mushhlove), Twitter, June 21, 2021, 3:24 p.m., https://twitter.com
/Mushhlove/status/1407056809383313412; @nsxttommy, Twitter, May 10,
2022, 10:17 p.m., https://twitter.com/nsxttommy/status/1527473535085465601;
Wxxdy (@_Wxxdy_), Twitter, January 10, 2023, 8:13 a.m., https://twitter
.com/_Wxxdy_/status/1612799719251607552.

37 **paid $1.3 million:** Aaron Mok, "Justin Bieber Bought a Bored Ape NFT
in January for $1.3 Million That's Likely Worth about $70,000 in the Wake of
the FTX Collapse," Yahoo! Finance, November 17, 2022, https://finance.yahoo
.com/news/justin-bieber-bought-bored-ape-190922945.html.

38 **custom diamond chain!:** Kyle Swenson, "Bored Ape Yacht Club Member
Neymar Rocked His Ape during Paris Fashion Week," Bored Ape Gazette,
September 30, 2022, https://www.theboredapegazette.com/post/bored-ape
-yacht-club-member-neymar-rocked-his-ape-during-paris-fashion-week.

39 **the community drives the brand:** See, e.g., Swoosie, "World's 2nd NFT
Restaurant | Bored Ape Yacht Club (BAYC) Members Eat Free, YouTube,"
https://www.youtube.com/watch?v=wWLNLGX9LZ4; Kyle Swenson, "This
Bored Ape Is Giving Every BAYC Member a Free Drink at His Ape Themed
Convenience Store," Bored Ape Gazette, updated October 30, 2022, https://
www.theboredapegazette.com/post/thisty-this-bored-ape-is-giving-every
-bayc-member-a-free-drink-at-his-ape-themed-convenience-store; Andrew
Hayward, "Why 137-Year-Old Brand Bicycle Is Making Bored Ape NFT
Playing Cards," Decrypt, October 18, 2022, https://decrypt.co/112202/why
-137-year-old-brand-bicycle-is-making-bored-ape-nft-playing-cards; "BAYC
Trezor Hunt: Will It Be IRL, and Who Is Applied Primate?," NFTevening,
updated January 17, 2023, https://nftevening.com/bayc-trezor-hunt-will-it
-be-irl-and-who-is-applied-primate; Truth Labs (@truth), "If you own a
@BoredApeYC you can add yourself to the whitelist now:," Twitter,
December 10, 2021, 10:20 p.m., https://twitter.com/truth/status
/1469507369231126532; Kyle Swenson, "BOOK PEOPLE: Jenkins The Valet's
Book 'Bored & Dangerous' Is Now Available," Bored Ape Gazette, July 11,
2022, https://www.theboredapegazette.com/post/book-people-jenkins-the
-valet-s-book-bored-dangerous-is-now-available; Kyle Swenson, "Pixel Vault
Announced A New Bored Ape Themed Comic. Here's How to Claim It:,"
Bored Ape Gazette, updated July 20, 2022, https://www.theboredapegazette
.com/post/pixel-vault-announced-a-new-bored-ape-themed-comic-here-s
-how-to-claim-it; AppliedPrimate (@AppliedPrimate), "We're thrilled to

officially announce our collaboration with @247ComicsHQ and Applied Primate: Origins!," Twitter, July 28, 2023, 12:39 p.m., https://twitter.com /AppliedPrimate/status/1684966758627872769.

40 **can sell their tokens:** BAYC NFTs are freely transferable, and have been frequently bought and sold on NFT marketplaces such as OpenSea: https:// opensea.io/collection/boredapeyachtclub.

40 **back to the parent company:** Creator royalties accrued for transactions on most NFT marketplaces; for example, at the time of this writing, royalties on BAYC NFT trades on OpenSea were set at 2.5% of the transaction price; see https://opensea.io/collection/boredapeyachtclub.

40 **robust secondary market:** Zeynep Geylan, "Yuga Labs' NFT Royalty Income Hits $107.8M in 2022," CryptoSlate, updated January 3, 2023, https://cryptoslate.com/yuga-labs-nft-royalty-income-hits-107-8m-in-2022; Luke Huigsloot, "Bored Apes Founders Propose New Model for NFT Creator Royalties," Cointelegraph, November 9, 2022, https://cointelegraph.com /news/bored-apes-founders-propose-new-model-for-nft-creator-royalties.

41 **people are calling *Web3*:** Jad Esber and Scott Duke Kominers, "Why Build in Web3," *Harvard Business Review*, May 16, 2022, https://hbr.org/2022 /05/why-build-in-web3; Chris Dixon, "Why Web3 Matters," a16z crypto, September 26, 2021, https://a16zcrypto.com/posts/article/why-web3-matters.

4. THE BUSINESS OF WEB3

42 **expanding across the world:** "A Short History of the Internet," Science+Media Museum, December 3, 2020, https://www.scienceandmediamuseum.org.uk /objects-and-stories/short-history-internet; "World Wide Web Timeline," Pew Research Center," March 11, 2014, https://www.pewresearch.org/internet /2014/03/11/world-wide-web-timeline.

42 **AOL online CDs, anyone?:** Phil Edwards, "In Memoriam: AOL CDs, History's Greatest Junk Mail," *Vox*, May 12, 2015, https://www.vox.com /2015/5/12/8594049/aol-free-trial-cds.

42 **"surfing the web":** "The Origins of the Ubiquitous 'Surfing the Internet,'" Internet Hall of Fame, October 10, 2019, https://www.internethalloffame .org/2019/10/10/origins-ubiquitous-surfing-internet.

42 **the "social web":** Danah M. Boyd and Nicole B. Ellison, "Social Network Sites: Definition, History, and Scholarship," *Journal of Computer-Mediated Communication* 13, no. 1 (October 1, 2007): 210–30, https://academic.oup .com/jcmc/article/13/1/210/4583062; "Social Media," Encyclopedia Britannica, https://www.britannica.com/topic/social-media.

43 **remember Yahoo! and Friendster?:** Robert McMillan, "The Friendster
    Autopsy: How a Social Network Dies," *Wired*, February 27, 2013,
    https://www.wired.com/2013/02/friendster-autopsy.

43 **many forward-thinking entrepreneurs:** Ngozi Nwanji, "Pharrell Williams
    Speaks on the Potential Power of Web3: 'It's Unlocking Something That Is
    Scaring the System,'" Afrotech, May 26, 2022, https://afrotech.com/pharrell
    -veecon-blockchain-technology-web3; "Part 1: The Limitless Potential of
    Web3: A Conversation with Alexis Ohanian," Milken Institute, May 3, 2022,
    https://milkeninstitute.org/video/alexis-ohanian-web3; "Reese Witherspoon
    on Onboarding Women to Web3," podcast interview on *NFT Now*, season 1,
    episode 46, February 16, 2022, https://nftnow.com/podcasts/reese
    -witherspoon-on-onboarding-women-to-web3; "Web3 Explained by Gary
    Vaynerchuk," Yahoo! Finance, June 6, 2022, https://news.yahoo.com/web3
    -explained-gary-vaynerchuk-203552540.html.

44 **fighting its own users and partners:** Chris Dixon, "Why Web3 Matters,"
    a16z crypto, September 26, 2021, https://a16zcrypto.com/posts/article
    /why-web3-matters; see also Chris Dixon, *Read Write Own* (New York:
    Penguin Random House, January 2024).

45 **show you targeted advertising:** See, e.g., Mark Hachman, "The Price of Free:
    How Apple, Facebook, Microsoft and Google Sell You to Advertisers,"
    PCWorld, October 1, 2015, https://www.pcworld.com/article/423747/the
    -price-of-free-how-apple-facebook-microsoft-and-google-sell-you-to
    -advertisers.html; Scott Duke Kominers, "Facebook Knows It Can't Offer More
    Privacy," Bloomberg.com, April 26, 2018, https://www.bloomberg.com/view
    /articles/2018-04-26/facebook-knows-it-can-t-offer-more-privacy; Paul Karp,
    "Meta Warns Australia's Plan to Limit Targeted Ads Could Push Free
    Platforms towards Subscription Fees," *The Guardian*, May 17, 2023, https://
    www.theguardian.com/technology/2023/may/18/meta-warns-australia
    -platforms-facebook-instagram-harmed-by-limiting-targeted-ads; Cameron F.
    Kerry and Mishaela Robison, "Rulemaking in Privacy Legislation Can Help
    Dial In Ad Regulation," Brookings, December 5, 2022, https://www.brookings
    .edu/blog/techtank/2022/12/05/rulemaking-in-privacy-legislation-can-help
    -dial-in-ad-regulation.

45 **if you're not paying:** "You're Not the Customer; You're the Product," Quote
    Investigator, https://quoteinvestigator.com/2017/07/16/product. See also the
    middle panel of the classic xkcd comic "Advertising": https://xkcd.com/870.

46 **a form of digital currency:** Satoshi Nakamoto, "Bitcoin: A Peer-to-Peer
    Electronic Cash System," Bitcoin.org, https://bitcoin.org/bitcoin.pdf.

46 **appreciate in value significantly:** There have been some pretty massive

Pokémon card sales; see, e.g., Tom Bowen, "The 30 Most Expensive Pokemon Cards Ever Sold (& How Many of Them Are Out There)," Gamerant, updated August 24, 2022, https://gamerant.com/most-expensive-pokemon-cards-ever -sold.

47   **the concept has been around:** The term was introduced by Neal Stephenson in his 1992 novel *Snow Crash*, although the concept had been discussed previously. See, e.g., Erik Gregersen, "Metaverse," Encyclopedia Britannica, https://www.britannica.com/topic/metaverse.

47   **where people can interact with one another:** Elizabeth Harkavy, Eddy Lazzarin, and Arianna Simpson, "7 Essential Ingredients of a Metaverse," a16z crypto, May 6, 2022, https://a16zcrypto.com/posts/article/7-essential -ingredients-of-a-metaverse.

47   *Snow Crash:* Neal Stephenson, *Snow Crash* (New York: Del Rey, 2000).

47   *Ready Player One:* Ernest Cline, *Ready Player One* (New York: Ballantine Books, 2011). For information about the film, see "Ready Player One," Warner Bros, https://www.warnerbros.com/movies/ready-player-one. And see also Scott Duke Kominers and Nicole Tempest Keller, "Halliday's OASIS," Harvard Business Publishing, February 26, 2019, https://hbsp.harvard.edu/product /819106-PDF-ENG.

47   **different affordances and functionalities:** "MUD," Jargon.net, http://jargon .net/jargonfile/m/MUD.html; Justin Olivetti, "The Game Archaeologist: A Brief History of Multi-User Dungeons," MassivelyOP, October 26, 2019, https://massivelyop.com/2019/10/26/the-game-archaeologist-a-brief-history -of-multi-user-dungeons.

47   **have expanded dramatically:** Herman Narula, *Virtual Society* (New York: Currency, 2022); Elena Burger, "Virtual Society, Blockchains, and the Metaverse," a16z crypto, October 9, 2022, https://a16zcrypto.com/posts /article/virtual-society-the-metaverse-blockchains; Scott Duke Kominers, "Metaverse Land: What Makes Digital Real Estate Valuable," a16z crypto, June 2, 2022, https://a16zcrypto.com/posts/article/metaverse-real-estate -digital-land-value-to-users.

48   **hard to use and too expensive:** See, e.g., "Paul Krugman's Poor Prediction," *Lapham's Quarterly*, https://www.laphamsquarterly.org/revolutions /miscellany/paul-krugmans-poor-prediction; David Emery, "Did Paul Krugman Say the Internet's Effect on the World Economy Would Be 'No Greater Than the Fax Machine's'?," Snopes, June 7, 2018, https://www.snopes .com/fact-check/paul-krugman-internets-effect-economy; David Cushman and Phil Fersht, "The Metaverse: Reports of 'Meh' Are Greatly Exaggerated," Horses for Sources, April 15, 2023, https://www.horsesforsources.com

/metaverse-meh-greatly-exaggerated_041523; Clifford Stoll, "Why the Web Won't Be Nirvana," *Newsweek*, February 26, 1995, https://www.newsweek .com/clifford-stoll-why-web-wont-be-nirvana-185306.

5. ESTABLISHING OWNERSHIP

53 **"Pocket Monsters" you've caught:** "Pokémon at 25: A History—From Pocket Monsters, to TCG and Pokémon GO," BBC, February 28, 2021, https://www .bbc.co.uk/newsround/56167405.

54 **George Orwell's famous novel *1984*:** Brad Stone, "Amazon Erases Orwell Books from Kindle," *The New York Times*, July 17, 2009, https://www.nytimes .com/2009/07/18/technology/companies/18amazon.html.

54 **Petaverse (an NFT company):** Petaverse Network, https://petaverse.network; "Our Team," Petaverse Network, https://petaverse.network/team.

54 **how to sell *physical* wallets:** Benjamin Edelman and Scott Duke Kominers, "Online Marketing at Big Skinny," Harvard Business Publishing, February 8, 2011, https://hbsp.harvard.edu/product/911033-PDF-ENG.

55 **confined to the Nintendo DS:** "Bandai Namco Group Fact Book 2021," Bandai Namco, https://www.bandainamco.co.jp/cgi-bin/releases/index.cgi /file/view/10492?entry_id=7280; "Top Selling Titles Sales Units," Nintendo, https://www.nintendo.co.jp/ir/en/finance/software/ds.html.

56 **a Broadway show:** Scott particularly recommends the musical *She Loves Me*; see for example a trailer for the 2016 Roundabout Theatre Company production at Playbill, "She Loves Me – Broadway," YouTube, https://www.youtube.com /watch?v=ubZ045hpeyg.

56 **easy to reference and immutable:** See, for example, the "Can't Be Evil" NFT licenses introduced by Scott's colleagues at a16z crypto: Miles Jennings and Chris Dixon, "The Can't Be Evil NFT Licenses," a16z crypto, August 31, 2022, https://a16zcrypto.com/content/article/introducing-nft-licenses.

57 **stays with you:** Gary S. Becker, *Human Capital* (Chicago: University of Chicago Press, 1993).

57 ***soul-bound* tokens:** Vitalik Buterin, "Soulbound," vitalik.ca, https://vitalik .ca/general/2022/01/26/soulbound.html; E. Glen Weyl, Puja Ohlhaver, and Vitalik Buterin, "Decentralized Society: Finding Web3's Soul," Social Science Research Network (working paper), May 10, 2022, https://papers.ssrn.com /sol3/papers.cfm?abstract_id=4105763; Andrey Sergeenkov, "What Are Soulbound Tokens? The Non-Transferrable NFT Explained," CoinDesk, updated May 11, 2023, https://www.coindesk.com/learn/what-are-soulbound -tokens-the-non-transferrable-nft-explained.

57   **Unless you're Bart Simpson:** *The Simpsons*, season 7, episode 4, "Bart Sells His Soul," aired October 8, 1995 on Fox; "Recap/The Simpsons S7 E4 'Bart Sells His Soul,'" TVTropes, https://tvtropes.org/pmwiki/pmwiki.php/Recap /TheSimpsonsS7E4BartSellsHisSoul.

58   **Meta made $113 billion:** "Meta Reports Fourth Quarter and Full Year 2022 Results," Meta Investor Relations, https://investor.fb.com/investor-news /press-release-details/2023/Meta-Reports-Fourth-Quarter-and-Full-Year -2022-Results/default.aspx.

59   **populated and available for trading:** See, e.g., Scott Duke Kominers, Shai Bernstein, and George Gonzalez, "LooksRare: The Decentralized, Tokenized, NFT Marketplace," Harvard Business Publishing, March 14, 2022, https:// hbsp.harvard.edu/product/822119-PDF-ENG.

59   **more willing to join:** Marco Reuter, "When Is Decentralizing on a Blockchain Valuable?," a16z crypto, January 13, 2023, https://a16zcrypto.com/content /article/when-is-decentralizing-on-a-blockchain-valuable; Marco Reuter, "The Value of Decentralization Using the Blockchain," Social Science Research Network (working paper), last updated July 20, 2023, https://papers .ssrn.com/sol3/papers.cfm?abstract_id=4219840.

60   **breaks down this intuition as follows:** The quote here is Adam's own slight adaptation of a version of the explanation he gave in an interview with Matt Prichard on KUSI News. For a video clip of the interview, see Adam Hollander (@HollanderAdam), "I was on the news tonight talking about #NFTs," Twitter, November 28, 2021, 11:47 p.m., https://twitter.com /HollanderAdam/status/1465180680418205697.

62   **featuring their pricey primates:** Bored and Hungry, https://justboredand hungry.com; Tim Hakki, "Snoop Dogg and Eminem Become Bored Apes in New Music Video," Decrypt, June 24, 2022, https://decrypt.co/103757/snoop -dogg-and-eminem-become-bored-apes-in-new-music-video; Kyle Swenson, "Timbaland Released A New Bored Ape Yacht Club Themed Music Video Today," Bored Ape Gazette, June 30, 2022, https://www.theboredapegazette .com/post/timbaland-released-a-new-bored-ape-yacht-club-themed-music -video-today-watch-it-here; Anna Chan, "Bored Ape #9797 Becomes the First NFT to Drop a Music Video: First Look," *Billboard*, https://www.billboard .com/music/music-news/bored-ape-9797-first-nft-music-video-exclusive -1235007900; "Bored Ape Recording Artist Shilly Releases First Single and Video for Pop-Punk Anthem, 'I'm Boring,'" NFTCulture, December 15, 2022, https://www.nftculture.com/nft-news/bored-ape-recording-artist-shilly -releases-first-single-and-video-for-pop-punk-anthemim-boring.

62   ***human capital*, in economese:** Becker, *Human Capital*.

63   **secret top loyalty level:** Richard Kerr, "Marriott Has a Secret 'Cobalt Elite' Program—TPG Has the Details," The Points Guy, August 6, 2019, https://thepointsguy.com/guide/marriott-secret-cobalt-elite-status.

64   **multiple academic papers:** John William Hatfield and Scott Duke Kominers, "A Simple Theory of Vampire Attacks," Social Science Research Network (working paper), last updated August 8, 2023, https://papers.ssrn.com/sol3/papers.cfm?abstract_id=4377561; Christian Catalini and Scott Duke Kominers, "Can WEB3 Bring Back Competition to Digital Platforms?," *TechREG Chronicle*, February 23, 2022, https://www.competitionpolicyinternational.com/can-web3-bring-back-competition-to-digital-platforms.

66   **"your possession and promotion":** The Hundreds Staff, "Loyalty Is Royalty," Adam Bomb Squad, January 30, 2022, https://web.archive.org/web/20220201154241/https://www.adambombsquad.com/updateds/loyalty-is-royalty; see also Adam Bomb Squad (@AdamBombSquad), "A big part of ABS is disrupting the traditional purveyor/consumer relationship," Twitter, January 30, 2022, 4:10 p.m., https://twitter.com/AdamBombSquad/status/1487896130977337347.

66   **created their own custom "Bombs":** See BombDAO (@thebombDAO), "Dolphin Discord channel members of @AdamBombSquad have been stealth minting," Twitter, February 14, 2022, 11:59 p.m., https://twitter.com/thebombDAO/status/1493283648044371970; "Dolphin Adam Bombs (Unofficial)" OpenSea, https://opensea.io/collection/dolphin-adam-bombs-unofficial; "Whale Adam Bombs Unofficial," OpenSea, https://opensea.io/collection/whale-adam-bombs-unofficial.

66   **recognized and encouraged:** Bobby Hundreds, "Bomb Talk 210: Season Finale with Ethan Lin," June 16, 2022, in *Bomb Talk* with Bobby Hundreds, podcast, https://podcasts.apple.com/ca/podcast/adam-bomb-squad-presents-bomb-talk-with-bobby-hundreds/id1589827434.

67   **the Bomb-licensing announcement noted:** The Hundreds Staff, "Loyalty Is Royalty."

67   **all over social media:** See, e.g., the replies to Adam Bomb Squad (@AdamBombSquad), "A big part of ABS is disrupting the traditional purveyor/consumer relationship."

68   **"having my books tomorrow":** Stone, "Amazon Erases Orwell Books from Kindle."

68   **on the digital copy:** Stone, "Amazon Erases Orwell Books from Kindle."

68   **"Retailers of physical goods":** Stone, "Amazon Erases Orwell Books from Kindle."

69   **actually own and control:** Iiro Jussila et al., "Individual Psychological

Ownership: Concepts, Evidence, and Implications for Research in Marketing," *Journal of Marketing Theory and Practice* 23, no. 2 (March 25, 2015): 121–39, https://www.tandfonline.com/doi/abs/10.1080/10696679.2015.1002330.

69 **reinforce each other:** Li Jin, "Building Psychological Attachment—Not Just Ownership—Into Web3," *Harvard Business Review*, April 4, 2023, https://hbr .org/2023/04/building-psychological-attachment-not-just-ownership-into-web3.

69 **willingness to invest time and energy into the brand:** Joann Peck, Colleen P. Kirk, and Suzanne B. Shu, "Caring for the Commons: Using Psychological Ownership to Enhance Stewardship Behavior for Public Goods," *Journal of Marketing* 85, no. 2 (September 25, 2020), https://journals.sagepub.com/doi /10.1177/0022242920952084.

69 **"function as a sort of profile":** Scott Duke Kominers and Jad Esber, "Decentralized Identity: Your Reputation Travels with You," a16z crypto, November 18, 2021, https://a16zcrypto.com/posts/article/decentralized -identity-on-chain-reputation.

69 **"no matter the specific platform":** Kominers and Esber, "Decentralized Identity: Your Reputation Travels with You."

70 **Proof of Attendance Protocol (POAP):** "What is POAP?," POAP, https:// poap.xyz/about-the-protocol.

70 **activist music group Pussy Riot:** "The Crazy About Crypto Show with Pussy Riot," POAP Gallery, October 6, 2021, https://poap.gallery/event/9665.

70 **a mindfulness event:** "Zenft Garden Society: Genesis," POAP Gallery, May 28, 2021, https://poap.gallery/event/2514.

70 **commemorating lectures or attendance:** "Harvard Business School Case Study on Bored Ape Yacht Club," POAP Gallery, March 22, 2022, https:// poap.gallery/event/34447; "Coffee with Captain—LIVE AT VEECON 2023," POAP Gallery, May 18, 2023, https://poap.gallery/event/126676.

70 **collect at a conference:** "The 2023 ACM SIGecom Winter Meeting on Crypto & Web3," POAP Gallery, February 22, 2023, https://poap.gallery /event/102578; "You Met @NFTBark in NFT NYC 2022!," POAP Gallery, June 17, 2022, https://poap.gallery/event/50432.

70 **digital business cards:** "Brinkman at VeeCon 2023," POAP Scan, May 18, 2023, https://app.poap.xyz/token/6633510; "You Have Met Patricio in November 2022 (IRL)," POAP Scan, November 9, 2022, https://app.poap.xyz/token/5876107.

73 **ditched its fitness tracker:** Scott Duke Kominers, "Under Armour Dumped Its App, and Consumers Feel the Heartbreak," Bloomberg.com, February 5, 2020, https://www.bloomberg.com/opinion/articles/2020-02-05/under -armour-dumped-its-app-and-consumers-feel-the-heartbreak.

73 **company that makes Fortnite:** At the time we were writing this, Fortnite

was one of the most popular games out there, so the possibility that its parent company might go bankrupt seemed rather unlikely. But the game industry goes through cycles, and even games that have been extremely popular have later been shut down.

74 **sold these sorts of NFTs:** "Puma Expands Its Metaverse Web Destination, Black Station, with Immersive Digital Retail Experience," Puma, June 13, 2023, https://about.puma.com/en/newsroom/brand-and-product-news/2023/06-13-23-puma_blackstation2; "NFTiff Frequently Asked Questions," Tiffany & Co., https://nft.tiffany.com/faq; Sophie Waldman, "Azuki Twin Tigers NFT Can Now Be Redeemed for Physical Jacket," Hypebeast, https://hypebeast.com/2022/7/azuki-twin-tigers-nft-can-now-be-redeemed-for-physical-jacket.

75 **climate-controlled vault:** "Collect What's Next," StockX, https://stockx.com/lp/nfts; "What Are Vault NFTs," StockX Help Center, https://stockx.com/help/articles/What-are-Vault-NFTs.

75 **service for fine liquor:** "The Secure Way to Trade Wine and Spirits," BAXUS, https://baxus.co; BlockBar Marketplace, https://blockbar.com; Kathleen Willcox, "How BAXUS Offers a Comprehensive Solution to Spirits Collectors on the Blockchain," Alcohol Professor, July 12, 2022, https://www.alcoholprofessor.com/blog-posts/baxus-spirits-nft; Randy Ginsburg, "How BlockBar Is Using NFTs to Disrupt the World of Luxury Spirits," NFT Now, September 20, 2022, https://nftnow.com/sponsored/how-blockbar-is-using-nfts-to-disrupt-the-world-of-luxury-spirits.

75 **for trading cards:** Jason Koeppel, "Enter the World of Physical Backed NFTs with Courtyard.io," One37PM, updated March 17, 2022, https://www.one37pm.com/popular-culture/courtyard-physical-collectible-backed-nfts.

75 **come with associated NFTs:** Jacquelyn Melinek, "Pudgy Penguins Wants to Use Its NFT-Inspired Toys to Bring IP to the Real World," TechCrunch, May 18, 2023, https://techcrunch.com/2023/05/18/pudgy-penguins-nft-toys-ip.

76 **Luca Netz, explained:** Luca Netz, "Pudgy Penguins with Luca Netz," podcast interview on *Coffee with Captain*, May 26, 2023, https://podcasts.apple.com/zw/podcast/pudgy-penguins-with-luca-netz/id1666919062?i=1000614617308.

76 **pretty much any product:** IYK, https://iyk.app; Aventurine.eth, "Meet IYK, The Team behind Your Favorite Drops and Activations," One37PM, updated January 10, 2023, https://www.one37pm.com/nft/iyk-near-field-technology.

6. ENHANCING OWNERSHIP WITH UTILITY

79 **average email open rate:** "Achieving a Good Email Open Rate," Constant Contact, updated October 19, 2020, https://knowledgebase.constantcontact.com

/email-digital-marketing/articles/KnowledgeBase/22856-What-s-a-Good-Open
-Rate?lang=en_US.

80 **admission to exclusive concerts:** Vismaya V., "BAYC Teams Up with
Tokenproof for ApeFest 2022," *Crypto Times*, June 3, 2022, https://www
.cryptotimes.io/bayc-teams-up-with-tokenproof-for-apefest-2022.

80 **top-tier speakers and media personalities:** "About VeeFriends," VeeFriends,
https://veefriends.com/faq.

81 **allocation of charitable donations:** "OnChainMonkey Raises ~$185,000 for
Ukrainian Humanitarian Aid with Charity NFT," OnChainMonkey, https://
news.onchainmonkey.com/2022/03/18/onchainmonkey-raises-185000-for
-ukrainian-humanitarian-aid-with-charity-nft.

81 **characters and key plot points:** "The Writer's Room: How It Works," Jenkins
the Valet, https://www.jenkinsthevalet.com/how-it-works.

81 **special access to driving tracks:** See, e.g., PorschΞ (@Eth_Porsche), "From
Downtown to A-town in #Atlanta bridged street art, reinvented fast food
and delivered modern track experiences for our holders this week," Twitter,
May 28, 2023, 10:00 a.m., https://twitter.com/eth_porsche/status
/1662821022847111170; PorschΞ (@Eth_Porsche), "A race day at the
@HungaroringF1 for our Pioneers?," Twitter, May 11, 2023, 9:00 a.m.,
https://twitter.com/eth_porsche/status/1656645331046498306; PorschΞ
(@Eth_Porsche), "A full-day track experience on #PECAtlanta?," Twitter,
May 26, 2023, 10:09 a.m., https://twitter.com/eth_porsche/status
/1662098584563511296.

81 **use NFT imagery:** "Terms & Conditions," Bored Ape Yacht Club,
https://boredapeyachtclub.com/#/terms; "Azuki NFT License Agreement,"
https://www.azuki.com/en/license; "SupDucks NFT Ownership & IP Rights,"
MegaVolt, https://megavolt.notion.site/ownership-ip-rights-09dc4f0ab82646d
7a56c7b49b05fe9ad.

81 **own music compositions:** "Kits AI Voice Models," Kits, https://www.kits.io.

81 **access to paywalled media:** "Knights of Degen Launches Partnership with
Action Network, Better Collective," Action Network, updated July 25, 2022,
https://www.actionnetwork.com/press/knightsdegen-launches-partnership
-with-action-network-better-collective.

81 **across-the-board price reductions:** "Our Newest Creation Has Arrived,"
Bugatti Group NFT, https://bugatticollectionsnft.com.

81 **wear in the metaverse:** Energii, "Adida Metaverse: Everything You Need
to Know," *NFTevening*, December 18, 2022, https://nftevening.com/adidas
-metaverse-everything-you-need-to-know/#What_ is_ Adidas_Virtual_Gear.

81 **use in online games:** The Sandbox (@TheSandboxGame), "The Aoki Avatars will be released in 3 waves," Twitter, July 19, 2022, 11:10 a.m., https://twitter .com/TheSandboxGame/status/1549411251972890624.

81 **acquire exclusive apparel:** Arthur Parkhouse, "Clone X to Release Physical Nike Air Force 1s," Hypebeast, August 30, 2022, https://hypebeast.com/2022/8 /clone-x-nike-air-force-1-rtfkt-nft; Emma Roth, "Tiffany Is Selling Custom CryptoPunk Pendants for $50,000," *The Verge*, August 1, 2022, https://www .theverge.com/2022/8/1/23287775/tiffany-custom-cryptopunk-pendants -nfts-nftiff.

81 **figurines (the littles, Thingdoms):** "Limited Edition—Jojo Street Cred," the littles, https://shop.thelittles.io/products/ac005-figure-colored-version; "Thingdoms," TC Print Shop, https://tcprintshop.com/pages/thingdoms-collab.

81 **and tumblers (Starbucks):** Steve (@NFTbark), "EPIC MAIL DAY!!," Twitter, June 11, 2023, 11:25 a.m., https://twitter.com/NFTbark/status/ 1667915905416716290.

82 **a number of them:** "The Lumsden Collection of Antique & Vintage Lawnmowers," Picton Castle Gardens, https://www.pictoncastle.co.uk /about/the-lumsden-lawnmower-museum.

84 **ride around in:** As of when we were writing, at least, this hypothetical looked likely to become a reality—the Goblintown/Truth Labs team announced a collaboration with Atari X to produce a game called "Goblin Crash"; see Atari X (@AtariX), "Hey @goblintown we fixed your poster," Twitter, November 8, 2022, 8:04 p.m., https://twitter.com/AtariX/status/1592684921218543616.

84 **play longer than 41 yards:** "Devonta Smith X Endstate," Endstate, https:// mint.endstate.io/devontasmith.

85 **gave out free burrito coupons:** Mark Brandau, "Qdoba Calls 'Burrito Boredom' Campaign a Successful Operation," Nation's Restaurant News, October 18, 2010, https://www.nrn.com/archive/qdoba-calls-burrito-boredom-campaign -successful-operation.

86 **experimenting with token-gated ticket sales:** "Unlock the Power of Your Brand's Community," Shopify, https://www.shopify.com/tokengated -commerce; "Ticketmaster Launches Token-Gated Sales, Enabling Artists to Reward Fans with Prioritized Ticket Access and Concert Experiences Through NFTs," Ticketmaster Business, March 27, 2023, https://business .ticketmaster.com/business-solutions/nft-token-gated-sales.

86 **sold whiskey and hot sauce:** @stacikanderson1, "Bourbon: Bottled," Twitter, April 22, 2022, 5:10 p.m., https://twitter.com/stacikanderson1/status /1517611793727770626; tab-hot-sauce, https://tab-hot-sauce.myshopify.com.

87 **introduced a mechanism:** "Nesting Rewards," Moonbirds, https://www
.proof.xyz/rewards.

89 **free one-year membership:** "Knights of Degen Launches Partnership with
Action Network, Better Collective," Action Network, updated July 25, 2022,
https://www.actionnetwork.com/press/knights-of-degen-launches
-partnership-with-action-network-better-collective.

89 **released in June 2021:** "Own a piece of Celtics history," Celtics Heritage
Collection, https://nft.celticsdigital.com.

90 **numerous gaming sponsorships:** See, e.g., Adam Stern, "NRG Signs
Partnership Deal with Hot Pockets Brand," March 19, 2021, Esports Observer,
https://archive.esportsobserver.com/nrg-hot-pockets-deal.

90 **self-identifying as brand enthusiasts:** Jad Esber and Scott Duke Kominers,
"Inverting the Internet's Personal Data Model," Social Science Research
Network (working paper), in preparation.

92 **United status NFTs:** Marriott and United have offered reciprocal status
benefits for years, in fact, but the Web 2 implementation of this is
extraordinarily cumbersome, requiring the two companies to coordinate
with each other and have their customers individually link their loyalty
accounts. See J. T. Genter and Elina Geller, "How United and Marriott
Elites Can Status Match," NerdWallet, updated July 25, 2023, https://www
.nerdwallet.com/article/travel/how-united-and-marriott-elites-can-get
-status-matching.

93 **roughly eleven million per year:** Megan Leonhardt, "About 12 Percent of
People Buying Concert Tickets Get Scammed," CNBC, September 14, 2018,
https://www.cnbc.com/2018/09/13/about-12-percent-of-people-buying
-concert-ticketsget-scammed-.html.

94 **testing out NFT-based ticket sales:** Ivan Mehta, "Ticketmaster Taps the
Flow Blockchain to Let Event Organizers Issue NFTs Tied to Tickets,"
TechCrunch, August 31, 2022, https://techcrunch.com/2022/08/31
/ticketmaster-taps-the-flow-blockchain-to-let-event-organizers-issue-nfts
-tied-to-tickets; "Ticketmaster Launches Token-Gated Sales, Enabling Artists
to Reward Fans with Prioritized Ticket Access and Concert Experiences
Through NFTs"; Anthon Ha, "YellowHeart Allows Musicians and Concert
Organizers to Take More Control of Resold Tickets," October 18, 2019,
https://techcrunch.com/2019/10/18/yellowheart.

95 **tokenproof to verify:** Joseph Genest, "Can Tokenproof Make Adidas'
Confirmed the Future of Sneaker Shopping?," HighSnobiety, https://www
.highsnobiety.com/p/tokenproof-adidas-confirmed.

7. BUILDING AND REINFORCING IDENTITY

102 **sense of brand attachment:** See, e.g., C. Whan Park, Deborah J. MacInnis, and Joseph Priester, "Brand Attachment: Constructs, Consequences, and Causes," *Foundations and Trends in Marketing* 1, no. 3 (January 22, 2008), 191–230, https://www.nowpublishers.com/article/Details/MKT-006.

103 **potential to speedrun:** The term *speedrun* originated in the context of video games, and means what it sounds like; see "speedrun," Merriam Webster Online, https://www.merriam-webster.com/dictionary/speedrun.

103 **think of as *virtual fashion*:** For further discussion, see Bobby Hundreds, *NFTs Are a Scam / NFTs Are the Future* (New York: Macmillan, 2023).

103 **rare patterning on digital racehorses:** Cathy Hackl, "Stella Artois Gallops into the Metaverse with Horse Racing NFTs," *Forbes*, June 18, 2021, https://www.forbes.com/sites/cathyhackl/2021/06/18/stella-artois-gallops-into-the-metaverse-with-horse-racing-nfts.

103 **virtual backpacks, and the like:** See, e.g., "10KTF: Collection: Ape daypack," OpenSea, https://opensea.io/collection/10ktf?search%5bstringTraits%5d%5b0%5d%5bname%5d=Collection&search%5bstringTraits%5d%5b0%5d%5bvalues%5d%5b0%5d=Ape%20Daypack.

103 **NFTs made it possible:** For a fantastic exposition of this, see Bobby Hundreds's essay, "The Street Does Not Really Exist," The Hundreds, August 12, 2021, https://thehundreds.com/blogs/monologue/thestreet; see also Bobby Hundreds, *This Is Not a T-Shirt: A Brand, a Culture, a Community* (New York: MCD, 2019).

103 **luxury car brands:** "The Epic Road Trip," Lamborghini, https://nft.lamborghini.com; "Porsche R2D," Porsche, https://nft.porsche.com.

103 **nonprofits (Saisei Foundation, Disabled American Veterans):** Andrew Hayward, "Author Tim Ferriss Tops NFT Sales Charts with 'Cockpunch,'" Yahoo! Money, https://money.yahoo.com/author-tim-ferriss-tops-nft-212825797.html; "DAV Partners with DAB, Inc.," Disabled American Veterans, https://www.dav.org/learn-more/news/2023/dav-partners-with-dab-inc.

105 **leave that wall behind:** Jad Esber, "the bookshelf as a metaphor: cultural artifacts in the digital era," koodos labs, August 25, 2021, https://blog.koodos.com/p/-the-bookshelf-as-a-metaphor-cultural.

105 **leverage network effects:** See, e.g., Feng Zhu and Marco Iansiti, "Why Some Platforms Thrive and Others Don't," *Harvard Business Review*, January–February 2019, https://hbr.org/2019/01/why-some-platforms

-thrive-and-others-dont; Thomas R. Eisenmann, "Managing Networked Businesses: Course Overview for Students," Harvard Business Publishing, January 10, 2006, https://hbsp.harvard.edu/product/806103-PDF-ENG; James Currier, "The Network Effects Manual: 16 Different Network Effects (And Counting)," NFX, June 2021, https://www.nfx.com/post/network-effects -manual.

106 **siloed and disjoined:** Scott Duke Kominers and Liang Wu, "Threads Foreshadows a Big—and Surprising—Shift in Social Media," *Harvard Business Review*, July 13, 2023, https://hbr.org/2023/07/threads-foreshadows -a-big-and-surprising-shift-in-social-media.

106 **time-consuming and difficult:** Kominers and Wu, "Threads Foreshadows a Big—and Surprising—Shift in Social Media."

106 **interoperable by design:** See Kominers and Wu, "Threads Foreshadows a Big—and Surprising—Shift in Social Media."

106 **extends his photo-wall metaphor:** Esber, "the bookshelf as a metaphor: cultural artifacts in the digital era."

107 **more competition among tech platforms:** Christian Catalini and Scott Duke Kominers, "Can WEB3 Bring Back Competition to Digital Platforms?," *TechREG Chronicle*, February 23, 2022, https://www.competitionpolicy international.com/can-web3-bring-back-competition-to-digital-platforms.

107 **Bluesky, Farcaster, and Lens:** "The AT Protocol," Bluesky, October 18, 2022, https://blueskyweb.xyz/blog/10-18-2022-the-at-protocol; "Farcaster: A Protocol for Building Sufficiently Decentralized Social Networks," Farcaster, https://www.farcaster.xyz; Sasha Shilina, "What Is Lens Protocol, and How Does It Work?," *Cointelegraph*, October 7, 2022, https://cointelegraph.com /news/what-is-lens-protocol-and-how-does-it-work; see also Kominers and Wu, "Threads Foreshadows a Big—and Surprising—Shift in Social Media."

109 **unlimited shelf space:** Chris Anderson, "The Long Tail," *Wired*, October 1, 2004, https://www.wired.com/2004/10/tail.

111 **instead of accruing to the *platform*:** See, e.g., Catalini and Kominers, "Can WEB3 Bring Back Competition to Digital Platforms?"

111 **from platform to platform:** Catalini and Kominers, "Can WEB3 Bring Back Competition to Digital Platforms?"

111 **BORED has argued:** BORED (@BoredElonMusk), "The next generation of game consoles will probably be the last," Twitter, April 2, 2023, 3:47 p.m., https://twitter.com/BoredElonMusk/status/1642614740299182081.

111 **on *community cohesion*:** Catalini and Kominers, "Can WEB3 Bring Back Competition to Digital Platforms?"; Jad Esber and Scott Duke Kominers,

"Why Build in Web3," *Harvard Business Review*, May 16, 2022, https://hbr
.org/2022/05/why-build-in-web3.

112 **car registrations on the blockchain:** Sergio Goschenko, "California DMV Is
Putting Its Titles on the Blockchain," Bitcoin.com, https://news.bitcoin.com
/california-dmv-is-putting-its-titles-on-the-blockchain.

113 **verified, public badge of honor:** In the Web 2 world, Facebook experimented
with digital "I Voted" stickers as a way of driving civic participation; see Dara
Lind, "Facebook's 'I Voted' Sticker Was a Secret Experiment on Its Users,"
Vox, updated November 4, 2014, https://www.vox.com/2014/11/4/7154641
/midterm-elections-2014-voted-facebook-friends-vote-polls.

113 **Presidential Fitness certificates:** "Presidential Physical Fitness Award
Badges, Certificates & Tests to Make the Team (1966–1987)," Click
Americana, https://clickamericana.com/topics/culture-and-lifestyle/school
-education/presidential-physical-fitness-award-1968-1981; "Presidential Youth
Fitness Program," Health.gov, https://health.gov/our-work/nutrition-physical
-activity/presidents-council/programs-awards/presidential-youth-fitness
-program.

114 **make use of consumer health data:** See, e.g., Serenity Gibbons, "5 Companies
Connecting Consumers to Custom Healthcare," February 16, 2023, https://
www.forbes.com/sites/serenitygibbons/2023/02/16/5-companies-connecting
-consumers-to-custom-healthcare/?sh=5079c4044b18.

114 **in pharmaceutical studies:** Darcy Jimenez, "Profit for Patients: Can NFTs
Allow People to Monetise Their Health Data?," Pharmaceutical Technology,
February 25, 2022, https://www.pharmaceutical-technology.com/features
/profit-patients-monetise-health-data-nfts.

115 **can curate around:** Jad Esber and Scott Duke Kominers, "Inverting the
Internet's Personal Data Model," Social Science Research Network (working
paper), in preparation.

8. CONNECTING THE COMMUNITY

117 **Alabama fans will yell:** AL.com, "Ask Alabama: Where Does 'Roll Tide'
Come From?," YouTube, https://www.youtube.com/watch?v=RXsEBs_hfsM.

118 **"PR you pray for":** This is a slight rephrasing of a quote originally attributed
to the famous advertising executive Helen Woodward; see Helen Woodward,
It's an Art (New York: Harcourt, Brace and Company, 1938).

120 **using Bored Ape NFT imagery:** "Cases of Ape Water," Ape Beverages,
https://apebeverages.com/products/ape-5382?selling_plan=3811016957.

120 **produced a card series:** AppliedPrimate(@AppliedPrimate), "Introducing

the Mega Mutant Melee Deck!," Twitter, June 8, 2023, 12:06 p.m., https://
twitter.com/AppliedPrimate/status/1666839173859516417; see also
AppliedPrimate, https://www.appliedprimate.com.

120 **custom mini skate decks:** Zookit (@CaptainZookit), "And . . . Here it is!
Zookit Customs - Skaters of the Internet," Twitter, May 10, 2023, 2:17 p.m.,
https://twitter.com/CaptainZookit/status/1656362755715133441.

120 **Women and Weapons NFT image:** @Girl_InTheVerse, Twitter feed, January
2022, https://twitter.com/girl_intheverse; see also GIRLintheVERSE.eth,
Linktree feed, https://linktr.ee/girlintheverse.

122 **Creative Commons Zero (CC0) licensing:** "CC0," Creative Commons,
https://creativecommons.org/share-your-work/public-domain/cc0.

122 **article with the pseudonymous NFT collector Flashrekt:** Flashrekt and
Scott Duke Kominers, "Why NFT Creators Are Going cc0," a16z crypto,
August 3, 2022, https://a16zcrypto.com/posts/article/cc0-nft-creative
-commons-zero-license-rights.

122 **pioneered by crypto artist Stellabelle:** Stellabelle/slothicorn, "Slothicorn
Philosophy: Preview to the Off-White Paper," Steemit.com, December 7, 2017,
https://steemit.com/slothicorn/@slothicorn/slothicorn-philosophy-preview
-to-the-off-white-paper.

122 **toy creators David Horvath and Sun-Min Kim:** Sun-Min and David,
"Uma No Copyright," OpenSea, May 2021, https://opensea.io/collection
/uma-no-copyright; Nicole Carter, "How to Build an Empire," *Inc.*, May 23,
2011, https://www.inc.com/articles/201105/small-business-success
-stories-pretty-ugly.html; Gendy Alimurung, "David Horvath and Sun
-Min Kim: The Doll Makers," *LA Weekly*, May 22, 2012, https://www
.laweekly.com/david-horvath-and-sun-min-kim-the-doll-makers.

123 **NFT collection called Nouns:** Nouns DAO, https://www.nouns.wtf.

123 **physical glasses in the Nouns shape:** "The Iconic Nouns Glasses Have
Come to Life," Nounsvision, https://nounsvision.com; "Bigshot Noggles in
Classic Red," Bigshot Toyshop, https://bigshottoyshop.com/products
/functional-nounish-funglasses-red.

123 **Super Bowl commercial:** Andrew Hayward, "Bud Light Super Bowl Ad
Includes Nouns Ethereum NFT Imagery," Decrypt, February 7, 2022, https://
decrypt.co/92239/bud-light-super-bowl-ad-includes-nouns-ethereum-nft
-imagery.

123 **roughly $45,000 each day:** A new Noun NFT is randomly generated and
sold at auction each day; in June 2023, the auction clearing prices were
generally around 27 ETH, which was roughly $45,000 at the time; see
https://nouns.wtf.

123   **some of their characters' hats:** Chain Runners, https://www.chainrunners
.xyz; Blitmap, https://www.blitmap.com; "#84—Logo," OpenSea, https://
opensea.io/assets/ethereum/0x8d04a8c79ceb0889bdd12acdf3fa9d207ed3ff63
/84; "Chain Runners," OpenSea, https://opensea.io/collection/chain-runners
-nft?search[stringTraits][0][name]=Head%20Above&search[stringTraits][0]
[values][0]=Blitmap%20Hat.

123   **including the hat:** "Blitmap Logo Hat (Dad Cap Style)," Blitstore, https://
blitstore.com/products/blitmap-logo-hat.

123   **an entire NFT series:** 1337 Skulls, https://1337skulls.xyz.

124   **bag of adventure game items:** "Resources," Loot, https://www.lootproject
.com/resources; "Loot (for Adventurers)," OpenSea, https://opensea.io/collection
/lootproject.

124   **borrowing the aesthetic:** Goblintown, https://goblintown.wtf; Jex Exmundo,
"Goblintown WTF? Meet the World's Strangest NFT Project," NFT Now,
https://nftnow.com/guides/how-goblintown-broke-the-nft-community;
"Adventurous Halflings," OpenSea, https://opensea.io/collection
/adventuroushalflings; "dirtbirds.wtf," OpenSea, https://opensea.io/collection
/dirtbirdswtf; "Ice Cream Sandwhich Shop," OpenSea, https://opensea
.io/collection/icecreamsandwhichshop.

125   **3D exploration game:** Andrew Hayward, "Twitch's New Favorite Game
'Only Up' Is Loaded with Goblintown NFT Art," Decrypt, June 15, 2023,
https://decrypt.co/144815/twitch-new-game-only-up-goblintown-nft.

126   **garnered so much interest that:** "CAA Signs Jenkins the Valet: Is This a
Sign That Hollywood Is Embracing NFTs?," *Forbes*, September 25, 2021,
https://www.forbes.com/sites/cathyhackl/2021/09/25/caa-signs-jenkins-the
-valet-is-this-a-sign-that-hollywood-is-embracing-nfts/?sh=23afb85e3b02;
Jenkins the Valet, "Tally Labs' $12m Fundraise: The Who, What, When,
Where, Why," Medium, May 18, 2022, https://jenkinsthevalet.medium.com
/tally-labs-12m-fundraise-the-who-what-when-where-why-25a5fae64b41.

126   **raised almost $1.9 million:** Jenkins the Valet, "Everything You Need to
Know about the Bored & Dangerous Fund Claim: Mechanics, Alternatives,
and Timeline," Medium, April 7, 2023, https://jenkinsthevalet.medium.com
/everything-you-need-to-know-about-the-bored-dangerous-fund-claim
-mechanics-alternatives-and-48652091d85c.

126   **made more than $2,100:** Jenkins the Valet, "An Update on Bored & Dangerous
Royalties, Podcast Licensing, and More," Medium, January 27, 2023, https://
jenkinsthevalet.medium.com/an-update-on-bored-dangerous-royalties
-podcast-licensing-and-more-8a0b4943a5ec.

127   ***decentralized autonomous organizations:*** Sonal Chokshi, Zoran Basich,

and Guy Wuollet, "DAOs, a Canon," a16z crypto, November 20, 2021, https://a16zcrypto.com/posts/article/dao-canon.

127 **a roughly $22 million treasury:** See "Nouns DAO Token Holdings," Etherscan, accessed September 19, 2023, https://etherscan.io/tokenholdings?a=0x0BC3807Ec262cB779b38D65b38158acC3bfedE10.

130 **world record for handshaking:** "Most People Shaking Hands," Guinness World Records, https://www.guinnessworldrecords.com/world-records/most-people-shaking-hands.

132 **new Forsythe choreography:** Scott is a huge Forsythe fan. See, e.g., "William Forsythe: Choreographic Objects," William Forsythe, https://www.williamforsythe.com/biography.html; "Full on Forsythe," Boston Ballet, https://www.bostonballet.org/performance/full-on-forsythe; "William Forsythe: Choreographic Objects," Institute of Contemporary Art, Boston, https://www.icaboston.org/exhibitions/william-forsythe-choreographic-objects.

132 **Scott gave out a POAP:** "Harvard Business School Case Study on Bored Ape Yacht Club—First Teach," POAP Scan, March 22, 2022, https://app.poap.xyz/token/4478535.

132 **handed out POAPs:** Gmoney, "Manifesto," Gmoney, https://g.money/manifesto.

132 **mint his Admit One NFT:** Gmoney, "Manifesto."

132 **selling for almost $25,000:** See "Admit One (ADMIT)," CoinGecko, https://www.coingecko.com/en/nft/admit-one.

133 **Drew Austin's house:** @BunchuBets, "I quit my six figure job to go to a party," Twitter, May 6, 2022, 5:10 p.m., https://twitter.com/BunchuBets/status/1522685191004770305.

133 **clients like Starbucks:** "Brand Building. Reimagined," Forum3, https://www.forum3.com.

133 **ultimately hired him:** "Mike Chavez," LinkedIn, https://www.linkedin.com/in/mikechavez3.

134 **fiction writer groups to elite hacker collectives:** See, e.g., Story Protocol, https://www.storyprotocol.xyz; "Lore," Divine Anarchy, https://divineanarchy.com/lore; Inkugami, https://www.inkugami.com; Chain Runners, https://www.chainrunners.xyz.

134 **comic series with high-quality storytelling:** E.g., Inkugami; @ForgottenRunes, "Forgotten Runes Comic Issue #1 is now on sale," Twitter, August 31, 2023, 2:36 p.m., https://twitter.com/forgottenrunes/status/1697317395218706797; "Comics," Nuclear Nerds, https://www.nuclearnerds.io/comics/0.

135 **NFT-based fantasy game:** EtherOrcs, https://www.etherorcs.com.

136   **a Cool Cat:** Cool Cats, https://coolcatsnft.com.

137   **social & community lead:** "Ish Verduzco," LinkedIn, https://www.linkedin
.com/in/ishverduzco.

137   **Nicholas Corso serves:** "Nicholas Corso," LinkedIn, https://www.linkedin
.com/in/nicholascorso5.

137   *director of vibes:* Erika Lee, "Becoming Threadguy: The Unseen Side of
the Prolific NFT Commentator," NFT Now, June 2, 2023, https://nftnow
.com/features/becoming-threadguy-the-unseen-side-of-the-prolific-nft
-commentator.

137   **embarrassed about the CDO title:** Brotman told the story during an
unrecorded *Conversations over Coffee* session in the Starbucks Odyssey
Discord Server.

138   **a degree of leadership:** See, e.g., Jon L. Pierce, Tatiana Kostova, and Kurt T.
Dirks, "Toward a Theory of Psychological Ownership in Organizations,"
Academy of Management Review 26, no. 2 (April 1, 2001), https://journals
.aom.org/doi/abs/10.5465/AMR.2001.4378028.

9. DRIVING BRAND EVOLUTION

141   **a semipermeable membrane:** "semipermeable membrane," Encyclopedia
Britannica, https://www.britannica.com/science/semipermeable-membrane.

141   **manage their community initiatives:** Erika Lee, "Becoming Threadguy:
The Unseen Side of the Prolific NFT Commentator," NFT Now, June 2, 2023,
https://nftnow.com/features/becoming-threadguy-the-unseen-side-of-the
-prolific-nft-commentator.

141   **designed a new collection:** Amanda Terry (@amandaterry), "Sharing how
@onchainmonkey Karma (mint on 6/29) was created," Twitter, June 10, 2022,
9:11 a.m., https://twitter.com/amandaterry/status/1535248239246692354.

141   **the company's own brand iconography:** The Hundreds Staff, "Adam Bomb
Squad and the Great Logo Search Logo Design Contest," Adam Bomb Squad,
May 9, 2022, https://web.archive.org/web/20220509191732/https://www
.adambombsquad.com/updates/adam-bomb-squad-and-the-great-logo-search
-logo-design-contest.

141   **a "tailor shop":** Bread, "Weekly(ish) Supdate #3," Medium, September 23,
2021, https://medium.com/supducks/weekly-ish-supdate-3-de4663a64839.

142   **cartoon and comic series:** "Forgotten Runes Book of Lore," Forgotten
Runes, https://www.forgottenrunes.com/lore; @ForgottenRunes, "Forgotten
Runes Comic Issue #1 is now on sale," Twitter, August 31, 2023, 2:36 p.m.,
https://twitter.com/forgottenrunes/status/1697317395218706797; "Our Media

Ecosystem," Forgotten Runes, https://www.forgottenrunes.com/#show
-section.

142   **so poorly received:** Eli Tan, "Azurbala NFT Mint Postponed after Art Goes
Viral for Wrong Reasons," CoinDesk, updated May 11, 2023, https://www
.coindesk.com/business/2022/10/03/azurbala-nft-mint-postponed-after-art
-goes-viral-for-wrong-reasons.

142   **real-time, useful feedback:** Jenkins the Valet (@JenkinsTheValet), "We're
excited to prove to you all that we can learn from our mistake and not make
it again," Twitter, October 2, 2022, 1:43 p.m., https://twitter.com
/jenkinsthevalet/status/1576629037060923392; Tom Farren, "Jenkins the
Valet: The Rise, Fall, and Rebirth of the Azurian PFP," NFT Now, April 26,
2023, https://nftnow.com/features/jenkins-the-valet-the-rise-fall-and-rebirth
-of-the-azurian-pfp.

142   **an action plan:** Jenkins the Valet, "Tally Labs Update: The Future of Writers
Room; The Status of Azurbala; and an Introduction to Avenue," Medium,
April 10, 2023, https://jenkinsthevalet.medium.com/tally-labs-update-the
-future-of-writers-room-the-status-of-azurbala-and-an-introduction-to
-e3e80f8a92f1.

142   **received extremely well:** See "Azurian," OpenSea, https://opensea.io
/collection/azurian.

142   **more deeply integrated:** Jenkins the Valet, "Azurbala PFPs: Working with
a Community Council," Medium, October 20, 2022, https://medium.com
/@jenkinsthevalet/azurbala-pfps-working-with-a-community-council
-a6a5d2d34773.

144   **Activist customers have pushed:** Stephie Grob Plante, "Shopping Has
Become a Political Act. Here's How It Happened," *Vox*, October 7, 2019,
https://www.vox.com/the-goods/2019/10/7/20894134/consumer-activism
-conscious-consumerism-explained; Simon Birch, "How Activism Forced
Nike to Change Its Ethical Game," *The Guardian*, July 6, 2012, https://www
.theguardian.com/environment/green-living-blog/2012/jul/06/activism-nike;
Connie Roser-Renouf, Edward Maibach, and Anthony Leiserowitz,
"Consumer Activism on Global Warming," Yale Program for Climate Change
Communication, October 14, 2016, https://climatecommunication.yale.edu
/publications/consumer-activism-global-warming.

144   **3,750-year-old cuneiform tablet:** Chris Baraniuk, "Ancient Customer-
Feedback Technology Lasts Millennia," *New Scientist*, March 2, 2015,
https://www.newscientist.com/article/dn27063-ancient-customer-feedback
-technology-lasts-millennia; "The First Customer Service Complaint in

Recorded History (1750 B.C.)," Open Culture, March 7, 2015, https://www
.openculture.com/2015/03/the-first-recorded-customer-service-complaint
-from-1750-b-c.html.

145 **how focus groups work:** The focus group model is often credited to the
twentieth-century sociologist Robert Merton: see "focus group," Encyclopedia
Britannica, https://www.britannica.com/topic/focus-group; "The Vocabularist:
Where Did the Term Focus Group Come From?," BBC, April 2, 2015, https://
www.bbc.com/news/blogs-magazine-monitor-32141190; Michael T. Kaufman,
"Robert K. Merton, Versatile Sociologist and Father of the Focus Group, Dies
at 92," *The New York Times*, February 24, 2003, https://www.nytimes.com/2003
/02/24/nyregion/robert-k-merton-versatile-sociologist-and-father-of-the
-focus-group-dies-at-92.html.

147 **upscale shop-and-play retailer:** "Introducing: Doodles x CAMP," Doodles,
May 31, 2023, https://www.doodles.app/blog/doodles-x-camp.

147 **Nike, Disney, and Teletubbies:** "Nike Kids Camp," CAMP, https://camp
.com/nike-kids-camp; "Disney: Mickey and Friends x CAMP," CAMP,
https://camp.com/disney-mickey-and-friends; "Disney: Encanto x CAMP,"
CAMP, https://camp.com/disney-encanto; "We're Proud to Have the
Teletubbies at Camp!," CAMP, https://camp.com/teletubbies-pride.

147 **too much supply:** Jon Hayes, "NBA Top Shot: Feel the Burn," OTMNFT,
March 26, 2022, https://www.otmnft.com/content/nba-top-shot-feel-the
-burn.

148 **NFL All Day:** "Own the Game Like Never Before," NFL All Day, https://
nflallday.com.

148 **secondary-sales volume:** Madeline Garfinkle, "Starbucks Odyssey NFTs
Sell Out in Just 18 Minutes," *Entrepreneur*, March 10, 2023, https://www
.entrepreneur.com/business-news/starbucks-odyssey-nfts-sell-out-in
-minutes-reselling-for/447372.

148 **implemented both suggestions:** Logan Hitchcock, "Starbucks Dropping
First Store Stamp," Lucky Trader, April 18, 2023, https://luckytrader.com
/news/starbucks-dropping-first-store-stamp.

149 **to the leadership level immediately:** The VP of Loyalty sent an email the
day of the drop and was plugged into the community feedback.

150 **"Parenting Guide" series:** "Target Parenting Guide," Target, https://www
.target.com/c/parenting-guide/-/N-ss9h9.

150 **Disney Parks superfans provide personalized advice:** "About planDisney,"
Disney Parks, https://plandisney.disney.go.com/about-plandisney; "Become a
Panelist," Disney Parks, https://plandisney.disney.go.com/recruiting.

10. THE STAIRCASE IN ACTION

153 **NFT-based loyalty program:** "Starbucks Brewing Revolutionary Web3 Experience for its Starbucks Rewards Members," *Starbucks Stories & News*, September 12, 2022, https://stories.starbucks.com/press/2022/starbucks -brewing-revolutionary-web3-experience-for-its-starbucks-rewards -members.

154 **"Starbucks has always served":** "Starbucks Brewing Revolutionary Web3 Experience for its Starbucks Rewards Members."

155 **official community moderator:** John D. (@JohnDWeb3), "GM! Excited to share some Professional/Web3 News!," Twitter, January 30, 2023, 5:10 a.m., https://twitter.com/JohnDWeb3/status/1620001373470195712.

156 **fans like Chris Jourdan:** Jourdan is the host of the daily Twitter Space *Coffee with Captain*, where he told this story to over two hundred listeners.

157 **forty-two thousand years ago:** "Earliest Musical Instruments Found," BBC, May 25, 2012, https://www.bbc.com/news/science-environment-18196349.

157 **dominated by intermediaries:** See, e.g., Timothy D. Taylor, *Music and Capitalism* (Chicago: University of Chicago Press, 2015).

157 **platforms like Bandcamp and Kickstarter:** Taylor, *Music and Capitalism.*

157 **new ways to reach their fans:** Taylor, *Music and Capitalism.*

157 **remained in place:** Taylor, *Music and Capitalism*; see also Scott's review of Taylor's *Music and Capitalism* in *Ethnomusicology* 65, no. 2 (2021): 397–98, https://scholarlypublishingcollective.org/uip/etm/article-abstract/65/2/396 /283916/Music-and-Capitalism-A-History-of-the-Present.

157 **estimated to be paying:** Ennica Jacob, "How Much Does Spotify Pay per Stream? What You'll Earn per Song, and How to Get Paid More for Your Music," *Insider*, February 24, 2021, https://www.businessinsider.com/guides /streaming/how-much-does-spotify-pay-per-stream.

158 **started as a country singer?:** "Life and Career," Taylor Swift Museum, https://www.theswiftmuseum.com/life-and-career.

159 **selling in the thousand-dollar range:** See, e.g., Matt Levy, "You Won't Believe Ticket Prices to See Taylor Swift at MetLife Stadium," *New York Post*, May 22, 2023, https://nypost.com/2023/05/22/how-to-get-last-minute-taylor -swift-eras-tickets-in-new-jersey; Joshua Medintz, "Tickets for Taylor Swift's Cincinnati Shows Ranging from $1,282 to Over $82K," *Cincinnati Enquirer*, June 16, 2023, https://www.cincinnati.com/story/entertainment/music/2023 /06/16/taylor-swift-cincinnati-tickets-eras-tour/70325359007.

159 **this was a great idea:** Scott Duke Kominers, "Fans Watch Taylor Swift. Economists Watch the Fans," Bloomberg.com, August 29, 2017, https://www

.bloomberg.com/view/articles/2017-08-29/fans-watch-taylor-swift-economists
-watch-the-fans.

159 **Ticketmaster has decided to test:** "Ticketmaster Launches Token-Gated
Sales, Enabling Artists to Reward Fans with Prioritized Ticket Access and
Concert Experiences Through NFTs," Ticketmaster Business, March 27, 2023,
https://business.ticketmaster.com/business-solutions/nft-token-gated-sales.

159 **all positions on the *Billboard* Top 10:** Gary Trust, "Taylor Swift Makes
History as First Artist with Entire Top 10 on *Billboard* Hot 100, Led by
'Anti-Hero' at No. 1," *Billboard*, October 31, 2022, https://www.billboard.com
/music/chart-beat/taylor-swift-all-hot-100-top-10-anti-hero-1235163664.

160 **a few breakout music stars:** Benjamin James, "Is NFT Star Daniel Allan
Web3's First Breakout Music Act?," *Billboard*, August 23, 2022, https://www
.billboard.com/pro/daniel-allan-nft-web3-music; Adam Protz, "Violetta
Zironi: 'Off the Back of NFTs, My Music Career Survived,'" Headliner, July 10,
2022, https://headlinermagazine.net/violetta-zironi-off-the-back-of-nfts-my
-music-career-survived.html.

160 **The theory is as follows:** "What Is Sound?," Sound, https://help.sound.xyz
/hc/en-us/articles/5304493670939-What-is-Sound-xyz-.

161 **most popular frozen pizza brand:** Nils-Gerrit Wunsch, "Dollar Sales of
Leading Frozen Pizza Brands in the United States in 2022," Statista, June 23,
2023, https://www.statista.com/statistics/915572/leading-frozen-pizza
-brands-us-dollar-sales.

161 **placement in popular movies:** Sergey, "DiGiorno Rising Crust Pizza in
Secret Headquarters (2022)," *Product Placement* (blog), August 12, 2022,
https://productplacementblog.com/movies/digiorno-rising-crust-pizza
-in-secret-headquarters-2022.

161 **"It's not delivery, it's DiGiorno":** Jaya Saxena, "The Meaning Changed, but
DiGiorno's Slogan Stays the Same," Eater, June 24, 2019, https://www.eater
.com/2019/6/24/18715848/digiorno-pizza-slogan-its-not-delivery-its
-digiorno.

162 **spirit of the Ninja Turtles:** The Ninja Turtles were really into pizza, although
they had some questionable taste in flavors. See Erik Germ, "8 Weirdest
'Teenage Mutant Ninja Turtles' Pizza Combos Taste Tested," Cracked,
March 3, 2022, https://www.cracked.com/article_32839_8-weirdest-teenage
-mutant-ninja-turtles-pizza-combos-taste-tested.html.

164 **puzzle-solving and long-distance biking:** If you're interested in puzzles,
you might find something noteworthy hidden in the next chapter ✦✦.

165 **carries more credibility:** "Nielsen: Global Consumers More Likely to Buy
New Products from Familiar Brands," Business Wire, January 22, 2013,

https://www.businesswire.com/news/home/20130121005056/en/Nielsen
-Global-Consumers-More-Likely-to-Buy-New-Products-from-Familiar
-Brands.

165 **the first six months:** See, e.g., Vicki J. (@VickiJEth), "30 days of @Starbucks
odyssey," Twitter, June 15, 2023, 4:45 p.m., https://twitter.com/vickijeth
/status/1669446032436985856; @Teacher96_Katie, "Just arrived! Here's
my @Starbucks custom @miir travel mug," Twitter, June 12, 2023, 4:28 p.m.,
https://twitter.com/Teacher96_Katie. Starbucks Odyssey members also
frequently talk about the program in the Starbucks Cups Hunters Facebook
group; see https://www.facebook.com/groups/705157900283853.

165 **similar forms of engagement:** See, e.g., Steve the Suit (@SteveTheSuit6),
"Mega-Thread," Twitter, June 20, 2023, 2:18 a.m., https://twitter.com
/SteveTheSuit6/status/1671039725086580736.

11. FINDING THE PROPER PRICE AND SCALE

170 **Reddit and Nike:** Martin Young, "Reddit Collectible Avatars Onboard Nearly
10M into the Crypto, NFT Space," Cointelegraph, May 29, 2023, https://
cointelegraph.com/news/reddit-collectible-avatars-onboard-millions-crypto
-nft; Rosie Perper, "Nike OF1 NFT Sale Surpasses $1M Despite Delays, Tech
Issues," CoinDesk, May 25, 2023, https://www.coindesk.com/web3/2023/05
/25/nike-of1-nft-sale-surpasses-1m-despite-delays-tech-issues.

170 **simply exploring the technology:** Jolene Creighton, "NFT Timeline: The
Beginnings and History of NFTs," NFT Now, December 15, 2022, https://
nftnow.com/guides/nft-timeline-the-beginnings-and-history-of-nfts.

170 **Dapper Labs's CryptoKitties:** Nellie Bowles, "CryptoKitties, Explained . . .
Mostly," *The New York Times*, December 28, 2017, https://www.nytimes.com
/2017/12/28/style/cryptokitties-want-a-blockchain-snuggle.html.

170 **decline in public interest:** See, e.g., Jon Russell, "Bitcoin and Almost Every
Other Cryptocurrency Crashed Hard Today," TechCrunch, December 22,
2017, https://techcrunch.com/2017/12/22/bitcoin-crypto-crashed-hard.

170 **having a resurgence:** Shanti Escalante-De Mattei, "The Year of the NFT:
How an Emerging Medium Went Mainstream in 2021," ARTnews, December
21, 2021, https://www.artnews.com/list/art-news/artists/2021-year-of-the-nft
-1234614022; "The Year of the NFT," *The Verge*, https://www.theverge.com
/23141561/nft-boom-token-mint-artists-collectors-auction; Ryan Browne,
"Trading in NFTs Spiked 21,000% to More Than $17 Billion in 2021, Report
Says," CNBC, March 10, 2022, https://www.cnbc.com/2022/03/10/trading-in
-nfts-spiked-21000percent-to-top-17-billion-in-2021-report.html.

171 **tens or hundreds of thousands of dollars:** Elizabeth Howcroft, "Set of 'Bored Ape' NFTs Sells for $24.4 mln in Sotheby's Online Auction," Reuters, September 9, 2021, https://www.reuters.com/lifestyle/set-bored-ape-nfts-sell -244-mln-sothebys-online-auction-2021-09-09; see also the transaction history listed on "Bored Ape Yacht Club," OpenSea, https://opensea.io /collection/boredapeyachtclub/activity.

171 **over sixty million:** "Roblox Reports First Quarter 2023 Financial Results," Roblox, May 10, 2023, https://ir.roblox.com/news/news-details/2023/Roblox -Reports-First-Quarter-2023-Financial-Results/default.aspx.

172 **more than ten million:** "Reddit Collectible Avatars," Dune, https://dune .com/polygon_analytics/reddit-collectible-avatars.

172 **and Nike's .SWOOSH:** "About .SWOOSH," Nike, https://www.swoosh .nike.

172 **Star Wars figurines:** Indeed, NFT Star Wars figurines already exist, in the form of "Cryptoys"; see "A Fun New Way To Collect Star Wars™ Digital Toys," Cryptoys, https://cryptoys.com/starwars.

173 **spin outward from there:** Christian Catalini, Ravi Jagadeesan, and Scott Duke Kominers, "Bitcoin and Beyond," Project Syndicate, April 23, 2021, https://www.project-syndicate.org/onpoint/bitcoin-and-new-digital-ledger -applications-by-christian-catalini-et-al-2021-04.

173 **made it possible:** See, e.g., Toni Fitzgerald, "5 Ways Streaming Changed Television Forever in the Last Decade," *Forbes*, December 24, 2019, https:// www.forbes.com/sites/tonifitzgerald/2019/12/24/5-ways-streaming-changed -television-forever-in-the-last-decade.

173 **well-established platforms:** See, e.g., Kyle Pierce (@zehpierce), "5 Best NFT Generators to Create an NFT Collection (No Code)," Hackernoon, March 11, 2022, https://hackernoon.com/5-best-nft-generators-to-create-an-nft -collection-no-code; Aasif Khan (@aasif-khan), "7 NFT Makers to Create Your NFT Art Collection with No Code," Hackernoon, February 15, 2022, https://hackernoon.com/7-nft-makers-to-create-your-nft-art-collection-with -no-code; Manifold, https://manifold.xyz/; Zora, https://zora.co.

173 **Billy Joel's earliest supporters:** Even just access to the famous Shea Stadium concert would have been pretty significant utility; see Fred Schruers, *Billy Joel: The Definitive Biography* (New York: Crown, 2014), https://www .penguinrandomhouse.com/books/236036/billy-joel-by-fred-schruers.

173 **"1,000 True Fans":** Kevin Kelly, "1,000 True Fans," *The Technium* (blog), https://kk.org/thetechnium/1000-true-fans.

174 **puzzle creators:** Great job! You found the hidden puzzle 🧩👀. If you correctly unscramble the instructions below and then follow them on

EverythingToken.io, you can receive a special NFT and/or bookplate while supplies last.

CKT CLI EEV ENE EPH ERY ETH GET HEP HER
IEC LEP NGC NTE OME RAS RTH STO THI UZZ.

(Special thanks to Paul Kominers for helping Scott assemble this puzzle!)

174 **hundred mega-megafans:** Li Jin, "100 True Fans," *Li Jin* (blog), February 19, 2020, https://li-jin.co/2020/02/19/100-true-fans.

175 **a €39,000 NFT "Treasure Trunk":** "Louis Vuitton Unveils Via," Louis Vuitton, https://us.louisvuitton.com/eng-us/stories/louis-vuitton-via; Maghan McDowell, "Louis Vuitton to Sell $39,000 NFTs," *Vogue*, June 6, 2023, https://www.vogue.com/article/louis-vuitton-to-sell-dollar41000-nfts; Sarah Elson, "Louis Vuitton to Sell €39,000 NFTs," Business of Fashion, June 6, 2023, https://www.businessoffashion.com/news/technology/louis-vuitton-to-sell -39000-nfts; Stephanie Hirschmiller, "Unpacking The Web3 Strategy behind Louis Vuitton's €39k Digital Treasure Trunk NFTs," *Forbes*, June 7, 2023, https://www.forbes.com/sites/stephaniehirschmiller/2023/06/07/unpacking -the-strategy-behind-louis-vuittons-39k-digital-treasure-trunk-nfts.

175 **purchase via application:** "Louis Vuitton Unveils Via."

175 **buy a pass:** See, e.g., Yume Wo Katare, "One year passes are LIVE!," Facebook, January 2, 2018, https://www.facebook.com/YumeWoKatare/posts/one-year -passes-are-live-a-few-guidelines-only-one-pass-holder-non-transferable -/1789979727740240; Rachel Leah Blumenthal, "Acclaimed Udon Shop Yume Ga Arukara Offers Never-Ending-Noodle Pass for $900," Eater Boston, October 21, 2019, https://boston.eater.com/2019/10/21/20924231/yuma-ga -arukara-annual-udon-pass-news.

176 **the restaurants' top evangelists:** You can even see Scott evangelize the brand in this *Insider Food* video: "Why People Wait for Hours to Eat at This Tiny Boston Ramen Workshop," YouTube, https://www.youtube.com /watch?v=H030kvQqrDA.

176 **The "dream for the year":** *Insider Food*, "Why People Wait for Hours to Eat at This Tiny Boston Ramen Workshop."

12. DESIGNING YOUR NFT STRATEGY

179 **identify market failures:** Thomas R. Eisenmann and Scott Duke Kominers, "Making Markets," Harvard Business Publishing, January 24, 2018, https:// hbsp.harvard.edu/product/818096-PDF-ENG; Scott Duke Kominers, "A

Three-Part Framework for Entrepreneurial Marketplace Design," Harvard Business Publishing, January 4, 2021, https://hbsp.harvard.edu/product /821065-PDF-ENG.

180 **focus on the reason:** Eisenmann and Kominers, "Making Markets."

180 **"buy more used bicycles":** There are a number of marketplace platforms working to improve the efficiency of the used bike market, such as BicycleBlueBook.com, https://www.bicyclebluebook.com/marketplace; BikeFair.org, https://bikefair.org; and BikeExchange, https://www.bike exchange.com.

183 **Reignmakers NFT platform:** "Reignmakers," DraftKings, https://www .draftkings.com/reignmakers.

183 *daily fantasy sports:* "Daily Fantasy Sports," DraftKings, https://www .draftkings.com/about/daily-fantasy-sports.

184 **the StockX Vault:** "Collect What's Next," StockX, https://stockx.com/lp/nfts; "What Are Vault NFTs," StockX Help Center, https://stockx.com/help /articles/what-are-vault-nfts.

187 **existing communities and networks:** See, e.g., Megan DeMatteo, "Minting Your First NFT: A Beginner's Guide to Creating an NFT," CoinDesk, updated January 12, 2023, https://www.coindesk.com/learn/minting-your-first-nft-a -beginners-guide-to-creating-an-nft; Scott Duke Kominers and 1337 Skulls Sers, "A New NFT Launch Strategy: The Wave Mint," a16z crypto, April 6, 2023, https://a16zcrypto.com/posts/article/a-new-nft-launch-strategy-the -wave-mint.

188 **private Discord chat server:** Langston Thomas, "The Ultimate Guide to Doodles NFTs: Everything You Need to Know," NFT Now, April 19, 2023, https://nftnow.com/guides/doodles-guide.

188 **a few referrals:** See, e.g., @cokemethzine, "Indiana Jones going after the treasure 'The Long Lost Doodle Discord Invites,'" Twitter, October 10, 2021, 1:46 p.m., https://twitter.com/cokemethzine/status/1447257206202802180.

188 **a significant share of the NFTs:** See "Doodles Transactions," Etherscan, https://etherscan.io/txs?a=0x8a90cab2b38dba80c64b7734e58ee1db38b8992e &p=1554.

188 **When Adidas launched:** Isabelle Lee, "Adidas Wades into the Metaverse in Partnership with Bored Ape Yacht Club and Other NFT Communities," *Markets Insider,* December 3, 2021, https://markets.businessinsider.com /news/currencies/metaverse-adidas-bored-ape-yacht-club-nft-punks-comic -gmoney-2021-12.

189 **gave mint access to holders:** Jay Peters, "Adidas Sold More Than $22 Million

in NFTs, but It Hit a Few Snags along the Way," *The Verge*, December 17, 2021, https://www.theverge.com/2021/12/17/22843104/adidas-nfts-metaverse-sold-bored-ape.

189 **primary sale price of $765:** Jay Peters, "Adidas Sold More Than $22 Million in NFTs, but It Hit a Few Snags along the Way."

189 **a bug during the launch:** Yolo, "Adidas Pauses and Re-Opens Minting after MAYC Holders Are Unable to Mint," *NFTevening*, December 18, 2021, https://nftevening.com/adidas-pauses-and-re-opens-minting-after-mayc-holders-are-unable-to-mint.

189 **almost entirely non-NFT-native:** Ivan Mehta, "Reddit Is Launching a New NFT Avatar Marketplace," TechCrunch, July 7, 2022, https://techcrunch.com/2022/07/07/reddit-is-launching-a-new-nft-avatar-marketplace.

189 **sold at fixed costs:** Mehta, "Reddit Is Launching a New NFT Avatar Marketplace."

191 **his NFT project VeeFriends:** VeeFriends, https://veefriends.com.

191 **began creating content:** @JeremyKnowsVF, "I hope you like the sound of my voice," Twitter, November 19, 2021, 5:01 p.m., https://twitter.com/jeremy knowsVF/status/1461816960203776006.

191 **he encouraged it:** Vaynerchuk retweeted Jeremy's content to his millions of followers and gave him a shout-out during the opening keynote of his conference.

191 **unofficial community events and meetups:** @JeremyKnowsVF, "It's a big day for the @veefriends community," Twitter, November 11, 2022, 10:12 a.m., https://twitter.com/jeremyknowsVF/status/1591086507963875328.

191 **hired to the official team:** @JeremyKnowsVF, "I landed my dream job at @veefriends," Twitter, February 16, 2023, 10:41 a.m., https://twitter.com/jeremyknowsVF/status/1626245433088409600.

192 **double as access passes:** "About VeeFriends," VeeFriends, https://veefriends.com/faq.

192 **A-list speakers:** "Veecon 2023 Confirmed Lineup; Over 200 Speakers and Panelists," Veecon, https://www.veecon.co/veecon-speakers-2023.

192 **implemented a community stage:** "Announcing the VeeCon Community Stage!" *VeeFriends* (blog), April 6, 2023, https://blog.veefriends.com/announcing-the-veecon-community-stage-bce5e323803f.

192 **raved about it:** See, e.g., @VonFrontin, "Epic session on content creation," Twitter, May 18, 2023, 6:45 p.m., https://twitter.com/VonFrontin/status/1659329339291213825.

192 **an unofficial BAYC community event:** OtherBlock, "OtherBlock: Miami Art Basel 2022 | Ape Basel," YouTube, https://www.youtube.com/watch?v=fkEkTq3YMAM.

192 **The party, called OtherBlock:** OtherBlock, https://www.otherblock.io
/home-1.

193 **BAYC founders showed up:** @TheOtherBlock, "Welcome to @TheOtherBlock,
@GordonGoner & @CryptoGarga!," Twitter, December 6, 2022, 9:58 p.m.,
https://twitter.com/TheOtherBlock/status/1600323784283545601.

193 **appearing in the movie *ET*:** Joe Bergren, "Steven Spielberg on 'E.T.'s Reese's
Pieces Scene and How It Changed from Script to Screen (Flashback)," *ET*,
June 13, 2022, https://www.etonline.com/steven-spielberg-on-ets-reeses
-pieces-scene-and-how-it-changed-from-script-to-screen-flashback; Calum
Russell, "The Real Reason Why E.T. Eats Reece's Pieces," Far Out, February 5,
2023, https://faroutmagazine.co.uk/the-reason-why-et-eats-reeces-pieces.

193 **acquire a SupDucks NFT, or license one:** "SupDucks NFT Ownership & IP
Rights," MegaVolt, https://megavolt.notion.site/Ownership-IP-Rights
-09dc4f0ab82646d7a56c7b49b05fe9ad.

193 **"Wait a minute":** Universal Pictures, "Back to the Future | The Very First
DeLorean Time Travel Scene," YouTube, https://www.youtube.com/watch
?v=FWG3Dfss3Jc.

194 **"No hate speech":** For an illustration of how this could work in practice, see,
e.g., Miles Jennings and Chris Dixon, "The Can't Be Evil NFT Licenses," a16z
crypto, August 31, 2022, https://a16zcrypto.com/posts/article/introducing
-nft-licenses; a16z/a16z-contracts, https://github.com/a16z/a16z-contracts
/blob/master/licenses/pdf/03%20-%20a16z%20CBE%20Form%20License%20
(CBE-Commercial-No-Hate).pdf.

13. ONGOING CHALLENGES

196 **as much as 0.34%:** @VitalikButerin, "The merge will reduce worldwide
electricity consumption by 0.2%," Twitter, September 15, 2022, 2:30 a.m.,
https://twitter.com/VitalikButerin/status/1570299062800510976; Daniel
Kuhn, "Did the Ethereum Merge Drop 'Worldwide Electricity Consumption'
by 0.2%?," CoinDesk, September 19, 2022, https://www.coindesk.com/layer2
/2022/09/19/did-the-ethereum-merge-drop-worldwide-electricity-consumption
-by-02.

196 **more than 99%:** Bhaskar Kashyap (@bskrksyp9), "Proof-of-Stake (POS),"
Ethereum, last updated May 12, 2023, https://ethereum.org/en/developers
/docs/consensus-mechanisms/pos; "What Is Proof of Stake," McKinsey &
Company, January 3, 2023, https://www.mckinsey.com/featured-insights
/mckinsey-explainers/what-is-proof-of-stake; see also Vitalik Buterin, *Proof of
Stake* (New York: Seven Stories Press, 2022); "Ethereum's Energy Expenditure,"

Ethereum, last updated June 15, 2023, https://ethereum.org/en/energy
-consumption; Arijit Sarkar, "The Merge Brings Down Ethereum's Network
Power Consumption by Over 99.0%," Cointelegraph, October 29, 2022,
https://cointelegraph.com/news/the-merge-brings-down-ethereum-s-network
-power-consumption-by-over-99-9; "Ethereum Blockchain Eliminates 99.99%
of Its Carbon Footprint Overnight after a Successful Merge According to
New Report," Consensys, September 15, 2022, https://consensys.net/blog
/press-release/ethereum-blockchain-eliminates-99-99-of-its-carbon-footprint
-overnight-after-a-successful-merge-according-to-new-report.

196 **transaction costs for something:** Randy Ginsburg, "What Are Gas Fees and
How Can We Fix Them?," NFT Now, June 1, 2022, https://nftnow.com/guides
/what-are-gas-fees-and-how-can-we-fix-them.

196 **thousands of transactions per second:** See, e.g., "Global Brand Card
Networks Worldwide—Purchase Transactions," Nilson Report, https://
nilsonreport.com/newsletters/1241.

196 **starting to be addressed:** "Layer 2, Ethereum for Everyone," Ethereum,
https://ethereum.org/en/layer-2; Mason Marcobello, "What Are Layer 2s and
Why Are They Important?," CoinDesk, updated May 11, 2023, https://www
.coindesk.com/learn/what-are-layer-2s-and-why-are-they-important;
Ginsburg, "What are Gas Fees and How Can We Fix Them?"

197 **were "self-custodial":** See, e.g., Sasha Shilina, "Custodial vs Non-Custodial
NFTs: Key Differences," Cointelegraph, January 23, 2022, https://cointelegraph
.com/explained/custodial-vs-non-custodial-nfts-key-differences.

198 **"All my apes are gone":** Eileen Kinsella, "'All My Apes Gone': An Art Dealer's
Despondent Tweet about the Theft of His NFTs Went Viral . . . and Has Now
Become an NFT," ARTnews, January 5, 2022, https://news.artnet.com/market
/kramer-nft-theft-turned-nft-2056489; "All My Apes Gone," Know Your Meme,
last updated 2022, https://knowyourmeme.com/memes/all-my-apes-gone.

198 **wallet service providers:** See, e.g., "A Powerful Web3 Auth Developer Platform,"
Dynamic, https://www.dynamic.xyz; "Products & Research Focused on the
Next Generation of the Internet," koodos labs, 2023, https://koodoslabs.xyz.

199 **Digital divides are pervasive:** See, e.g., Emily A. Vogels, "Digital Divide
Persists Even As Americans with Lower Incomes Make Gains in Tech
Adoption," Pew Research Center, June 22, 2021, https://www.pewresearch
.org/short-reads/2021/06/22/digital-divide-persists-even-as-americans
-with-lower-incomes-make-gains-in-tech-adoption; Landry Signé, "Fixing the
Global Digital Divide and Digital Access Gap," Brookings, July 5, 2023,
https://www.brookings.edu/articles/fixing-the-global-digital-divide-and
-digital-access-gap.

199   **Web3 is no different:** See, e.g., Jessica Apotheker, Joël Hazan, Pierre-François Marteau, Peter Cho, Suchi Srinivasan, Simone Berry, and Akbar Hamid, "Web3 Already Has a Gender Diversity Problem," BCG, February 16, 2023, https://www.bcg.com/publications/2023/how-to-unravel-lack-of-gender-diversity-web3; Judith Bannermanquist, "Women in Web3 Advocate for Increased Diversity in the Ecosystem," Cointelegraph, March 9, 2023, https://cointelegraph.com/news/women-in-web3-advocate-for-increased-diversity-in-the-ecosystem; Bianca Barratt, "How Female Creators Can Encourage More Women to Invest in NFTs," *Forbes*, May 20, 2022, https://www.forbes.com/sites/biancabarratt/2022/05/20/how-female-creators-can-encourage-more-women-to-invest-in-nfts/?sh=655ab5a510c6; and Audrey Handem, Adetola Olatunji, Michelle Dhansinghani, Sharlene Guiriba, Shazia Hasan, "Unlocking Inclusion for Women of Color in Web3," TechCrunch, March 18, 2022, https://techcrunch.com/2022/03/18/unlocking-inclusion-for-women-of-color-in-web3.

199   **in principle an opportunity:** See, e.g., Rebekah Bastian, "The Diversity, Equity and Inclusion Potential of NFTs," *Forbes*, October 24, 2021, https://www.forbes.com/sites/rebekahbastian/2021/10/24/the-diversity-equity-and-inclusion-potential-of-nfts.

199   **significant opportunities here as well:** Giselle Mota, "NFTs Offer Opportunity for Inclusion As Tech Accelerates from Harlem to Hollywood," *Harlem World Magazine*, https://www.harlemworldmagazine.com/nfts-offer-opportunity-for-inclusion-as-tech-accelerates-from-harlem-to-hollywood.

200   **to some degree:** See, e.g., Jason Greenberg and Ethan Mollick, "Activist Choice Homophily and the Crowdfunding of Female Founders," *Administrative Science Quarterly* 62, no. 2 (June 2017): 341–374, https://journals.sagepub.com/doi/full/10.1177/0001839216678847; Scott Duke Kominers and Alexandru Nichifor, "Birchal: Equity Crowdfunding in Australia," Harvard Business Publishing, September 20, 2021, https://hbsp.harvard.edu/product/822034-PDF-ENG.

201   **providing Web3 education and access:** House of First, https://houseoffirst.com; "WoW Foundation," World of Women, https://foundation.worldofwomen.art; People of Crypto, https://www.peopleofcrypto.io; Miss O Cool Girls, https://missocoolgirls.xyz.

201   **NFT collections have been created:** In addition to the NFT projects already cited in this section, see, e.g., Women and Weapons, https://womenandweapons.io; Langston Thomas and Unicorn DAO, "18 Queer Artists Spreading Pride Throughout Web3," NFT Now, June 26, 2023, https://nftnow.com/features/18-queer-artists-who-embody-the-meaning-of-pride;

Emma Sandler, "Nyx Cosmetics Introduces Non-Binary LGBTQIA+ Avatars into the Metaverse," Glossy.co, June 3, 2022, https://www.glossy.co/beauty/nyx-cosmetics-introduces-non-binary-lgbtqia-avatars-into-the-metaverse; Eric James Beyer, "5 Web3 Projects Fighting for Racial Justice," NFT Now, February 28, 2023, https://nftnow.com/features/web3-projects-fighting-for-racial-justice; "The Great Void NFT series," 400 Drums, https://www.400drums.com/drums; Keely Cat-Wells, "NFTs by Disabled Creatives Breaking Moulds and Making Profits," *Forbes*, December 2, 2021, https://www.forbes.com/sites/keelycatwells/2021/12/02/nfts-by-disabled-creatives-breaking-moulds-and-making-profits; ARTXV, https://www.artxv.org; Alejandra Villalobos and Reid Davis, "CARE Package NFT Project Delivers Urgent Humanitarian Aid to Afghan Families in Need," Care.org, October 11, 2021, https://www.care.org/news-and-stories/ideas/care-package-nft-project-delivers-urgent-humanitarian-aid-to-afghan-families-in-need; Soul of Ukraine, https://soulofukraine.io.

201 **Shannon Snow optimistically remarked:** "Shannon Snow on the Rosenzweig Report," Rosenzweig & Company, February 28, 2023, https://www.rosenzweigco.com/media-1/shannon-snow-on-the-rosenzweig-report.

201 **the specific functionalities it has:** Robert Stevens, "Securities vs. Commodities: Why It Matters for Crypto," CoinDesk, updated May 5, 2023, https://www.coindesk.com/learn/securities-vs-commodities-why-it-matters-for-crypto; Jacquelyn Melinek, "Are Cryptocurrencies Commodities or Securities? Depends on Which US Agency You Ask," TechCrunch, March 28, 2023, https://techcrunch.com/2023/03/28/are-cryptocurrencies-commodities-or-securities; Nicole D. Swartz, "Bursting the Bitcoin Bubble: The Case to Regulate Digital Currency as a Security or Commodity," *Tulane Journal of Technology and Intellectual Property* 17 (2014): 319–35, https://journals.tulane.edu/TIP/article/view/2644; Carol R. Goforth, "How Nifty! But Are NFTs Securities, Commodities, or Something Else?," *UMKC Law Review* 90 (2022): 775–800, https://heinonline.org/HOL/LandingPage?handle=hein.journals/umkc90&div=39; Brian Elzweig and Lawrence J. Trautman, "When Does a Non-Fungible Token (NFT) Become a Security?," *Georgia State University Law Review* 39, no. 2 (2023): 295–336, https://readingroom.law.gsu.edu/gsulr/vol39/iss2/8; Billy Abbott, "The Anything Asset: The Tax Classification of Cryptocurrency, NFTs, DAOs and Other Digital Assets," *Chapman Law Review* 26, no. 2 (May 1, 2023): 459–502, http://www.chapmanlawreview.com/wp-content/uploads/2023/05/clr_26-2-459-abbott.pdf; "NFTs as Commodities: Proposed Senate Bill Signals Regulatory Guidelines," JDSupra, June 14, 2022, https://www.jdsupra.com/legalnews/nfts-as-commodities-proposed-senate-4602413;

"Lummis-Gillibrand Responsible Financial Innovation Act," Cynthia Lummis, https://www.lummis.senate.gov/wp-content/uploads/Lummis -Gillibrand-Section-by-Section-Final.pdf.

202 **the broader crypto ecosystem:** The list was too long to enumerate in full, but for a few particularly salient examples, see, e.g., Aaron Klein, "The Future of Crypto Regulation: Highlights from the Brookings Event," Brookings, August 11, 2022, https://www.brookings.edu/2022/08/11/the-future-of -crypto-regulation-highlights-from-the-brookings-event.

202 **centralization in the infrastructure:** See, e.g. Shaurya Malwa, "70% of Ethereum Nodes Are Hosted on Centralized Services," Decrypt, October 8, 2020, https://decrypt.co/44321/70-of-ethereum-nodes-are-hosted-on -centralized-services; Brayden Lindrea, "3 Cloud Providers Accounting for Over Two-Thirds of Ethereum Nodes: Data," Cointelegraph, August 18, 2022, https://cointelegraph.com/news/3-cloud-providers-accounting-for-over-two -thirds-of-ethereum-nodes-data; and see also Hanna Halaburda and Christoph Mueller-Bloch, "Will We Realize Blockchain's Promise of Decentralization?," *Harvard Business Review*, September 4, 2019, https://hbr.org/2019/09/will-we -realize-blockchains-promise-of-decentralization.

203 **at the application layer:** See Christian Catalini and Scott Duke Kominers, "Can WEB3 Bring Back Competition to Digital Platforms?," *TechREG Chronicle*, February 23, 2022, https://www.competitionpolicyinternational .com/can-web3-bring-back-competition-to-digital-platforms.

203 **Some have speculated that:** See, e.g., Scott Nover, "The Decentralized Web Is Not Decentralized," *Quartz*, January 19, 2022, https://qz.com/2112965 /web3-is-not-decentralized.

203 **attempting to lead the charge:** See, e.g., Scott Nover, "Why Facebook Changed Its Name," *Quartz*, October 29, 2021, https://qz.com/2081663/why-facebook -changed-its-name-to-meta.

203 **observed in late 2021:** Moxie Marlinspike (@moxie), "I created an NFT, but the image renders differently based on who's looking at it," Twitter, October 12, 2021, 7:22 p.m., https://twitter.com/moxie/status/1448066579611234305; Moxie Marlinspike, "My First Impressions of Web3," *Moxie* (blog), January 7, 2022, https://moxie.org/2022/01/07/web3-first-impressions.html.

203 **several major competitors:** See, e.g., "Marketplaces," The Block, https:// www.theblock.co/data/nft-non-fungible-tokens/marketplaces.

204 **open its platform up:** Scott Duke Kominers, "Why Facebook and Twitter Opened the Door to NFTs," Bloomberg.com, January 25, 2022, https://www .bloomberg.com/opinion/articles/2022-01-25/why-facebook-and-twitter -opened-the-door-to-nfts.

204 **futurist Francisco Alarcon:** "FAR," FAR, https://0xfar.com.

205 **"The Street Does Not Really Exist":** Bobby Hundreds, "The Street Does Not Really Exist," The Hundreds, August 12, 2021, https://thehundreds.com /blogs/monologue/thestreet; see also Bobby Hundreds, *NFTs Are a Scam / NFTs Are the Future* (New York: Macmillan, 2023).

206 **"Fashion doesn't have to just be":** Hundreds, "The Street Does Not Really Exist"; see also Hundreds, *NFTs Are a Scam / NFTs Are the Future.*

206 **Ready Player Me:** "The World's Leading Avatar Platform," Ready Player Me, https://readyplayer.me.

207 **many different digital spaces:** Scott Duke Kominers, "Metaverse Land: What Makes Digital Real Estate Valuable," a16z crypto, June 2, 2022, https://a16zcrypto.com/posts/article/metaverse-real-estate-digital-land -value-to-users.

INDEX

Note: Italicized page numbers indicate photographs or illustrations.